COMMUNISM
Its Faith
and Fallacies

COMMUNISM
Its Faith
and Fallacies

An Exposition and Criticism

by James D. Bales

Baker Book House
Grand Rapids 6, Michigan
1962

Library of Congress Catalog Card Number 61-17544
Copyright, 1962 by James D. Bales

Appreciation is expressed to the following publishers
for permission to quote from the following books:

Yale University Press. Karl W. A. Wittfogel, *Oriental Despotism: A Comparative Study of Total Power,* 1957.

Paternoster Press. Robert E. D. Clark, *The Universe: Plan or Accident?,* 1961.

Grand Rapids International Publications. Jan Lever, *Creation and Evolution,* 1958.

Farrar, Straus & Cudahy, Inc. Chiang Kai-shek, *Soviet Russia in China,* 1957.

Doubleday & Company, Inc. Sir Charles Sherrington, *Man on His Nature,* 1953.

David McKay Company, Inc. Lecomte du Noüy, *Human Destiny,* 1948.

First printing, February 1962

Second printing, March 1962

DEDICATED
To J. B. and Ruth
in
Appreciation
and with
Affection

Foreword

by Herbert A. Philbrick

For nine years I was a "member" of the communist conspiracy. I learned about communism from the teachings of the communists themselves. I studied their training manuals and textbooks in leadership training courses. Today I am appalled to read and to hear, in books and magazines, in sermons and conversations, some of the utterly fantastic opinions on communism. I am convinced that in no other area of study can there be found so much misinformation, confusion, and just plain balderdash as in the area of communism and religion.

It is for that reason that I am thrilled with the scholarly and masterful study on *Communism: Its Faith and Fallacies* as set forth by Dr. J. D. Bales. Obviously Dr. Bales sternly put aside any and all opinions he may have held concerning communism, and diligently set out to present, factually and precisely, what the communists do believe, teach and advocate.

There is a task not as easy as it might seem. For example, it is indeed, as Dr. Bales points out, "difficult for some people to believe the truth about the ethical code of communism."

Dr. Bales has not been content to compile a description of the surface appearances of the communists, or of communist behavior. He has gone to the very root, the heart and soul of communism itself, to learn not only *what* a communist does, but *why* a communist behaves as he does.

In this I am certain Dr. Bales has reached a new plateau of intellectual understanding of the communist faith. In his research, he has travelled throughout the world; he has conferred directly with the best minds he could seek out, both in the free world and indeed within the communist apparatus itself (he attended, for example, courses at the communist "Jefferson School" in New York). He has ruthlessly culled out all that could not be verified, documented, and proved. *This* is communism, stripped to its essence.

Further pitfalls were to be overcome. Harry and Bonaro Overstreet (*What We Must Know About Communism* and *The War Called Peace*) point out that the structure of communist theory is a patchwork mountain of nearly nothing; an impressive

7

facade which seems to overwhelm many viewers, who approach it in fear and trembling. Undaunted, Dr. Bales attacks this structure and proceeds to take it apart, exposing its utter emptiness.

Finally, having advanced this far, what is one to do with the shamble? Fortunately, in his forage in the morass of communist ideology, Dr. Bales does not become unhinged from his own firm, fixed point of reference. Too many others, alas, otherwise excellent scholars and students of communist ideology appear to not have a firm standard, a yardstick, with which to evaluate the evils of communism. Thus we are given, in the end, a fuzzy picture, an indistinct, out-of-focus gray. But the image of communism so accurately outlined by Dr. Bales is sharply defined against his own faith in the reality of the living, personal God, the value of the human soul and the nature of man as a spiritual and moral being.

Certainly this is a book which has been sorely needed, and it will fill a yawning gap in our understanding and evaluation of the faith and fallacies of communism.

Herbert A. Philbrick

Rye Beach, New Hampshire
September 6, 1961

Preface

by Hollington K. Tong

Dr. James D. Bales, Professor of Christian Doctrine at Harding College in Searcy, Arkansas, is a great authority on communism, well known among Chinese students of communism. His book, *Communism: Its Faith and Fallacies,* deserves intensive reading, for it contains information of historical importance. To my knowledge, few other books so brilliantly explain what communism means to the free world, and none better portrays as utterly inexcusable, even criminal, the possibility of co-existence between communism and democracy or of Communism and Christianity.

There is no better summary of the significance of communism than the one given by Dr. Bales. "Briefly defined," he says, "Communism today is a Marx inspired, Moscow directed, international criminal conspiracy against civilization, based on a God-denying philosophy of life, sustained by faith in the dialectic, backed by the devotion of its fanatical believers and to an uncertain extent by the armed might of the Red armies." This definition epitomizes the studied opinions of all outstanding authorities on communist doctrine, to whom the author gives due credit.

Following his definition of communism, Dr. Bales offers a scholarly review of the philosophy of communism, of atheism and theism, dialectical and historical materialism, the communist concept of class and class struggle, the communist attitude toward religion, communist persecution, communist infiltration of religious organizations and the communist objective of final destruction of religion. The review is worthy of serious study.

The author draws liberally from both communist and non-communist sources, thereby increasing the value of his book and strengthening his conclusion on the great evil communism poses to the free world. Let us hope he will stimulate a full understanding by men and women of the true nature of communism and inspire them to devise antidotes for their own protection.

The author, who has made a thorough study of the Chinese

communist domination of the China mainland, supports his conclusion by quotations from the Chinese communist leaders on their ultimate intentions. In a sense, unhappy Asia is today a mirror reflecting to the free world how naked is the communist plan for world conquest. What has happened in Asia during the last 15 years, while the West was marking time, is a pattern of what can happen to Europe, Africa and the Americas if free men should become so unwary as to succumb to communist political traps.

The immediate problem that confronts the free world is the projected disarmament conference. Unless the free world enters it with an iron will, it could very well be the last world conference in which the West would meet Soviet Russia on a basis of equal power and equal solidarity. While the West continues to deliberate on how to deal with them, the communists the world over are marching on to their final objective, welcoming as they advance new signs of a split in the free world and weakening of its moral stamina.

Dr. Bales cautions the leaders of the democratic camp with these pungent words: "When man in the free world viewed the communist in the light of our philosophy of life we became disarmed psychologically. But the communist in viewing us in the light of his philosophy of life armed himself psychologically and physically." How true!

Professor Gerhart Niemeyer, author of *An Inquiry Into Soviet Mentality*, supports Dr. Bales' conclusion and says that "the communist mind has so defined its world that it shares neither truth nor logic nor morality with the rest of mankind." So, "when dealing with a communist," Dr. Bales concludes, "one is dealing with an individual who regards himself as involved in a war to death with the non-communist. His actions whether in peace or in war, are but a part of his total war against civilization. He does not come to the conference table to work out a just arrangement but rather to use the conference table as a means of furthering the destruction of his enemies."

According to Dr. Bales, President Chiang Kai-shek, of the Republic of China, in his book on *Soviet Russia in China*, backs by personal experience the conclusion drawn by Dr. Bales. President Chiang says: "What we did not realize was that Communists are Communists, first, last and always. They were traitorous and treacherous all the time. Everywhere they went they set traps for others. Any weak spot in our organization or a loophole in our precautionary measures would give them a chance to start trouble. In our war against Communism we made the mistake of judging the Communists by the same yardstick of national consciousness and democratic and ethical concepts."

In the light of these various statements made by the anti-communist leaders, what the communists have been doing in international conferences make sense. The regrettable thing is that statesmen of the free world still indulge in wishful thinking.

Unfortunately, some of the world's leading churchmen have been doing the same thing in urging cooperation between Christianity in the West and the controlled church in the communist area, this despite the fact that the communist denies the existence of God and affirms the eternal existence of matter. Dr. Bales rightly points out that to the communists God is the symbol of man's self-abnegation, a reflection of man's enslavement to the economic system. "The communists," he adds, "believe that the destruction of the religious consciousness is essential to man's complete mastery of the world." It is well worthwhile to note the warning in Whittaker Chamber's book that "the crisis of the Western world exists to the degree that it is indifferent to God."

Dr. Bales has done well in putting forward the Christian's belief in the existence of God, the naturalness of faith in God, the fact of conscience, the existence of moral law and order. Without answering the communists in regard to the existence or non-existence of God, the book would have been incomplete. There is no better Christian than Dr. Bales to give this answer. His book, *Atheism's Faith and Fruits*, still stands as an authoritative work on the subject.

It is hoped that the timely publication of his new book will awaken non-communists to think in terms of taking the offensive in a struggle for freedom, which would roll back the engulfing tide of communism and saving in a positive way all those suffering under communist slavery.

If this tide is not stopped in time, today's wealth may be tomorrow's poverty, today's freedom may be tomorrow's slavery, although today's God will still be tomorrow's God. It pays to read Dr. Bales' book. It gives the correct direction to be taken to prevent the world from being gradually dominated by the communists.

Hollington K. Tong

Taipei, 1961

Table of Contents

PROLOGUE

"The real culprit is the Communist ideology itself." *New York Times,* June 5, 1956.

"It is difficult, but necessary, to recognize that the communist ideology has no resources within it for coming to terms with other systems of thought." Reinhold Niebuhr, *The Moral Implications of Loyalty to the United Nations!,* July 1952, p. 7.

"It made philosophy into a revolutionary weapon of the working people, an instrument, a method of understanding the world so as to change it." Maurice Cornforth, *Materialism and the Dialectical Method,* New York: International Publishers, 1953, p. 54.

"Stalin and the present Khrushchev leadership which he created and trained are certainly criminal desperadoes. But the Communist system which breeds and rears such criminal types as the rulers and leaders of its society is even more horribly criminal." Jay Lovestone, *AFL-CIO American Federationist,* August 1956, p. 11.

"Communist theory and practice hang together more closely than in other ideologies, but it is possible to exaggerate their monolithic unity." Sidney Hook, "The Import of Ideological Diversity," *Problems of Communism,* November-December 1957, p. 11.

CHAPTER ONE

What Is Communism?

In defining communism, three different aspects of it must be kept in mind if we are to see it in its entirety. It is an idea or philosophy of life, a highly organized and well disciplined international conspiracy and armed might. Today this term designates not only a theoretical future society wherein men will work according to their ability and will be rewarded according to their need, but also the entire philosophy of life which includes the economic life as only one of its facets.

What is communism? Is it as Lenin said, "The Soviet power, plus electrification"? Or is it as Earl Browder maintains, "Twentieth Century Americanism"?[1] Hardly!

The word communism is not of recent origin, since communistic societies of one type or another existed or were proposed long before. The "Bible Communists" had a community in America in the early nineteenth century.[2] The word was coined by some secret revolutionary societies in Paris around 1837. Karl Marx used it in the *Communist Manifesto*. From 1840 to 1872 it described some movements which demanded the revolutionary overthrow of society. Since around 1917 it has been the label for Marxism as advocated by Lenin and his successors in Russia.[3]

The *Oxford English Dictionary* defines communism as: "A theory which advocates a state of society in which there should be no private ownership, all property being vested in the community and labour organized for the common benefit of all members." The definition, however, is not only inadequate but also misleading if it is applied to what is commonly known today as communism. It goes far beyond this definition. Com-

---

[1] *What Is Communism?* New York: Workers' Library Publishers, 1936, pp. 174, 188.

[2] Benjamin B. Warfield, *Perfectionism*, Vol. II, Philadelphia: Presbyterian and Reformed Publishing Company.

[3] Max Beer, "Communism," *Encyclopedia of the Social Sciences*, Vol. IV, New York: The Macmillan Company, 1942, p. 81.

munism is a philosophy of life, a call to revolutionary action, an organization, armed might, an international conspiracy and a goal.

As a philosophy of life, communism endeavors to explain the universe, life, history, and the future. It embraces atheism, dialectical materialism and class struggle as integral parts of its explanation. Its concern is not only with theory but also with action. Thus Marx emphasized that he was not interested simply in understanding the world, but in changing it. As a philosophy of life communism endeavors to dominate and to control the outer and the inner life of its devotees[4] who "accept its discipline in every part of their private and professional lives."[5] Thus it has been called a religion or a religion-substitute by some.[6] In fact, Bertrand Russell labels communism, as it has developed in Russia, as "a political religion analogous to Islam."[7]

As a philosophy of life, communism must be evaluated by its inner consistencies or contradictions, its attitude toward certain facts of human experience, by its harmony or lack of harmony with well-established truths and by its fruits.

As a goal, communism refers to that ideal state of society which, according to Marxism, will follow socialism. It is claimed

---

[4] Bishop Fulton J. Sheen, *Communism and the Conscience of the West*, New York: The Bobbs—Merrill Company, 1948, p. 58.

[5] Hugh Seton-Watson, *From Lenin to Malenkov*, New York: Frederick A. Praeger, p. vii. See also Liu Shao-chi, *How to Be a Good Communist*, Peking: Foreign Languages Press, 1952, pp. 49-59.

[6] See the quotation in Corliss Lamont, *Soviet Civilization*, New York: Philosophical Library, 1952, p. 225.

[7] Lester E. Denonn, Editor, *Bertrand Russell's Dictionary of Mind, Matter and Morals*, p. 30. Today whenever possible, communists are using interviews with Russell to further some of their objectives—such as using the Sobell and the Matusow cases to discredit American justice. See the interview with Russell by Cedric Belfrage in the *National Guardian*, June 18, 1956. This is in spite of earlier statements by Russell that he would prefer a new world war to a "universal communist empire," "To Turn Us from Madness," *Reader's Digest*, Dec. 1953, p. 3. "Man's Peril From Hydrogen Bomb," *The Listener*, Dec. 30, 1954, p. 2. For some of his latest statements see his correspondence with Sidney Hook, *The New Leader*, Aug. 18, 1958, p. 13, and with Alfred Kohlberg. Also the open letter of Norman Thomas to Mr. Russell, *The New Leader*, Jan. 7, 1957. Some social scientists say that communism is not a religion, although the response of the communists to communism may be religious, Douglas Jackson in Merrimon Cuninggim, Editor, *Christianity and Communism*, p. 32. Sidney Hook spoke of "The totalitarian Communist Church."

that in this society there will be no coercive state, no classes and no private ownership of means of production and distribution. Men will work for the common good; each will so live as to call forth the best in others. In as far as work and wages are concerned it will be: "From each according to his ability, to each according to his needs." Corliss Lamont, a veteran supporter of procommunist causes, says that "real communism, as Marxism understands it, has at no time existed in the Soviet Union."[8]

However, the term communism is used today, not so much with reference to the goal, as with reference to the Soviet system and to all those parties, in every country, which advocate Marxism and look to Moscow for leadership. Thus a House Report maintained that "communism may be defined as an organized movement which works for the overthrow by force or violence of the governments of countries which are not yet under the control of the communists, and establishment in place thereof (a) a regime termed proletarian dictatorship, and (b) an economic system based upon the substitution of communal ownership of property for private ownership."

This report then goes on to say that "Communism is a worldwide political organization advocating: (1) the abolition of all forms of religion; (2) the destruction of private property and the abolition of inheritance; (3) absolute social and racial equality; (4) revolution under the leadership of the Communist International; (5) engaging in activities in foreign countries in order to cause strikes, riots, sabotage, bloodshed, and civil war; (6) destruction of all forms of representative or democratic government, including civil liberties such as freedom of speech, of the press, and of assemblage; (7) the ultimate objective of world revolution to establish the dictatorship of the so-called proletariat into a universal union of soviet socialist republics with

---

[8] *Soviet Civilization*, p. 53. For some information on Lamont see Medford Evans, "Hypocrisy against the Devil," *National Review*, May 2, 1956, pp. 20-21; June 6, 1956, p. 22; Sidney Hook, "Corliss Lamont: 'Friend of the G.P.U.,'" *The Modern Monthly*, March, 1938, pp. 5-8, which is a reply to Lamont's defense of the Moscow trials against the verdict of the Dewey Commission report. Of course, Khrushchev now agrees that Stalin was a ruthless murderer in those very trials, "A Summary of the Secret Khrushchev Report on Stalin," *National Guardian*, 1956. See the entire speech in the *Congressional Record*, June 4, 1956, pp. 8465-8479. "Proceedings Against Corliss Lamont for Contempt of the Senate," 83rd Congress, 2nd Session, Senate Report No. 1813, July 16, 1954; *Congressional Record*, Aug. 11, 1954, pp. 13406-13407; *Newsweek*, Oct. 29, 1951, p. 61.

its capital at Moscow; (8) the achievement of these ends through extreme appeals to hatred."[9]

Concerning point number (3), it must be observed that although their propaganda takes this position, communists today actually are interested only in exploiting the grievances of each group or race as a means of dividing a country and of rising to power in the ensuing confusion. There are new classes in Russia today which have arisen since the revolution; and as for racial equality, they will murder one of their own race and Party as quickly as they will murder an individual of another race if that individual is in their way and his destruction will promote communism! Khrushchev verified this when he pointed out that under Stalin there were "mass deportations from their native places of whole nations, together with all communists and Komsomols without any exception; this deportation action was not dictated by any military consideration."[10]

Briefly defined, Communism today is a Marx inspired, Moscow directed,[11] international criminal[12] conspiracy[13] against civilization,[14] based on a God-denying philosophy of life, sustained by faith in the dialectic, backed by the devotion of its fanatical believers and to an uncertain extent by the armed might of the Red Armies.[15] This definition is in line with the position of George

---

[9] *Investigation of Un-American Activities and Propaganda,* House Resolution 282, Union Calendar No. 2, House Report, No. 2, 1939, p. 12.

[10] Speech of February 25, 1956 before their 20th Congress, The *Congressional Record,* June 4, 1956, p. 8473.

[11] See the reaffirmation by the Subversive Activities Control Board of the subservience of the Communist Party of the United States to Moscow in the Modified Report of the Board, Dec. 18, 1956. Herbert Brownell, Jr., Attorney General of the United States, Petitioner, *vs.* the Communist Party of the United States of America, Respondent. Washington, D.C.: Government Printing Office, 1957. See also the Recommended Decision of Board member, Frances A. Cherry on Second Remand Proceedings issued September 19, 1958.

[12] Sir M. Findlay in his report to the British Government on September 17, 1918 said that the "whole Soviet Government has sunk to the level of a criminal organization." *A Collection of Reports on Bolshevism in Russia.* Presented to Parliament by Command of His Majesty, April 1919. London: Published by His Majesty's Stationary Office, 1919, p. 5.

[13] Jay Lovestone, *AFL-CIO American Federationist,* Aug. 1956, p. 10-11.

[14] Augur, *Soviet Versus Civilization,* New York: D. Appelton and Company, 1927.

[15] Compare *The Commonweal,* Aug. 6, 1954, as reprinted in the *Congressional Record,* 1954, A 5793. "Marxist-Leninist Communism is a system of analytic and interpretive ideas and a cluster of organizational and

Meany that it "takes just as little sense, and spells out just as much nonsense, to refuse to call an enemy of freedom what he really is, as it would do to refuse to call a spade a spade."[16]

A communist is one who has accepted the Marxian philosophy of life as it is expounded by the Party and who is under some degree of Party discipline.

The philosophy of communism is expressed in the writings of Karl Marx, Frederick Engels, V. I. Lenin,[17] Joseph Stalin and some other writers. Marx and Engels are so closely interwoven that they themselves sometimes found it difficult to determine who had thought out what first.[18]

It has been thought by some that Lenin and Stalin changed the philosophy of Marx and Engels. For example, Robert V.

---

strategic devices for the establishment and maintenance of total political, economic and idealogical power" (Karl A. Wittfogel, "Peking's 'Independence,' " *The New Leader,* July 20, 1959).

[16] George Meany, President of the AFL-CIO, *Congressional Record,* June 25, 1956, p. A5007. " . . . The Russians are up to no good . . . they are committed to a fundamental campaign against Western civilization . . . this is so obvious by now that it needs no further discussion" (Arthur Schlesinger, Jr., in "Is Co-Existence Possible?" New York: The Taminent Institute, 1955, p. 15).

[17] The destalinization program brought an increased emphasis on Lenin. See the last three issues of *"For a Lasting Peace, For a People's Democracy,"* 1956. For a current evaluation of the contributions of Lenin to Marxism see William Z. Foster, *History of the Communist Party of the United States,* New York: International Publishers, 1952, pp. 149-156. For a brief presentation by Lenin of Marx's teaching see the Little Lenin Library, Vol. 1, *The Teachings of Karl Marx,* New York: International Publishers, 1930. For Stalin's estimate of Lenin's contributions to Marxism see his answer to the first question of an "American Labor Delegation," Sept. 9, 1927. Also printed in *On the Theory of Marxism,* Little Lenin Library, Vol. 31, pp. 27-31.

The denunciation of Stalin did not mean the repudiation of Stalin. Communists said that he made some mistakes but these "mistakes were only secondary compared with his great merits." Stalin "was boundlessly loyal to the cause of the proletarian revolution. . . " (Ai Szu-chi, "The 80th Anniversary of the Birth of J. V. Stalin," *Peking Review,* Dec. 29, 1959, p. 10).

A. Mikoyan once praised Stalin as the Lenin of his day. See his *Stalin-The Lenin of Our Day,* New York: Workers Library, 1940. With Stalin at the helm there was "an unshakable belief in the infallibility of the general line of the Party. . . " (p. 60).

[18] M. M. Bober, *Karl Marx's Interpretation of History,* Cambridge: Harvard University Press, 1950, Preface to First Edition. For a brief discussion of some of the principal writings of Marx and Engels see R. N. Carew Hunt, *The Theory and Practice of Communism,* New York: The Macmillan Company, 1951, pp. 12-13.

Daniels speaks of "the manifold differences between Marx's theories and Stalin's interpretation of them" and of Lenin and Stalin butchering the notion of historical materialism.[19] It is true that some changes have been made, but it must not be forgotten that the philosophy of Marx and of Engels made provisions for some modifications by its very concept of the dialectic and of the importance of the particular time and place. Some students of the subject now maintain that there is greater unity between Marx and Stalin than they had once thought.[20]

It is unnecessary, however, for our purposes to resolve this debate as to the extent of the Russian modifications of Marx. Regardless of the unity or lack of complete unity between Marx and his successors we are justified in viewing their writings as official interpretations of the philosophy of communism. Although communists maintain that Marxism undergoes developments to meet changed conditions and times, yet since they regard Marxism as a science they also maintain that there are basic concepts which do not undergo change. They also believe that even the changes are "right" and "true" for the times and circumstances. As the National Committee of the Communist Party recently stated: "The principles of scientific socialism were first put forward by Marx and Engels. They were further developed in the imperialist era by Lenin. They were later enriched by contemporary Marxists in many countries. Basing ourselves on these Marxist-Leninist principles as interpreted by the Communist Party of our country, we must learn much better how to extract from the rich body of this theory that which is universally valid, combining it with the specific experiences of the American working class in the struggle for socialism in the United States. The Party must distinguish better between the additions to Marxist theory made by Lenin which are valid for all countries and those specific aspects of Lenin's writings which reflect exclusively certain unique features of the Russian revolution or of Soviet society."[21]

---

[19] *Problems of Communism*, Vol. IV, No. 6, Nov.-Dec., 1955, p. 44.

[20] R. N. Carew Hunt, *Marxism Past and Present*, New York: Macmillan Company, 1954. "The form which Lenin was to give it, and which Stalin inherited was naturally influenced by the problems raised by the October revolution, and this has become the orthodox form which is accepted by communists in all countries. Yet it was a legitimate interpretation of principles, which had never been disavowed" (p. 3).

[21] *Draft Resolution for the 16th National Convention of the Communist Party, U.S.A.*, New York: New Century Publishers, Sept. 1956, pp. 55-56.

It is also clear that there are certain concepts which have been adhered to by communists since the days of Marx. Some of them are atheism, dialectical materialism and the class struggle.

Does not the statement of the National Committee convey to non-communists the importance of understanding the basic philosophy of communism and the current interpretation and application of that basic philosophy?

CHAPTER TWO

The Importance of Understanding the Philosophy of Communism

There are those who argue that the men in the Kremlin do not believe the philosophy of communism, but that it is a hypocritical cloak for Russian imperialism. Thus they must be dealt with as simply another power group. Is this the whole story? Or are they a power group which adheres to a definite philosophy of life which has an influence on their actions? Even if the philosophy is but a cloak, is it possible that through a process of rationalization it has become far more than a cloak for some of them? Under Stalin was theory "entirely subordinated to practice," without "any appreciable long-run guiding or inhibiting effect on the policies of the government"?[1] Or do the communists think that they are applying a scientific philosophy to political situations?[2] Must the philosophy be dealt with in order to destroy communism?[3]

In endeavoring to solve this problem we must deal with such questions as: Do the communists themselves claim that their

---

[1] Robert V. Daniels in his review of Alfred G. Meyer, *Marxism. The Unity of Theory and Practice* in *Problems of Communism*, Vol. IV, 1955, pp. 47-48. Gustav A. Wetter thinks that in the Soviet Union "there is little left of real dialectics, and that it consists, rather, of a materialistic evolutionism, decked out in dialectical terminology" (*Dialectical Materialism*, New York: Frederick A. Praeger, 1958, p. xi). However, he stated that the Soviets do view it as a method by which they think. *Ibid.*, p. 5. This, in itself, would be sufficient to justify a study of dialectical materialism.

[2] R. N. Carew Hunt, *The Theory and Practice of Communism*, p. v; see also p. 87. "Communist theory and practice hang together more closely than in other ideologies, but it is possible to exaggerate their monolithic unity" (Sidney Hook, "The Import of Ideological Diversity," *Problems of Communism*, Vol. V, Nov.-Dec. 1957, p. 11).

[3] As maintained by Walter C. Jaskievicz in Bill Duke, "Reading, Writing and Russian," *The American Mecury*, July, 1955, p. 35.

philosophy is important? Do they stress it? Do they often act as if the philosophy were true? What is the testimony of those who have been in contact with some of the top leaders of communism?

COMMUNISM—AND MARX AND LENIN

Dr. Wilhelm Starlinger was for six years confined with Russian political prisoners. He served them as a doctor. It was his judgment that there was a "decline of the Marxist-Leninist dialectical materialism as a pseudo religion." The vocabulary of dialectical materialism was still employed, but he was of the opinion that an "emotional, fanatical nationalism," the "glorification of messianic Great Russian nationalism," was replacing it. However, he maintained that it would be disastrous to conclude "from these incipient mutations that dialectical materialism and its present instruments of power—the Bolshevik Party, church and state" had lost their significance and were no longer a threat to civilization.[4]

Khrushchev himself claims to be a believer in Marxism. On September 17, 1955, he said to the East German delegation: "We always tell the truth to our friends as well as to our enemies. We are in favor of a detente, but if anybody thinks that for this reason we shall forget about Marx, Engels, and Lenin, he is mistaken. This will happen when shrimps learn to whistle. . . ."[5] We have heard no whistling shrimps! Have you?

Jurij Gudim-Levkovich, who once associated with Khrushchev,

---

[4] "Limits of Soviet Power," *U.S. News and World Report*, Nov. 4, 1955, pp. 145-146.

[5] Denis Healey, " 'When Shrimps Learn to Whistle,' " *International Affairs*, Vol. 32, Jan. 1956, p. 2, published by the Royal Institute of International Affairs, London. See also *St. Louis Post-Dispatch*, Sept. 18, 1955.

Khrushchev is a "true believer in Communism" (Richard Nixon, University of Chicago Law School Dedicatory Address, Oct. 5, 1959).

Khrushchev "devoutly believes in the Marxist gospel," A. Harriman, "Peace With Russia?" New York: Simon and Schuster, 1960. As quoted in *The New Leader*, June 6, 1960, p. 28.

Allen W. Dulles, Director of Central Intelligence, pointed out that although there are time-servers, and that in some revolutionary ferver may show some signs of diminishing, yet there are many fanatically dedicated communists. It is not only a conspiracy but also a way of life, *U.S. News and World Report*, Sept. 5, 1960, p. 89. Stefan T. Possony thinks that "Communists remain true believers" but that they do manipulate their ideology and use it as a weapon, *National Review*, Sept. 24, 1960, p. 188.

maintained that Khrushchev is an orthodox party man "one hundred per cent. His belief starts with Marx and ends with Stalin. That determines his general outlook. He is a fanatic about the idealogy of communism."[6]

Marguerite Higgins, an American correspondent, has visited Russia twice within the past few years, staying three months each time. She has talked with the leading men in the Soviet government, including Khrushchev. Of Khrushchev she said that she thinks that he is a true believer in communism and that he has cut off all doubt in his mind. She is convinced that to him communism represents an absolute good. She believes him to be a totally uncomplicated, thoroughly dedicated communist who is not intellectual enough to have any doubts. She reports that Khrushchev on one occasion bluntly stated ". . . if you think that means we're going to give up communism, you're crazy."[7]

THE PHILOSOPHY EMPHASIZED BY COMMUNISTS

The communists have long emphasized the importance of their philosophy. M. I. Kalinin, one of the leading educationalists in Russia, spoke of the need for mastering and applying the Marxist method.[8] *The History of the Communist Party of the Soviet Union* (*Bolsheviks*), a very important text, stated that "it is the duty of every active member of our Party to know these principles" of dialectical and historical materialism.[9]

In his pamphlet on *How to Be a Good Communist*, Liu Shaochi emphasized that in order to be a good communist one must be completely *indoctrinated* in the theory of Marx, Engels, Lenin

---

[6] *U.S. News and World Report*, Dec. 16, 1955, p. 54. For Eugene Lyons' evaluation of Khrushchev see *Reader's Digest*, Aug. 1959, pp. 49-54.

[7] Compare *U.S. News and World Report*, Jan. 6, 1956, p. 64. William E. Bohn, "Nikita Khrushchev's Vulgar Marxism," *The New Leader*, Oct. 12, 1959, p. 5.

[8] *On Communist Education*, Moscow: Foreign Language Publishing House, 1950, p. 469.

[9] While Herbert A. Philbrick was in the Party, as an undercover agent for the F.B.I., he "studied revolution through the voluminous *History of the Communist Party of the Soviet Union* (*Bolsheviks*), the 'bible' of communism, edited and authorized by the Central Committee of the Russian Communist party," *I Led Three Lives*, New York: McGraw-Hill Book Company, Inc., 1952, p. 110. Gabriel A. Almond wrote that it "was the most important training text used in the schools of the Communist movement at the time this study was conducted. Every militant was still required to read and study it." It has recently been replaced with a new history.

principles for christians (handwritten annotation)

and Stalin; thoroughly *dedicated* to the Party and *willing to participate* in whatever work the Party may assign to him.

In 1955 the National Conference of the Communist Party of China issued the following directive: "The fourth basic lesson is that the Party must intensify education in Marxist-Leninist and Communist ideology within the Party, improve its ideological-political work and carry on a ceaseless and systematic struggle against all shades of bourgeois ideas that tend to corrode our Party. . . . The Party demands that all members who can do so, should systematically and diligently study the theories of Marxism-Leninism, dialectical materialism and historical materialism."[10] This is in line with the observation of Shau Wing Chan and Yuan-Li Wu that "Since 1950 so much importance has been attached to the so-called 'thought remodeling campaign' that it has become one of the principle activities throughout the country, involving practically the whole population."[11]

In his report to the 20th Congress of the Communist Party, Khrushchev emphasized the importance of an intensification of the teaching and practice of Marxism-Leninism. There was, he said, a pressing need for "a popular exposition of the fundamentals of Marxist philosophy."[12] He closed his 1956 report by saying: "The future is with us, for we are confidently marching forward along the only correct path, the path charted for us by our teacher, the great Lenin. . . . Under the banner of Marxism-Leninism, which is transforming the world, the Communist Party of the Soviet Union will lead the Soviet people to the complete triumph of Communism."[13] His speech denouncing Stalin closed with: "We are absolutely certain that our party, armed with the historical resolutions of the 20th Congress, will lead the Soviet people along the Leninist path to new successes,

---

[10]*Documents of the National Conference of the Communist Party of China*, Peking: Foreign Languages Press, 1955, pp. 55-56. Robert Guillain, "What I Saw inside Red China," *Reader's Digest*, Sept. 1956, p. 33, speaks of the "tidal wave of Russian Marxism" which is drowning Chinese intellectual life. The Central Committee of the Communist Party, USSR, has called for increasing emphasis on their philosophy, *World Marxist Review*, Mar. 1960, p. 67.

[11] "Popular Discontent in Communist China," *Problems of Communism*, Vol. IV., Nov. 4, 1955, p. 15.

[12]*Report of the Central Committee, CPSU to the 20th Congress of The Communist Party of the Soviet Union*, New York: New Century Publishers, 1956, p. 119.

[13] *Ibid.*, p. 125.

to new victories. [Tumultuous, prolonged applause.] Long live
the victorious banner of our Party—Leninism! [Tumultuous, prolonged applause ending in ovation. All rise.]"[14]

STALIN NOT ABANDONED

In his interpretation of the 20th Congress of the Communist
Party of the Soviet Union, Max Weiss, the Educational Director
of the Communist Party in the United States, pointed out that
they were still Marxist-Leninists. They were obligated to study
Marxism-Leninism and the American scene in order to know
how best to apply Marxism-Leninism in their fight against
capitalism.[15]

The denunciation of Stalin did not imply that communism
was wrong; in fact, it did not even imply that Stalin was basically wrong or that he did not make contributions to the theory
of Marxism-Leninism. Thus Max Weiss told the National Committee of the Communist Party that "Stalin who despite his
serious mistakes stood to the end on the correct general line of
the CPSU with result that we all know insofar as the con-
struction of Socialism is concerned."[16]

The Political Bureau of the Central Committee of the China's
Communist Party met in Peking and issued a 17,000 word summary of a meeting in Peking in the December 29, 1956, issue of
the newspaper, *Jen Min Jih Pao*. This was summarized by the
Soviet news agency Tass and the summary was published in the
National Guardian.[17] It stated: "Despite errors, Stalin 'creatively
applied and developed Marxism-Leninism . . . expressed the will
of the people and was a worthy and outstanding fighter for
Marxism-Leninism.'" "Stalin and those who made similar mistakes must be treated 'as comrades, not as enemies.' Since their
mistakes have historic and social roots, other leaders similarly
placed could have committed them." "Pointing out that the

---

[14]Boris I. Nicolaevsky, annotater, "The Crimes of the Stalin Era. Special
Report to the 20th Congress of the Communist Party of the Soviet Union,
by Nikata S. Khrushchev," New York: *The New Leader*, 1956, p. S65. The
Senate Internal Security Subcommittee also published a copy of Khrushchev's speech.

[15] *The Meaning of the 20th Congress of the Communist Party of The
Soviet Union*, New York: New Century Publishers, 1956, pp. 16-19.

[16] *Ibid.*, p. 24.

[17] Jan. 28, 1957, p. 6.

main target of imperialists and revisionists is the Soviet Union, the Chinese sum up the 39-year old history of the first socialist state as a 'grand' success, the first triumphant hymn of Marxism-Leninism in the History of mankind, that has resounded throughout the universe."[18]

Khrushchev puts it this way: ". . . we do not criticize Stalin as a bad Communist as far as the interests of the working classes are concerned . . . in the things that counted, that is in the interests of the working class, God grant that every Communist should fight for the interest of the working class as Stalin did."[19] On the fourth anniversary of his death, Stalin was described by *Pravda* as, "an outstanding revolutionary, a devoted Marxist-Leninist theoretician and great organizer." In fact, Khrushchev now describes him as a "model Communist."[20]

THE PARTY USES THE PHILOSOPHY

The importance of an understanding of the philosophy of communism is also emphasized by the fact that the Communist Party *still recruits on the basis of Marxism*. Although the history of the Communist Party has been attended by the apostasy of many disillusioned recruits, yet more and more the Party has built in safeguards to keep the initiates from unbelief. The ultimate "end of Communism—the classless society—has always been vague and remote." The convert's faith is in the Party and its leadership. He is not to think against its decisions, for it is the bearer of truth. Thus he is without standards to determine whether or not the Party has really deviated from its supposed purpose, or whether it is but a tactical deviation. But since the Party can do no evil, its actions must be right.[21] Then, too, he has been taught that the arguments used by opponents of communism are but reflections and rationalizations of their class

---

[18] See also the *Peiping People's Daily*, Dec. 29, 1956, as cited in the *Chinese News Service*, Jan. 15, 1957, p. 4.

[19] AP Dispatch, *Arkansas Gazette*, Jan. 18, 1957, p. 1.

[20] AP, Moscow, Mar. 5, 1957 in the *Arkansas Gazette*, Mar. 6, 1957, p. 9a. Stalin is praised in the new official history of the Party. Leopold Labedz, "Khrushchev's New Party History," *The New Leader*, Oct. 12, 1959, p. 17. Oct. 27, 1961, Khrushchev further criticized Stalin in what seems to be a further drive to consolidate his power.

[21] Gabriel A. Almond, *The Appeals of Communism*, Princeton, N. J.: Princeton University Press, 1954, pp. 377-378.

interest, and therefore it is useless for him even to evaluate them.[22]

Finally, the communist is kept in the Party by the consequences which follow disassociation from the Party. To abandon the Party is to admit that he had given his soul into the hands of wicked and ruthless men. It means that he must go back into the world which he has been taught to view as a mass of corruption. He is led to believe that he must stay with communism as the only hope of man, or that he must return to and defend all of the abuses that exist in the present world. He must sever friendships, and leave the circle which has become his life. He must abandon the cause which has given him a purpose in life, and be left purposeless unless he has become converted to another faith. All of these things are designed to keep in the "faith" those who have been recruited on the basis of the communist philosophy of life.

It seems that the philosophy is one of the basic means used by the Russian leaders to control and to unite the various communist parties throughout the world. Surely the loyalty of communists in America to their Russian masters, the close cooperation between Russia and China and the attitude of the Chinese Reds toward Russia cannot be fully explained apart from assuming their common acceptance of the ideological bond of Marxism. "Perhaps the strongest cement in the Soviet-Chinese partnership is their common political aims. In addition to sharing profoundly a clear-cut communist philosophy of thought and action, their leaders are united in common interest and goals."[23]

A COMMON MOULD

Communists throughout the world are alike. Is this not because they share the same philosophy of life? A Chinese communist is like a Russian communist who is like a communist in America. Chiang Kai-shek tells of his sad but enlightening experiences with the communists in 1924 and in 1937. These experiences give concrete proof that in dealing with the communists one is

---

[22] *Communist Manifesto,* Moscow: Foreign Languages Publishing House, 1957, pp. 78-79, 83. See also the exchange between Eugene Lyons and Howard Fast in *The New Leader,* July 9, 1956; July 30, 1956. They seem to fail to realize that this also discredits their own "class thinking."

[23] Philip E. Mosley, *Russia After Stalin,* Headling Series, No. 111, Foreign Policy Association, May-June 1955, p. 51.

not dealing with people who share our values. Says Chiang Kai-shek: "In our dealings with the Chinese communists we have always set a great store by ethical considerations, good faith and righteousness. It was our belief that every Chinese cannot help feeling loyal to his own country first. That was why we had sincerely hoped to move forward together with the communists on the road of democracy to complete our task of national reconstruction.

"What we did not realize was that communists are communists, first, last and always. They were traitorous and treacherous all the time. Everywhere they went they set traps for others. Any weak spot in our organization or a loophole in our precautionary measures would give them a chance to start trouble. In our war against communism we made the mistake of judging the communists by the same yardstick of national consciousness and democratic and ethical concepts."[24]

Even if it should be true that communist theory is but a hypocritical cloak for the leaders of the Party, it is believed by millions of their subjects. Thus this philosophy is a "powerful political myth inspiring communists with fanatical zeal,"[25] and binding them to their masters.

---

[24] *Soviet Russia in China*, New York: Farrar, Straus and Cudahy, 1957, p. 213. See also Gabriel A. Almond. *The Appeals of Communism*, p. 377. Vice-Admiral Leslie C. Stevens thought that Russia "is more apt to act consistently with her ideology than with the manner in which Great Powers normally act," "The Russian Doctrine," *The Atlantic Monthly*, June, 1952, p. 55. For additional information on the importance of their philosophy to communists, see *Political Affairs*, Dec. 1949, p. 13; Waldemar Gurian, *Bolshevism*, p. 171; Herbert J. Muller, *The Uses of the Past*, p. 309; Marguerite J. Fisher, *Communist Doctrine and the Free World*, p. viii; Betty Gannett, *The Communist Party and You*, New York: Published by the C.P., 1947, p. 30; *Fortune*, April 1955, pp. 133, 135; Viliam Siroky, Prime Minister, Czechoslovak, *For a Lasting Peace, For a People's Democracy*, Nov. 4, 1955, p. 3; *U.S. News and World Report*, Dec. 2, 1955, p. 4; Joseph S. Roucek, Editor "Soviet Communism," *Twentieth Century Political Thought*, p. 18; George Catlin, *The Story of the Political Philosophers*, pp. 569-570; "Litvinov's Political Testament," *Problems of Communism*, No. 1, 1952, p. 16; Georgi Dimitroff, *The United Front against Fascism*, New York: New Century Publishers, p. 126; *History of the C.P.S.U. (B)*, p. 105; M. I. Kalinin, *On Communist Education*, p. 469; Turner, *Challenge to Karl Marx*, New York: Reynal and Hitchcock, 1941, p. 179.

[25] *U.S. News and World Report*, Jan. 6, 1956, p. 97. Some informed communists, who had been imprisoned, told John Noble that they thought that in the Party in Russia only about 500,000 were *fanatical* believers. Personal interview, March 1959.

To the extent the communist believes his philosophy to that extent we must take his philosophy seriously in any effort to understand the communist. The author is convinced that regardless of the possible attitude of some of the Soviet leaders, most communists believe in varying degrees their philosophy and that an understanding of the communist philosophy of life is necessary to an understanding of what the communists have done, are doing and plan to do. A common human tendency is to judge others by one's self. This is true with reference to one's weak points as well as with reference to one's strong points. Because certain actions of the communist do not seem reasonable, some people have refused to accept as true the reports of things which the communists have done, are doing, or plan to do. However, when viewed in the light of their philosophical outlook, that which would not be rational for us is seen to be a logical conclusion from their fundamental assumptions about history and life.

THE COMMUNIST MIND

To understand how the communist views us, we must understand his philosophy. And it is important for us to understand not only how he views himself but also how he regards us.

When we, in the non-communist world, view the communist in the light of our own philosophy of life we become psychologically disarmed. But the communist in viewing us in the light of his philosophy of life arms himself psychologically and physically.

Martin Dies maintained that "It is impossible to understand the tactics and statements of communists and their fellow travelers unless their very special code of ethics be kept constantly in mind."[26] And Benjamin Gitlow, one of the founders of the Communist Party in America who later left them and has worked against them, observed that "Getting the American communists to reject the ethical concepts of civilization constituted the central point in the campaign for the bolshevization of the American communists."[27]

Since their moral code cannot be understood unless their

---

[26] *The Trojan Horse in America*, p. 240.
[27] *The Whole of Their Lives*, New York: Charles Scribner's Sons, 1948, p. 81.

philosophy is understood, it is important to understand their philosophy. For example, it would be disastrous for leaders of the non-communist world to think that they can sit down at the conference table and talk with the leaders of the communist world as if these leaders were reasonable men who hold to our basic philosophy of life. To judge them by ourselves and our ideals and goals is to make them into our own image, when in reality they are not. "The Communist mind has so defined its world that it shares neither truth nor logic nor morality with the rest of mankind."[28]

When dealing with a communist one is dealing with an individual who regards himself as involved in a war to death with the non-communist. His actions whether in peace or in war, are but a part of his total war against civilization.[29] He does not come to the conference table to work out a just arrangement but rather to use the conference table as a means of furthering the destruction of his enemies. Furthermore, he does not regard himself as bound by the moral code of his opponent. Instead he is an agent of history who is authorized to use any means to destroy his opposition!

The communist judges others by himself. Therefore, when dealing with the non-communist he does not attribute to his opponent good will and a desire for the advancement of civilization. Instead he views the non-communist as an individual who is also but maneuvering for position at the conference table, and elsewhere. He views his opponent as an exponent of a class viewpoint whose very ideals and arguments are but a rationalization of his class interests and an effort to perpetuate and to extend these interests at the expense of other classes.

It is for such reasons as the above that Niemeyer concluded that only "to the degree that Westerners make themselves students of Marxist-Leninist dogma and develop a flair for dialectic can they be at all confident that they understand Soviet policies."[30] A very practical conclusion which Niemeyer draws is that "Above all, in this period of 'soft' Kremlin policy, we are tempted to fall into the error of believing that when Communists appear to be doing the same as other people, it actually *is* the

---

[28] Gerhart Niemeyer, *An Inquiry into Soviet Mentality*, New York: Frederick A. Praeger, 1956, p. 70.

[29] House Committee on Un-American Activities, *Soviet Total War*, Washington, D. C.: Government Printing Office, 1956, 2 Vols.

[30] *op. cit.*, p. 71.

same thing. The truth is that when Communists appear to be doing the same things as other people (in art, education, science, etc.), they are mostly doing just the opposite—actually pursuing their own destructive objectives through seemingly non-political means. When engaged in apparent cooperation with others, they are actually fighting the struggle which to them is 'the law of laws.' "[31]

THEORY AS GUIDE TO ACTION

The importance of an understanding of their philosophy is underscored by their continual emphasis on the idea that *theory must be a guide to action*. Marx insisted that they were not interested simply in interpreting the world, but in changing it.[32] This is echoed by Mao Tse-tung's statement that "what Marxist philosophy considers most important is not understanding the laws of the external world and thereby explaining it, but actively changing the world by applying the knowledge of objective laws."[33]

Since, however, circumstances differ, the communists believe that at different periods different aspects of Marxism-Leninism must be emphasized. Thus Khrushchev recently called for a re-emphasis on certain aspects of their philosophy. They must "return to and actually practice in all our ideological work, the most important theses of Marxist-Leninist science about the people as the creator of history and as the creator of all material and spiritual good of humanity, about the decisive role of the Marxist party in the revolutionary fight for the transformation of society, about the victory of communism."[34]

Such considerations as these lead the author to accept the conclusion that if "the philosophy of communism had been

---

[31] House Committee on Un-American Activities, *The Irrationality of Communism*, Washington, D.C.: Government Printing Office, 1958, p. 16. This is the Aug. 8, 1958 consultation with Dr. Gerhart Niemeyer.

[32] *Selected Works*, Moscow: Co-operative Publishing Society, 1935, Vol. I, p. 473.

[33] Mao Tse-Tung, *On Practice*, New York: International Publishers, p. 11. See also Earl Browder, *Theory As a Guide to Action*, New York: Workers Library Publications, Inc., Jan. 1939.

[34] Khrushchev, *Congressional Record*, June 4, 1956, p. 8478, from his speech on Stalin at the 20th Congress, Feb. 25, 1956. The authenticity of his speech is admitted by the communists. *National Guardian*, June 18, 1956, p. 4.

seriously examined, we might have avoided many well-meant but disastrous moves. Too many Americans felt that communism was undoubtedly 'foreign' and perhaps even on the screwball side, but were not yet sufficiently oriented to the ideological age to believe that the future of the world might actually be dependent on the abstruse dialectics found in dull, barely readable Marxist tomes."[35] To illustrate this, consider a recent statement by Khrushchev which contained a threat to the West and a statement of his confidence in the triumph of communism. At a party in Moscow on Nov. 18, 1956, he told an audience, which included some Western diplomats, that "Whether you like it or not, history is on our side. We will bury you!"[36]

What did Khrushchev mean? His faith in dialectical materialism throws a flood of light on this assertion. The dialectic teaches that the thesis (capitalism) creates the antithesis (the proletariat under the leadership of the Communist Party) which becomes the grave-digger of the thesis. This is the way history must work and will work. On this seemingly abstract philosophical idea, the concept of the dialectic, rests Khrushchev's absolute confidence that they will bury us.

Let us now analyze and examine the philosophy of communism. First of all, let us consider its atheism.

---

[35] "The Idea of Communism," *The Commonweal*, Aug. 6, 1954, p. 427. Quoted in the *Congressional Record*, Aug. 14, 1954, p. 13768.

[36] AP Dispatch, *Arkansas Gazette*, Nov. 19, 1956, p. 1. See also *U.S. News and World Report*, Dec. 27, 1957, p. 32.

CHAPTER THREE

Atheism Versus Theism

"I was asked something about the economic problem of Communism. I answered, citing Dostoevsky: 'The problem of Communism is not an economic problem. The problem of Communism is the problem of atheism!' "[1]

Man, as a being who knows, is aware of his own existence and of the existence of the universe. He seeks for an answer concerning his origin and that of the universe. The possible answers are not many. There are but two possibilities: It is either God or matter. There is no other alternative explanation. The agnostic's position is not an alternative explanation. It is but a denial that there is sufficient evidence on which to decide between these two alternatives.

THE ATHEISM OF COMMUNISM

The communist's position concerning origins is atheistic. He denies the existence of God and affirms instead the eternal existence of matter. He maintains that it is reasonable to believe that matter created life and that life's manifold forms, including man, have evolved without the operation of any force or forces beyond those which we see working in matter today.

Karl Marx was an atheist before he developed the philosophy of communism.[2] In 1841 in the preface to his doctor's dissertation on *The Difference between the Democritean and Epicurean Philosophies of Nature*, he cited "Hume and two biting Texts from the *Prometheus Bound* of Aeschylus, his life-long favorite:

'In simple words, I hate the pack of gods.'
Be sure of this, I would not change my

---

[1] *Witness Whittaker Chambers*, New York: Random House, 1952, pp. 711-712.

[2] Otto Rühle, *Karl Marx*, New York: The Viking Press, 1928, pp. 26-33. John Spargo, *Karl Marx*, pp. 54-57. Franz Mehring, *Karl Marx*, New York: Humanities Press, Inc., pp. 43-59.

> State of evil fortune for your servitude.
> Better to be the servant of this rock
> Than to be faithful boy to Father Zeus."[3]

Marx made atheism such an essential part of Marxism that it "cannot be conceived without atheism."[4] In 1948 the Ten Commandments of communism were published for the Young Communist League. The league was told: "If you are not a convinced atheist, you cannot be a good Communist or a real Soviet citizen. Atheism is indissolubly bound to Communism. These two ideals are the pillars of the Soviet power."[5] Chou En-lai said at the Bandung Conference in April 1955: "We Communists are atheists. . . ."[6] The *Great Soviet Encyclopedia* contends that "atheism is the ideological weapon which enabled the 'progressive social classes' to put an end to the social, economic and political conditions which had 'hindered the evolution of productive powers, science and culture.' "[7]

One must not conclude, however, that atheism has always been placed openly in the foreground,[8] or that atheism has been a formal requirement for Party membership. William Z. Foster, the national chairman of the Communist Party in America, testified before the Fish Committee that atheism "is not laid down as a formal requirement for membership." But, Foster added, "a worker who will join the Communist Party, who understands the elementary principles of the Communist Party, must necessarily be in the process of liquidating his religious beliefs and, if he still has any lingerings when he joins the Party, he will soon get rid of them."[9] When they are in power, so says the Party: "It is

---

[3] Henry F. Mins, "Marx's Doctoral Dissertation," *Science and Society*, Winter 1948, p. 167.

[4] Introduction to Lenin, *Religion*, New York: International Publishers, p. 6.

[5] Quoted in Pedro Vazquez Lopez, *et. al.*, *A Christian's Handbook on Communism*, Revised Edition, New York: National Council of Churches, Apr. 1955, p. 31. A report from East Germany on Jan. 10, 1955, included a reference to the spreading of atheism as a part of the Party's Program. It was to be made the basis of public education.

[6] *The Christian Century*, May 11, 1955, p. 573.

[7] *Ibid.*, Jan. 18, 1956, p. 85.

[8] Lenin, *Religion*, p. 10.

[9] Quoted in *Investigation of Un-American Activities and Propaganda*, House Resolution 282, Union Calendar No. 2, House Report No. 2, 1939, p. 18. See also Stalin, "Interview with American Labor Delegation," *Leninism*, Moscow: Co-operative Publishing Society of Foreign Workers in the U.S.S.R., 1934, Vol. I, pp. 386-387.

not to be tolerated that even the smallest manifestation of religiousness should be observed among Communists."[10]

God, to the communist, is the symbol of man's self-abnegation. God is also a reflection of man's enslavement to the economic system. Faith in God is therefore viewed as incompatible
with the emancipation of humanity. Thus, the communists believe that the annihilation of religious consciousness is essential
to man's complete mastery of the world. "On the basis of the
inherent atheism of earthly self-reliance, Marx undertook his
radical criticism of the existing order with the purpose of
changing it."[11]

This idea was first advanced in Marx's essay on "The Jewish
Question." As summarized by Rühle: "Man is for man the
highest being, and as such—as individual and as a member of
the species rolled into one—has to mount the throne of human
history.

"The gods have been dethroned. Their existence has been
shown to be the outcome of men's attempts to find compensation
for their own defects and weaknesses. Ideas are but reflexions
of the soul's anxiety."

"Mankind will only be able to pursue its emancipatory ascent
successfully, when it becomes competent to make every individual willing and able to bring his subjective scheme of life into
harmony with the objective evolutionary scheme of society—
when the private individual is wholly merged in the member
of the species.

"Only the objectively socialized and subjectively communalized human being will be able to effect the emancipation of
mankind, thus becoming master of his own fate."[12]

This is an expression of the ancient desire of man to be the
sole architect of his own fate, the undisputed master of his own
life. The communist leader, however, does not explain that instead of submitting to God man must submit to the Gospel According to Karl Marx, surrender his individuality, become a

---

[10] Zarya Vostoka, *Dawn of the East*, Jan. 27-28, 1949. Quoted in *Notes:
Soviet Affairs*, March 28, 1956, p. 3.

[11] Karl Lowith, *Meaning in History*, Chicago: University of Chicago
Press, p. 47. See Chang Meng-Chen, "Freedom of Religious Belief in
China," *Peking Review*, July 21, 1959, p. 6.

[12] Otto Rühle, *Karl Marx: His Life and Works*, pp. 66-67. See the
"Jewish Question" in *Karl Marx, Selected Essays*, New York: International
Publishers, 1926. It is not in later editions. The concept of freedom in the
above quotation is identical with the Nazi concept of freedom.

communalized member of the beehive and let the Communist Party become the master of his fate!

Of course, not all atheists are communists, but all indoctrinated communists are atheists, interested in the spread of atheism,[13] since only when people's hearts have been voided of faith in God is it possible to instill faith in Marxism. As before pointed out, Karl Marx was an atheist before he developed and accepted the communist philosophy of life. In his teens William Z. Foster said that his religious faith was shattered, and "all I needed for a completely materialist outlook on life were the works of Marx and Engels, which I was to read some years later."[14] Some ex-communists, who have told of their conversion to communism, have testified that atheism prepared the way for their acceptance of communism. Charles David Blodgett told the House Un-American Activities Committee: "If young people don't have a firm foundation in God and church, they are Communist material. Once I didn't believe in God. I was an atheist . . . and the Communists got me, the way they get people who don't believe . . . who don't have faith."[15]

Since atheism is so essential to communism, Whittaker Chambers believed that the "crisis of the Western world exists to the degree in which it is indifferent to God."[16]

THE BELIEFS OF ATHEISM

The communist endeavors to discredit faith in God by insisting that in our scientific age we must walk by sight. This overlooks the fact that atheism involves faith. To deny the existence of God is not to be left without any beliefs. A system of denials often implies a system of affirmations. He who denies the existence of God is affirming that matter created our present world order and all life—including man and all his beliefs, both theistic and atheistic.

Atheism involves a number of articles of faith. These articles of faith are not only without adequate evidence but some of

---

[13] Lenin, *Religion*, p. 10.

[14] *The Twilight of World Capitalism*, New York: International Publishers, p. 158.

[15] Quoted in the *National Republic*, Jan. 1954, p. 27. This is similar to the testimony of Elizabeth Bentley, Professor Louis Budenz and Mrs. Budenz. Personal interviews.

[16] *Witness Whittaker Chambers*, p. 17. Notice that he said indifferent, and not just atheistic.

them are contrary to the available evidence. What does the communist have to believe in order to be an atheist?

(1) The Communist believes that *God does not exist*. To be sure, he cannot prove it. To *know* that God does not exist one would have to know everything and to be everywhere, for the thing which he did not know might prove God's existence. And the place where he was not might contain evidence of God's existence. He would have to know all the causes which have ever operated, for the one cause he did not know might be God. The person who possessed such characteristics would be a God himself! The atheist cannot reverse this argument and say that one must know all in order to have sufficient reason to believe in God. Several lines of evidence show that it is rational to accept God and irrational to reject God. We need to know at least some of the evidence, but we do not need to know everything.

Atheists sometimes find their own creed difficult to believe. Thus there are times when some communists are faced with doubts concerning their atheism. Some of them, after they have abandoned communism and atheism, have told us of these doubts.

(2) In fact, the communist finds atheism and materialism so hard to believe that he *has created his own god* and called it dialectical materialism. He regards Diamat[17] as controlling history and directing the course of history to a predetermined and certain end. To Diamat he offers his service. Diamat will finally bring the leap from the world of necessity into the communist world of freedom. This god works incessantly and inevitably for freedom. There is a power, then, which works for the triumph of truth, justice and good will. The communist has taken matter and idealized it into a Creator who is *benevolent* and *irresistible*. He believes that there is a force or power at work in human history which is irresistibly working for the emancipation of humanity. The ideal society of communism, where each will work for the greatest advancement of others, will come because Diamat cannot be defeated. Diamat works for the advancement of man stage by stage in dialectical progress until the state of peace and plenty has been reached.

However, Diamat is an idol, a creation of man. As Reinhold

---

[17] A contraction of Dialectical Materialism. Since, as applied to human history, it is called historical materialism, this god may also be called Hismat.

Niebuhr said of communism, "Its ostensible atheism is less significant than its idolatry. It worships a god who is the unqualified ally of one group in human society against all others."[18]

(3) The Communist scoffs at the idea of the Eternal God but he must believe in *the eternal existence of matter*. Something has always existed for something now exists. If in the beginning there was nothing, there would not be anything now since out of nothing comes nothing. Therefore, everyone must accept the fact that something has always existed. The only issue is whether it is reasonable to believe that God (Spirit) created matter, life, and mind; or whether matter created mind, consciousness, and intelligence.

(4) The communists must believe in *the spontaneous generation of life from non-life*. Scientists agree that this earth could not always have supported life. Therefore life has not forever existed on this earth. But life is now here. If atheism is true, life must have come into existence by a natural process. And yet, the scientific study of nature has shown that life comes from life. The creation of life, by the non-living and from the non-living, would be a greater miracle than a creation by a living Creator. The communist believes in a Creator, but he accepts the idea of a dead Creator, matter, instead of the living Creator—God.

Communists live in the hope that scientists will some day create life. Even if this were done, it would not prove that the non-living created life in the remote past. All that it would prove is that an intelligent being, in this case man, can create life.

(5) The communist must believe that the *order found in nature and in man is the result of chance or of something labeled fate or law*, which is non-intelligent and non-conscious. Atheists usually concede that there is at least "apparent design" and order in nature. The atheist must attribute it to a cause which is less than intelligent. This is extremely difficult to believe when an individual really faces the issue; so the communists crowd it out of their minds. Whittaker Chambers has pointed out that the

---

[18] *Faith and History*, New York: Charles Scribner's Sons, 1949, p. 211. See also his, *The Irony of American History*, New York: Charles Scribners Sons, p. 173. Charles Lowry called communism "a new religion" in *Communism and Christ*. See also House Committee on Un-American Activities, *The Ideology of Freedom vs. The Ideology of Communism*, Washington, D. C.: Government Printing Office, 1958. Consultation with Charles Wesley Lowry, p. 9. Also his letter in the *New Leader*, Oct. 22, 1956, p. 30. Martin D'Arcy viewed it as a "faith," *Communism and Christianity*, Penguin Books, 1956.

first crack in his communist armor came when, as he was look-ing at his little daughter in her high chair, he thought of her "intricate, perfect ears." "The thought passed through my mind: 'No, those ears were not created by any chance coming together of atoms in nature [the communist view]. They would have been created only by immense design.'" He crowded the thought out of his mind, although he never completely forgot it, for if he had completed the thought he would have concluded: "Design pre-supposes God."[19]

(6) The communist must believe that *consciousness arose out of a peculiar combination of non-conscious matter.* The creator of consciousness was non-conscious.

(7) The communist must believe that *man is a matter-machine without any power of choice,* and thus *without any real respon-sibility* for his conduct. How could matter, regardless of how refined it might be, decide between alternatives and be respon-sible for that decision? This doctrine of non-responsibility is further implied in the communist doctrines of economic deter-minism, class and ideology. The verdict we pass on morons, that they are not responsible, is passed by the communist on all mankind, including themselves. And yet, they write and act as if men have some responsibility, and thus accountability, for their conduct.

(8) The communist must believe that *non-moral matter created man with a moral sensitivity*—a sense of obligation or duty.

(9) The communist must believe that *mind and the power of rational thought were created* by the non-rational, *by that which is mindless.*

(10) The atheist must believe, in order to be consistent, that *all thought is irrational,* for it is all assumed to be *the inevitable by-product of irrational causes.* According to atheism, mental processes are wholly determined by the physical movement of atoms in the brain. As Woolsey Teller, a non-communist atheist, put it: Thought is "a form of vibration and sensation in the nerve fibers of the brain and of the nervous system . . . thought is matter in motion."[20] Marx said that matter thinks. This move-ment of matter is physically determined; there is nothing rational about it because physical forces cannot make rational decisions

---

[19] *Witness Whittaker Chambers,* p. 16.
[20] *The Atheism of Astronomy,* pp. 10-11.

between alternatives. One thinks the way that he does because matter makes matter move in a certain way in his brain. The self-styled "freethinker" is not really a free thinker, for all is determined, and nothing is free. There is, therefore, nothing rational about the arguments of the atheist against the believing in God. They are just the result of the inevitable vibrations of his brain! How strange it is that those who claim the name "rationalist" and maintain that theists are not rational, should end up with a position which implies that all thought is irrational.[21] To say "I think" no more implies rationality than to say "I itch." Both terms, according to materialism, describe physical sensations, since only the physical exists.

If this is the whole story about reasoning and thought, there is no way of knowing whether our thoughts actually represent reality. We cannot know whether or not they are true. Thus the communists could never know that Marxism is true, since Marxism is a system of thought arrived at by physical vibrations caused by internal and external material pressures. This is disastrous to their philosophy for, as Bradley put it, "no theory can be true which is inconsistent with the possibility of our knowing it to be true."[22]

(11) In order to be consistent the communists must believe that *their own philosophy is but the reflection of an irrational world.* For they maintain with Marx that the process of thinking is "nothing else than the material world reflected by the human mind, and translated into forms of thought."[23] In the "material world" Marx included the economic system as a basic element. This economic system he regarded as irrational since it supposedly had socialization of production without socialization of ownership. If the economic system is decisive[24] in shaping man's

---

[21] C. S. Lewis, *Miracles: A Preliminary Inquiry*, chapters on "Naturalism."

[22] As quoted in James B. Pratt, *Matter and Spirit*, p. 21.

[23] *Capital*, New York: Modern Library, p. 25.

[24] *Ibid.*, pp. 12-15. "But don't wrangle with us so long as you apply, to our intended abolition of bourgeois property, the standard of your bourgeois notions of freedom, culture, law, etc. Your very ideas are but the outgrowth of the conditions of your bourgeois production and bourgeois property, just as your jurisprudence is but the will of your class made into a law for all, a will, whose essential character and direction are determined by the economical conditions of existence of your class" (House Committee on Un-American Activities, *The Communist Conspiracy*, Part I, Section A, p. 60). The quotation is from their reprint of the *Communist Manifesto*. This quotation is on pages 78-79 of *Manifesto of the Communist Party*, 1957.

thinking, it follows that the forms of thought, which are but the reflection and translation of an irrational economic world, are irrational forms of thought. This means that Marx's own philosophy which includes the dialectic, atheistic, economic determinism and his vision of future communism are all an irrational reflection of an irrational world. For, according to his position, he lived in an irrational society. The communist position is therefore so contradictory that he must deny his basic position concerning thought in order to maintain that his own thoughts, his own condemnation of the existing order and his own justification of the coming order, are true. *Reality is such that when man sets out to deny God, man ends up accepting concepts which deny man's own rationality.* His own logic demands that he deny that his own arguments are rational.

The communist cannot reply that his thoughts, in contrast with the capitalistic thoughts, are not a reflection of the irrational world, but a reflection of the better world to come, i.e. the future world of communism. *For how can his thoughts,* which are but a reflection of the material world which surrounds him, *transcend this material world and reflect a world which does not yet exist?* Since the communist world order is not in existence, it could not be reflected in anyone's mind today, nor could it have been reflected in Karl Marx's mind in his day.

It must also be kept in mind that the thoughts of Marx and of Engels could not have been created by the class interests of the working class for they were brought up in a capitalistic environment. Engel's father was a wealthy industrialist. Karl Marx did not earn his living with the toiling masses of the world. He was a writer who usually was supported by others, chiefly by Engels. How, then, could their minds have reflected a system of thought contrary to the interest of their class!

So the communist is faced with a dilemma. If he maintains that Marx and Engels, and others, could have forms of thought which were not the reflection of the material world, he has denied the Marxist interpretation of thought. If he maintains that their interpretation of thought is correct, he is forced to deny the validity of their own philosophy and the arguments which are used to support it. For he has no grounds on which to maintain that his thinking is exempt from his characterization of the nature of thought itself.

(12) The communist also believes that *he and the Party are the agents which have been ordained* by Diamat *to be the bearers of the great hope of mankind.* The communists are the tools

of history, and their toil and sacrifices will help usher in the glorious age!

(13) Communists believe that *the Party is the official spokesman for Diamat,* and that its voice is the voice of "truth," the "truth" for the times.

These, then, are some of the articles of faith in the creed of the atheistic communists. It is amazing what they believe while they refuse to believe in God. It is strange how those who hold to such articles of faith can accuse the theists of being credulous.[25]

It is as unreasonable to believe in Marxism as it is to believe in atheism, for the communists agree that "Marxism cannot be conceived without atheism."[26]

The communist cannot deny that faith in God exists. How, then, do communists account for the origin of the idea of God?

ORIGIN OF THE IDEA OF GOD AND RELIGION

In writing on the question of the origin of faith in God, Engels took the position, common to his day, that it resulted from fallacious reasoning on natural phenomena. Said he, "the first gods arose through the personification of natural forces . . . out of the many more or less limited and mutually limiting gods there arose in the minds of men the idea of the one exclusive god of the monotheistic religions."[27] This concept of the origin of religion is still held by communists.[28]

It may even be said that Engels did not think that fallacious *reasoning* led man to believe in the supernatural, but that belief in God was simply a reflection in the mind of men. "All religion, however, is nothing but the fantastic reflection in men's minds of those external forces which control their daily life, a

---

[25] For a further discussion of atheism and of some of its fruits see James D. Bales, *Atheism's Faith and Fruits,* Boston, Mass.: W. A. Wilde Company, 1951.

[26] Introduction to Lenin, *Religion,* p. 6.

[27] *Ludwig Feuerbach,* New York: International Publishers, 1941, p. 20. Pages 30-31 in the earlier edition. This is the book concerning which Engels said: "About religion I have said the most necessary things in the last section of Feuerbach" (*Selected Correspondence,* New York: International Publishers, 1936, p. 484).

[28] Marcel Cachin, *Science and Religion,* New York: International Publishers, 1946, p. 18. Chang Meng-Chen, "Freedom of Religious Belief in China," *Peking Review,* July 21, 1959, p. 6.

reflection in which the terrestrial forces assume the form of supernatural forces. In the beginning of history it was the forces of nature which were at first so reflected."[29]

If this is the correct explanation of the origin of religion, its origin can not be explained by the economic system. Therefore, the economic interpretation of history can not account for religion which has been one of the most powerful forces in history. To this Engels agreed: "It would surely be pedantic to try and find economic causes for all this primitive nonsense."[30] It was not until after religion had arisen as a reflection of natural forces in men's mind, that "side by side with the forces of Nature, social forces begin to be active; forces which present themselves to man as equally extraneous and at first equally inexplicable, dominating them with the same apparent necessity as the forces of Nature themselves."[31]

This assumes, of course, that man could not really reason, but was just a dumb brute who had no understanding of nature or of his economic system. One can assume this if he so desires, but a mere assumption is a long way from proof.

After religion arose, so the communist believes, it changed with the changing economic systems since it is supposed to reflect the economic system.

This does not fit in with the facts. There was, for example, no economic revolution preceding the appearance of Christianity. Furthermore, the evidence shows that "the same form of production is associated with different types of religion, the same type of religion is associated with different forms of production, and that a change in religion can occur without benefit of an antecedent change in the productive order."[32]

Engels believed that religion originated as the result of two related concepts: (1) the doctrine of *uniformity* which demanded that everything must have a natural explanation, and (2) the doctrine of *evolution* which included the natural explanation and also maintained that the lowest form of religion came first, and the highest form last. Therefore, since the origin of the idea of God *had* to be explained naturally, the grossest forms

---

[29] *Herr Eugen Dühring's Revolution in Science (Anti-Dühring)*, New York: International Publishers, n.d., p. 353. Printed in the USSR.

[30] Dona Torr, Translater, *Marx-Engels Selected Correspondence*, p. 482.

[31] *Anti-Dühring*, pp. 353-354.

[32] M. M. Bober, *Karl Marx's Interpretation of History*, Cambridge: Harvard University Press, 1948, pp. 355-356.

of religion must have come first, and the highest form, faith in one God, must have come last. Having assumed these things, an individual can find all manner of religious beliefs which he can arbitrarily arrange in an evolutionary order, beginning with the lowest form and proceeding to the highest form. One can assign a belief to a late or to an early period according to where he thinks that it should fit in the evolutionary framework. But it would be just as simple to take the highest form and place it first and arrange the others in descending order, as it is to arrange them in an ascending order. And, unless one is willing to go by the evidence, one is as justified in doing the one arbitrarily as he is the other. The question is: *Which order is favored by the evidence.*[33]

In a study of the origin and history of religion one must distinguish between a possible psychological explanation as to how an idea may have arisen, and the historical evidence as to the actual origin and history of the idea.[34]

Some have claimed that the animism which exists among some "primitive" people today is the oldest form of religion. But a belief in a Supreme Being is found among animists.[35] Warneck said: "how could these religions, which represent the initial state of development, derive any nourishment in that initial stage from the idea of a Supreme God, who should be the last member of a long series of acquisitions, laboriously won? Why does the Indonesian, when in great distress, flee to God, of whom, according to that hypothesis, he should have no knowledge whatever? How is it that, in taking an oath, the Animist

---

[33] After speaking of the nature-mythologist view of the origin and history of religion, the anthropologist Schmidt, said: "All the other theories, however, came into being after the outbreak of Materialism and Darwinism, and their work was all done on the lines of Evolutionist natural science. This puts all that is low and simple at the beginning, all that is higher and of worth being regarded only as the product of a longer or shorter process of development. This they found easier to do, because the principal objects of their study were savages who had not yet made the acquaintance of any sort of writing on which to date the monuments of their culture. Hence the question of earlier and later, of the chronological sequence of religions and forms of religion, which must be settled before the causal interaction of the facts can be exactly determined, could be answered only by help of the Evolutionist method, which is really no method at all, as we shall see later" (Wilhelm Schmidt, *Origin and Growth of Religion*, pp. 13-14).

[34] *Ibid.*, p. 5.

[35] For example, the Miao tribe in Northern Thailand.

appeals to God? That is forestalling his development indeed. It is a fact that he has the idea of God: but the fact that this idea is but dimly apprehended proves that we are not dealing with a new idea, victoriously opening up new paths. . . . The Animism of today gives us the impression of a religion that carries the marks of a fall, of a worship no longer understood, and become an empty ceremony."[36]

According to the Apostle Paul devolution, not spontaneous evolution, has marked the religious history of mankind whenever men turned from a knowledge of the Creator. Sir William M. Ramsay, an archaeologist who started out as a devotee of the hypothesis of evolution in religion, asked: "Who is right, Paul or the moderns? For my own part, I confess that my experience and reading show nothing to confirm the modern assumptions in religious history, and a great deal to confirm Paul. Wherever evidence exists, with the rarest exceptions, the history of religion among men is a history of degeneration; and the development of a few Western nations in invention and in civilization during recent centuries should not blind us to the fact that among the vast majority of the nations the history of manners and civilization is a story of degeneration."[37]

The tendency in a religion is not toward automatic purification and refinement from within, but in the direction of falling from a higher standard to a lower. The history of Israel, as set forth in the Old Testament, embraces numerous apostasies.

Most critics of Christianity will at least acknowledge that Christianity in its purest form existed in the beginning of Christianity. Much of the criticism of the faults found in Christianity is in reality criticism of departures from Christianity. The simplicity of the worship and life of the early Christians became corrupted as time went on. In the case of Christianity the highest and purest form came first, not last.

"The very fact that all other nations (besides the Jews) have travelled along a line leading to polytheism, and that all have failed to get beyond it, constitutes a presumption that monotheism is not to be reached by the route that leads to polytheism. If it is possible to reach monotheism via polytheism, it is at

---

[36] J. Warneck, *The Living Forces of the Gospel.* London: Oliphant, Anderson and Ferrier, 1909, p. 99. Quoted by J. N. D. Anderson, *The World's Religions*, London: The Inter-Varsity Fellowship, 1950, p. 23.

[37] *The Cities of St. Paul*, Grand Rapids, Michigan: Baker Book House, 1949, p. 17. See also Romans, Chapter 1.

least a remarkable fact that of all the peoples of the world, no single one is known to have done so."[38]

Where is the example of a people spontaneously, without an influence from outside of their culture, laying aside polytheism for monotheism?[39]

When men are not hypnotized by the hypothesis of evolution, which demands that the historical facts be arranged in such a way as to fit the hypothesis, they realize that the further back into any culture they go the fewer gods that culture has. In his *The Religion of Ancient Egypt*, William W. F. Petrie wrote: "What we actually find is the contrary of this, monotheism is the first state traceable in theology. . . . Wherever we can trace back polytheism to its earliest stages we find that it results from combinations of monotheism. In Egypt even Osiris, Isis, and Horus (so familiar as a triad) are found at first as separate units in different places. . . ."[40] Professor Stephen Langdon set forth the evidence from the sources which convinced him that in the Semitic and Sumerian religion "monotheism preceded polytheism and belief in good and evil spirits."[41]

Modern research has been such that a recent Gifford Lecturer can speak of the utter demolition of "the simple evolutionary theory of Comte and Tylor." With but a few exceptions, the evidences show that "the most primitive levels of human life which we can reach by the soundest ethnological methods reveal a belief in one supreme deity or High God. . . ."[42]

After examination of some of the evidence, J. R. Swanton, then of the Bureau of American Ethnology of the Smithsonian Institution, wrote: "My conclusions . . . are, in brief, (a) that the deduction of religious concepts or emotions from natural phenomena, however closely it may be found associated, is unproved and improbable; (b) that the history of religion has probably consisted in the differentiation of various elements

---

[38] Frank Byron Jevons, *An Introduction to the History of Religion*, London: Metheun and Company, 1902, p. 388.

[39] Sir William Dawson, *Modern Science in Bible Lands*, pp. 31-32.

[40] *The Religion of Ancient Egypt*, London: Archibald Constable and Company, Ltd., 1906, pp. 3-4.

[41] *Semitic Mythology*, Boston: Marshall Jones Company, 1931, pp. xviii, 91, 93. See also his article on "Monotheism as the Predecessor of Polytheism in Sumerian Religion," reprinted in Sir Charles Marston, *The Bible Comes Alive*, pp. 295 ff.

[42] Herbert H. Farmer, *Revelation and Religion*, New York: Harper and Brothers, 1954, p. 106.

from an original complex and the varying stress placed upon
these elements rather than the successive introduction of new
elements."[43]

Let us now consider some of the reasons for faith in the existence of the Supreme Being.

IS FAITH IN GOD REASONABLE?

It is realized, of course, that God's existence cannot be proved
as one can prove a proposition in mathematics. However, one
cannot prove mathematically the reality of ideas. And surely
the communists have never mathematically established the truth
of communism.

The existence of God cannot be demonstrated as can a truth
in the realm of physical science. One cannot go into the laboratory, perform an experiment, and prove God's existence; but the
same is true of many facts of reality. What laboratory experiment can prove a fact of history? How could one demonstrate,
either mathematically, or scientifically by an experiment, the
fact that Marx once lived? Or that he wrote the book called
Capital? The communists have not attempted to give us a
laboratory demonstration of the truth or historical materialism,
nor has it been scientifically established that communism will
ultimately be achieved. The truth of falsity of these things must
be established by some other method of approach than by the
mathematical or laboratory approach.

The fact that we cannot pick up ideas with forceps is not an

---

[43] "Three Factors in Primitive Religion," *American Anthropologist*, Vol.
XXVI, p. 365. Quoted in Charles J. McFadden, *The Philosophy of Communism*, New York: Benziger Bros., Inc., 1939, p. 278. For additional
material see Andrew Lang, *The Making of Religion*, New York: Long-
mans, Green and Company, 1898. Wilhelm Schmidt, *High Gods in North
America.* Samuel M. Zwemer, "The Origin of Religion By Evolution or by
Revelation," *Transactions of the Victoria Institute*, 1935. Also his book on
The Origin of Religion, Nashville, Tennessee: Cokesbury Press, 1935. Pro-
fessor Fairbairn, *Studies in the Philosophy of Religion*, p. 22. James Orr,
The Problem of the Old Testament, p. 496. P. Schebesta, *Revisiting My
Pygmy Hosts*, London, 1933. R. P. Trilles, *Les Pygmees de la foret Equa-
toriale*, Paris, 1932. M. Vanoverbergh, "Negritos of Northern Luzon,"
Anthropos, Vol. XX, 1925, p. 436; Vol. XXV, 1930, pp. 550-551. Wilhelm
Schmidt, *Der Ursprung der Gottesidee*, Munster, 6 Vols., 1925-1935. G.
Murdock, *Our Primitive Contemporaries*, 1934, pp. 103, 185-256, 269. R.
Lowie, *Primitive Religion*, 1924. W. F. Albright, *The Archaeology of
Palestine*, p. 19.

argument against their reality or power. The fact that God cannot be placed under a microscope or seen through a telescope might be an argument against His materiality, but not against the reality of His existence as Spirit.

Faith is involved, but in light of the evidence, which we shall briefly outline, are we not justified in believing in God? The reader, of course, must make his own decision. We do not live in a mechanical or completely material world; therefore decisions cannot be forced on a person.

If God exists, Marxism is false, for then "a spiritual and not only an economic power" exists.[44] The ancient warrior wished that all his enemies had but one neck, since with one blow all of them could be dispatched. Communism is such an enemy. Once atheism, the neck of communism, is severed, communism as we know it today, expires. To this agree the communists—that without atheism there is no genuine Marxism.

We are faced with the existence of mind and of matter. Is it reasonable to explain all in terms of matter? Man, with his marvelous characteristics, is surely a better key to ultimate reality than is an atom. Why explain the highest (man) simply in terms of the lowest (matter)?

As has been stated, there are only two alternatives—either God or matter is the creator. Agnosticism is not an alternative explanation, but rather a denial that man can decide between the alternatives. Agnosticism would be defensible only if the atheistic explanation were as reasonable as the theistic explanation. But it has been shown that to accept atheism one must accept articles of faith, some of which are without evidence and some of which are contrary to evidence. On the other hand, a reasonable case can be made for theism.

FAITH IN GOD IS NATURAL

Faith in some Supreme Being is natural to man. This is shown by several lines of evidence.

First, faith in some Supreme Being or a supernatural being is universal both geographically and historically.[45]

---

[44] Berdyaev as quoted in Matthew Spinka, *Nicholas Berdyaev: Captive of Freedom*, Philadelphia: The Westminster Press, 1950, p. 18.

[45] J. N. D. Anderson, *The World's Religions*, Grand Rapids: William B. Eerdmans; Wilhelm Schmidt, *The Origin and Growth of Religion*; S. M. Zwemer, *The Origin of Religion*.

Second, it is natural for children to believe in God; as seen even in some cases in which there has been an effort to rear children without faith in God. Piaget and Clavier, as a result of their studies of children, concluded that the child inherently gives the facts of the world a theistic interpretation. When given a chance the child will naturally and almost inevitably arrive at a conception of God. Selbie in his *Psychology of Religion*, James Pratt, Jung and others have also set forth evidence which in one way or another helps sustain this position.[46]

The communists have discovered that even in the generation which they have reared in atheism, there are still millions who have faith in God.

Third, the experience of men who face danger and solitude helps show how natural faith in God is. On such occasions some men who did not normally give much thought to matters of religion seem, nevertheless, to have become aware of spiritual realities. This, for example, has been the experience of some of the polar explorers.[47] It has also been said, "There are no atheists in the foxholes of Bataan."

Fourth, it is so natural for man to believe in God, that when he denies the existence of the true God, he creates false gods. Diamat is one of the communist's gods. Then, too, the communists now admit, there were some who deified Stalin. In his speech before the Twentieth Party Congress in Moscow, February 25, 1956, Khrushchev said that for years the belief had been cultivated among them that Stalin was "a superman possessing supernatural characteristics akin to those of a god."[48]

Ekaterina Furtseva, one of the eight secretaries of the Central Committee of the Communist Party of the Soviet Union, thought that during the war the "deification of Stalin was understandable because Soviet soldiers went into battle with words for the Fatherland and for Stalin. This inspired their valor but raised the personality of Stalin too high. After the war, conditions were very hard and the deification of Stalin then, too, may have helped to inspire people."[49]

---

[46] Thomas Hywel Hughes, *Psychology and Religious Origins*, New York: Charles Scribner's Sons, 1937, pp. 118-148.

[47] James D. Bales, *The Thinking Christian*, Vol. I, No. 1, p. 36. Robert E. D. Clark, *Science and Religion*; James D. Bales, "Alone in the Antarctic," *Science and Religion*, 1949, p. 68.

[48] *U.S. News and World Report*, June 15, 1956, p. 34.

[49] Tabitha Petran, "High Soviet Official in Frank Interview: Denies

This illustrates man's need for something beyond himself in which to believe. It shows that he can find inspiration by looking to something above him, or that which he conceives to be above him. This need of man is not eliminated by the affirmation of atheism. Man is so incurably religious that when he loses faith in the true God he turns to false gods. *Man is theotropic.* This characteristic of man, when reflected on, indicates something about man which cannot be explained by materialism. Man's religious and spiritual needs point to something in his nature which is beyond the material.

The deification of Stalin also helps us to see that religious needs are not eliminated by a change in an economic system. The communists claim to have established socialism in Russia, and yet their "new men" included communists, who, although nurtured in the communist philosophy, still needed faith in some kind of god.

The communist has not squarely faced the issues which are raised by the question: *How is it possible for man, with his hunger for a god, to be wholly material and economic?* They have refused to think deeply on the question.

What must be the nature of the universe which has so overwhelmingly led men to believe in some god? Can it be that a universe which is wholly material, and utterly devoid of God and the spiritual, has continually and persistently worked out in the mind of man faith in some kind of supreme Being?

THE FIRST CAUSE

Some of the arguments for the existence of God are based on the concept of a First Cause. Said Herbert Spencer, "We cannot think at all about the impressions which the external world produces on us, without thinking of them as caused; and we cannot carry out an inquiry concerning their causation, without inevitably committing ourselves to the hypothesis of a First Cause."[50] "Every science except the purely mathematical sciences, affirms the truth of the law of causation. Every student of

---

Jewish Curbs," *National Guardian,* June 25, 1956, p. 4. This is a pro-Communist paper.

[50] *First Principles,* New York: D. Appleton and Co., 1897, p. 38. It should be kept in mind that Spencer was an agnostic. This makes his admission all the more significant. See page 51 of the edition published by The De Witt Revolving Fund, Inc., New York, 1958.

logic knows that this is the ultimate canon of the sciences."[51] To deny the reality of the law of causation is to deny the possibility of science, for science endeavors to trace cause and effect. For example, the science of medicine would be impossible if there were no causes of ill health.

Scientists today are more and more coming to the concept of a First Cause, a beginning, a prime cause, as a result of a study of some of the facts of astronomy and physics which point to an origin of the universe which represents "a discontinuity in, perhaps a beginning of, the action of the laws of nature as we know them."[52] This will be considered later in connection with the fact of entropy.

But why must one postulate a First Uncaused Cause? "As Aristotle pointed out in his Metaphysics (Book II, Chapter 2), 'If there is no first cause, there is not a cause at all.' If there is no first cause, then all things are effects [intermediates], but this denies the law of causation which is the basis of science. Or if there is no first cause, all things form an endless series; but this only multiplies the difficulty, and is contrary to both science and philosophy. Aristotle well said: 'the cause of things are neither an infinite series nor indefinitely various in kind' . . . in the realm of existence we must not be condemned forever to the mere treadmill exercise of an indefinite regress; but must come ultimately to the reality that is there, so to speak, in its own right, the conception of which does not need the conception of something else upon which it is dependent."[53]

The first Cause in order to be the First Cause had to be adequate to bring about the results or effects which we see. Experience teaches that a thing or power does not give rise to something of which there is no trace or cause in the originating power. Life comes from life; energy from something that possesses energy at least potentially. Energy is not spontaneously generated from nothing. How, then, can it be considered scientific to believe that man arose from matter, which had no trace of consciousness, intelligence or morality?

---

[51] W. T. Stace, *Critical History of Greek Philosophy*, New York: St. Martin's Press, Inc., p. 6.

[52] Henry Magenau, "Is There Purpose in the Universe," *American Scientist*, Vol. 38, No. 1, Jan. 1950, p. 172. See also the July 1949 article *Numerology*.

[53] G. D. Hicks, *The Philosophical Basis of Theism*, p. 165. Quoted from a manuscript of Dr. Pat Hardeman.

The First Cause by definition must have been an originating cause. This cause must have been capable of initiating action without first being acted on by some outside force. Our own experience shows that a living creature can be an originating cause. Man with his power of rational thought can originate action without waiting until he is acted upon by some physical force. *We know of no originating cause which is inanimate.* Why, then, should one consider it scientific to believe that the First Cause, the originating Cause, was impersonal and inanimate.[54]

Let us now look at some of the realities in life which indicate that it is unreasonable to view matter as the First Cause.

LIFE FROM LIFE

Scientists agree that life has not always existed on this earth. The condition of earth was once such that life was impossible. Life, however, is now here. How did it originate?

It has been suggested by some that life came to this earth from another planet on a speck of dust or on a meteor. This supposition does not solve the question of the origin of life; it simply places the problem on some other planet.[55]

Concerning the origin of life, there are only two possibilities. Life was created by a supernatural power or by a natural power. The only question is: Who is the creator of life, the living God or dead matter?

In spite of all the technical words which may be used to describe an hypothesis of the origin of life in natural terms, all the naturalistic explanations boil down to one form or another of the spontaneous generation of life from the non-living and by the non-living. The communists answer "yes" to the question: "Is living substance created and maintained as a result of the unaided action of matter on matter?"[56] The communist can-

---

[54] Ambrose Fleming, *The Origin of Mankind,* London: Marshall, Morgan and Scott, Ltd., p. 3. He was president of the Television Society, and Professor Emeritus of Electrical Engineering in the University of London.

[55] Robert W. Hegner, *College Zoology,* New York: Macmillan Company, p. 722. There are creationists who believe that God utilized natural processes, which we may someday discover, in creating life. Walter R. Hearn, "The Creation of Life," *Gordon Review,* Winter, 1958, pp. 156-165, Gordon Faculties, Beverly Farms, Mass.

[56] Professor Kapp asks this question in the *Journal of the Transactions of the Victoria Institute,* Vol. 81, p. 80. Kapp's answer is "no."

not answer otherwise since he believes that matter in motion is the sole reality. He is committed to the assumption that life had a natural, rather than a supernatural, origin. A theist can consider the possibility that God used natural forces to create life, but the atheist rules out the possibility that God created life.

Since the doctrine of spontaneous generation is essential to the philosophy of communism, communists have been very interested in trying to prove it.[57] After attending an international symposium on the origin of life in Moscow, Professor Melvin Calvin said that the communists seem to have been ordered to a crash program on the subject.[58] And yet, the communists themselves admit that they have not yet proved it. A. I. Oparin, a member of the USSR Academy of Science writes: ". . . We have every reason to *believe* that sooner or later we shall be able practically to demonstrate that life is nothing else but a special form of existence of matter. The successes scored recently by Soviet biology hold out the *promise* that the artificial creation of the simplest living beings is not only possible, but that it will be achieved in the not too distant future."[59] The communists evidently considered this book to be a worthy contribution to the subject of the origin of life or they would not have published it in English for circulation throughout the English speaking world. Thus their latest publication on the subject in English admits that they have not proved that life has come from the non-living.

O. B. Lepeshinskaya was a Stalin Prize Winner and a member of the Academy of Medical Sciences of the U.S.S.R. Her work on *The Origin of Cells from Living Substance* was published in Moscow in 1954 by the Foreign Languages Publishing House. She also admitted that the spontaneous generation of life has not been proved.[60] It must be true, she maintained, for it is taught by dialectical materialism.[61] Although claiming to be scientific, the communists reveal that they are blind believers in the antiquated theories of Marx and Engels. As she said:

---

[57] *Report of the Central Committee, CPSU to the 20th Congress,* New York: New Century Publishers, 1956, p. 87. The claim is here made that Communists are more interested in science than anyone else.

[58] AP Dispatch, *Montgomery Advertiser,* Aug. 25, 1957, pp. 8, 13.

[59] *The Origin of Life,* Moscow: Foreign Languages Publishing House, 1955, p. 101. Italics by J. D. B.

[60] pp. 39-40.

[61] *Ibid.,* pp. 38-39.

"Soviet biology, armed with the advanced theory of Marx-Engels-Lenin and Stalin, is distinguished by its creative, trans-forming spirit."[62] And Oparin wrote: ". . . Engels also determined the further channels of scientific investigations in this field, the roads along which Soviet biology is now successfully travel-ling."[63] This is an acknowledgment that the doctrine of the spontaneous generation of life is not a scientific doctrine, but a doctrine to which they hold, not only without scientific evidence, but contrary to scientific evidence. They try to dodge this by saying that since Marxism is scientific, therefore, the doctrine of spontaneous generation is scientific, for it is embraced in Marxism. We remind them that this is not a question for verbal argument, but for scientific demonstration, and this demonstra-tion is the very thing which they cannot give.

It has been established by everyday observation and by count-less scientific experimentations that life comes from life. All *scientific evidence* is against the assumption that life comes from the non-living. "It may now be stated definitely that all known living organisms arise from pre-existing living organisms."[64] Already in his day Pasteur challenged the world to prove spon-taneous generation. "The world has been trying to do so ever since on a colossal scale, for instance, through the fermented-liquor industries of the united world. But Pasteur's negative stands unshaken."[65]

In spite of this, one of the most firmly established of all laws in science, the communists agree with the assertion of Erasmus Darwin:

> "Without parents by spontaneous birth
> Rise the first specks of animated earth."

---

[62] *Ibid.*, p. 80.

[63] *The Origin of Life*, p. 14.

[64] *The Encyclopedia Britannica*, 1956, Vol. I, p. 48. See also: Sir Charles Sherrington, *Man on His Nature*, pp. 139, 142; Douglas Dewar, "Current Theories of the Origin of Living Organisms," *Journal of the Transactions of the Victoria Institute*, Vol. LXXXVI, pp. 53-93; R. J. C. Harris, "The Origin of Life," *Journal of the Transactions of the Victoria Institute*, Vol. LXXXI, pp. 58-84. For a discussion of some of the hypotheses held by those who try to give a naturalistic explanation see, M. L. Johnson, Editor, *New Biology*, No. 16, London: Penguin Books, April 1954; *New Biology*, No. 12, 1952; Arnold Lunn, *The Flight From Reason*, pp. XXXVIII-IX.

[65] Sir Charles Sherrington, *Man on His Nature*, New York: Doubleday Anchor Books, 1953, p. 96.

EVALUATING THE CONTENTIONS

Some maintain that things were different in the beginning, and that under those different conditions, life was created by the non-living, although it is not being done now. This is just an assertion. Furthermore, it represents an abandonment of a fundamental concept in atheism, i.e. that all must be explained in terms of the laws of nature which now operate. In addition to this, it is an admission that the doctrine of the spontaneous generation of life is not a subject of scientific investigation and confirmation. How can scientific confirmation be made of a phenomenon which is not now taking place, but which is supposed to have taken place under conditions which are entirely different from the conditions which now exist and the processes which now work?

Many who believe in the creation of the living by the non-living and from the non-living are not aware of the vast assumptions which they are making; assumptions for which they have no real evidence. They are postulating tremendous miracles with inanimate matter as the miracle worker. The following discussion shows something of the complicated nature of the problem and thus how difficult it is to believe that it all came about as a result of the blind working of non-intelligent forces of nature.

Scientists are not agreed on *the nature of the original environment* in which life is supposed to have arisen.[66] Of the diversity of ideas on this subject, N. W. Pirie observed: "All these, and many other views, are held by astronomers and physicists all of whom have an air of authority. We have, therefore, a plethora of miscellaneous information but as little knowledge of the environment in which life may have originated as Tyndall and Huxley had. The sceptical biochemist may be excused for thinking that dogmatism is not yet justified. In the last forty years the only significant new idea that has been contributed to the problem is Haldane's suggestion that the primitive atmosphere contained amonia and hydrocarbons, and that, in the period before living systems had evolved which could destroy them, a varied group of organic substances would accumulate as a result of the ultraviolet light from the sun acting on this gas

---

[66] "Unfortunately, the geochemists can't agree on whether the atmosphere of the earth was an ozidized one or a reduced one, or some intermediate stage between" (Melvin Calvin, "Chemical Evolution and the Origin of Life," *American Scientist,* July 1956, p. 249).

mixture and on the gas coming from volcanoes. Wisely he did not go into details; it will be time enough to try to draw detailed pictures of the origin of life when the experts have remained unanimous for ten years about at least the outlines of a picture of the environment. Physics is as fickle a science as any other and our picture is unlikely to be satisfactory if we rely much on the 'Stop Press' news. Until we know for certain whether the original atmosphere contained significant amounts of oxygen and whether there were carbon compounds beside CO_2, hypothesis will be indistinguishable from speculation."[67]

The new hypothesis about the origin of the earth brings new ideas about the nature of the primitive atmosphere. Unless there is scientific evidence as to the nature of the atmosphere one cannot arrive at a satisfactory hypothesis concerning the nature of the prebiotic condition of the surface of the earth. ". . . the factors that lead to different conclusions about the atmosphere lead also to different conclusions about the surface."[68]

Complex substances, involving complicated chains of atoms would be necessary for life to exist. And yet, apart from living organisms, and a few cases in the laboratory, complex substances cannot be built up from simple ones.[69]

Protein molecules are necessary for the existence of life. Lecomte du Noüy has estimated that the probability for a single protein "molecule of high dissymmetry to be formed by the action of chance and normal thermic agitation remains practically nil. Indeed, if we suppose 500 trillion shakings per second

---

[67] N. W. Pirie, "Vital Blarney," *New Biology*, No. 12, p. 109. Pirie's contribution to the discussion, an editorial introduction in *New Biology*, No. 16, said: "Pirie furthermore will never allow us to forget that our body of knowledge is much more provisional than, in the intellectual excitement, we sometimes like to admit" (p. 9). J. D. Bernal, a Marxist, also admits that the discussions on the origin of life involve "much speculation" (p. 28). As Pirie observed, "The framer of a hypothesis, or speculation, about the origin of life labours under the difficulty, not only that he does not know what raw material he has to work with, but also that he does not know what types of substance he must arrange to have synthesized" (No. 12, p. 109). For such reason as these, J. B. S. Haldane mentioned "how little we can afford to be dogmatic about the physico-chemical situation at the time when life originated" (No. 16, p. 23).

[68] N. W. Pirie, "On Making and Recognizing Life," *New Biology*, No. 16, p. 45.

[69] Melvin Calvin, "Chemical Evolution and the Origin of Life," *American Scientist*, July 1956, p. 251.

(5×10^{14}), which corresponds to the order of magnitude of light frequencies (wave lengths comprised between 0.4 and 0.8 microns), we find that the time needed to form, on an average, one such molecule (degree of dissymmetry 0.9) in a material volume equal to that of our terrestrial globe is about 10^{243} billions of years (1 followed by 243 zeroes).

"But we must not forget that the earth has only existed for two billion years and that life appeared about one billion years ago, as soon as the earth had cooled $(1 \times 10^9$ years)."[70]

Professor Jan Lever also raised the questions as to what "is the probability that from the free interplay of amino-acid molecules there originates a protein built up of 1000 amino acids in a definite arrangement as they always occur in normal proteins? It appears that by considering a great number of simplifications this probability amounts to 10^{-1360} if for instance 1000 kg. of amino acids gets the chance for this reaction during a billion years. This means thus a decimal fraction with 1359 zeros after the decimal point."[71]

Of course, it might be maintained that by chance it did happen right at the first. One case, however, would not be sufficient, for hundreds of millions of identical molecules would be necessary. Then, too, we are speaking here only of the origin of protein molecules necessary to life and not of life itself. If it is maintained that by chance hundreds of millions of molecules of protein were formed, one would be forced to conclude that it was not a game of chance after all, but that the dice had been loaded! We would then be faced with the question as to what power loaded the dice!

Of the organic molecules, which would be essential prerequisite for the creation of life, George Wald wrote: "... we must first of all explain how such complicated molecules could come into being. And that is only the beginning. To make an organism requires not only a tremendous variety of these substances, in adequate amounts and proper porportions, but also

---

[70] *Human Destiny*, New York: Longmans, Green and Company, 1948, p. 34. Regardless of how scientists differ on the age of the earth, they never postulate an infinite existence. Dr. Hans Gaffron of the University of Chicago, said that it took nature three billion years to create life, *Science News Letter*, Dec. 5, 1959, p. 380.

[71] *Creation and Evolution*, Grand Rapids, Michigan: Kregel's, 1958, p. 47. These calculations are those of Mr. Schultz as cited by Troll, *Das Virusproblem in ontologischer Sicht*, Wiesbaden, 1951.

just the right arrangement of them. Structure here is as important as composition—and what a complication of structure! The most complex machine man has devised—for example, an electronic brain—is child's play compared with the simplest of living organisms. The especially trying thing is that complexity here involves such small dimensions. It is on the molecular level; it consists of a detailed fitting of molecule to molecule such as no chemist can attempt."[72]

Not only did the right raw materials have to be present, but they also had to exist in just the right proportions,[73] and enter into the right arrangements.[74] "To form an organism, molecules must enter into intricate designs and connections; they must eventually form a self-repairing, self-constructing dynamic machine."[75]

In addition to the fact that the right materials would have to exist in the right proportions at the right time, they would also have to have been out of the reach of anti-vitamins which are potent poisons. Even if the molecules necessary to life were formed by nature, what right have we to maintain that anti-vitamins would not have been formed also? "We must not forget that a biological system of great complexity is easily put out of gear by a very few molecules of the wrong kind—a million combinations that are right and workable become useless if one happens to be of the wrong kind. And, of course, with the first living organisms, there would have been no time for the evolution of immuno-chemical and toxicological mechanisms to prevent harmful molecules from destroying life as soon as it came into existence."[76]

To complicate the problem still more, one is faced with the fact of spontaneous dissolution. As Wald admitted, "spontaneous dissolution is much more probable, and hence proceeds much more rapidly, than spontaneous synthesis."[77] Many of the compounds necessary to life, especially the co-enzymes, "are exceedingly unstable and, once formed, would have disappeared

---

[72] "The Origin of Life," *Scientific American*, Aug. 1954, p. 47.

[73] Herbert H. Farmer, *Towards Belief in God*, New York: Macmillan Company, 1943, p. 204.

[74] George Wald, "The Origin of Life," *Scientific American*, Aug. 1954, p. 46.

[75] *Ibid.*, p. 50.

[76] Robert E. D. Clark, *The Universe: Plan or Accident?* London: The Paternoster Press, 1949, pp. 101-102.

[77] George Wald, *op. cit.*, p. 49.

in half an hour. So it will not do to suggest that they might be formed one by one by chance—with long periods in between. Chance must produce all the molecules that are required concentrated together in a cell, within a matter of at most an hour or so."[78]

Furthermore, a living system must have a supply of energy. The first form of life would have to have a system of obtaining and delivering energy when it was needed and where it was needed. This mechanism is of great complexity whether in simple or complex organisms. Many different kinds of molecules are involved, and no single stage of the mechanism could be missing without rendering the entire thing useless. Besides, in order to obtain energy the cell first must have some energy. "The living cell, in fact, presents us with a stage of affairs which Malcolm Dixon, one of the greatest living authorities on enzymes, has compared to a factory designed to produce machine tools. Without machine tools the factory cannot even start production of machine tools—no matter how perfect its organization."[79]

It does not help matters to assume that the first form of life was so simple that its creation by matter is not difficult to believe. There is no *simple* form of life. The simple cell carries on highly complicated processes. A cell is a "coordination of complexity," and not a "chaotic complexity of a mixture of gases."[80] It is not a static but a dynamic system. "It is energy-cycles, suites of oxidation and reduction, concatenated ferment-actions. It is like a magic hive, the walls of whose chambered sponge-work are shifting veils of ordered molecules, and rend and renew as operations rise and cease. A world of surfaces and streams. We seem to watch battalions of specific catalysts, like Maxwell's 'demons,' lined up, each waiting, stop-watch in hand, for its moment to play the part assigned to it."[81]

The cell must carry on such fundamental reactions as protein synthesis—a "highly complex" process,[82] nitrogen fixation and photosynthesis.[83] ". . . the first form of living material must

---

[78] Robert E. D. Clark, *op. cit.*, p. 104.

[79] *Ibid.*, pp. 103-104.

[80] Lecomte du Noüy, *Human Destiny*, p. 37.

[81] Sir Charles Sherrington, *Man on His Nature*, 2nd Edition, p. 80.

[82] Ernest F. Gale, "Experiments in Protein Synthesis," *Scientific American*, March 1956, p. 46.

[83] R. J. C. Harris, "The Origin of Life," *Transaction of the Victoria Institute*, Vol. 81, p. 77.

have been a functional unit, and not merely a structural unit. Hence, it follows that those who try to account for the origin of life solely in terms of physicochemical phenomena must be prepared to explain the origin, not merely of a mass of unspecialized protoplasm, nor of 'the simplest living cell,' but of a complete organism."[84]

The first form of life would have to be exceedingly complicated because it would have had to subsist entirely on an inorganic environment.[85] It would not have had any other form of life on which to depend or with which to cooperate. This would have necessitated a much more complicated enzyme system than man has, since it would have had to make all necessary organic substances.

Such primitive forms of life would have to utilize whatever kind of materials might be at hand. "This puts a premium on biochemical efficiency and adaptability. An organism such as that needs the unspecialized genius of a successful Robinson Crusoe."[86]

The difficulty of the situation would be complicated by the fact that "almost every one of the great classes of chemical entities which we, quoting Dr. Needham, cited as together essential for the organized system of living substance was a something unknown to earth before life came."[87]

Not only would non-living matter have to create the first form of life, but it would have to create a form of life with the power to reproduce itself in some way. "That is to say, we should insist on the ability to reproduce as an essential quality in an eobiont."[88]

Some have suggested that the virus is the link between the living and the non-living. Several observations are in order here. *First*, the "proof of the origin of any virus is lacking."[89] Thus, here we do not find any scientific proof as to how life originated.

---

[84] G. E. Barnes, *Transactions of the Victoria Institute*, Vol. 81, p. 81.

[85] Frederic Wood-Jones, *Design and Purpose*, London: Kagan Paul, Trench, Trubner and Company, Ltd., 1942, p. 66.

[86] N. W. Pirie, "Some Assumptions Underlying Discussion on the Origins of Life," *Annals of the New York Academy of Sciences*, Aug. 30, 1957, p. 375.

[87] Sir. Charles Sherrington, *Man on His Nature*, p. 139.

[88] N. W. Pirie, "On Making and Recognizing Life," *New Biology*, No. 16, p. 51.

[89] Thomas M. Rivers, *Viral and Rickettsial Infections of Man*, 2nd Edition, New York: J. B. Lippincott, Company, 1952, p. 5.

Second, the authorities are not agreed on whether or not the virus is a living or a non-living system. *Third,* a virus "can live only in living cells. . . . It is a parasite."[90] It must have a living host, in order to multiply.[91] That which can function only in connection with a living host cannot be the *first* form of life.

Fourth, scientists, who believe in the spontaneous generation of life, are not agreed on whether the virus is an early form of life or whether it is a degenerate form, "the end stage of a long evolutionary development,"[92]—or rather devolution.

Fifth, Drs. Fraenkel-Conrat and Williams have put together "inert fragments of tobacco mosaic virus to produce disease-producing viruses." This is a case of tearing down and rebuilding a virus, but to what extent one can be torn down and rebuilt is another matter. "It is not claimed that this is an example of spontaneous generation despite the apparent mixing of two lifeless materials to produce a living virus."[93] It should be borne in mind that they started with a virus, and we cannot be positive as to the extent to which damage was done when they divided this virus into the nucleic acid and the enveloping protein.

In view of these facts, it is not scientifically established that the virus is the first form of life.

The hypotheses which are framed to explain life's origin must also take into consideration that scientists do not believe that the earth, nor conditions on it favorable to the existence of life, has existed forever. So whatever hypothesis they frame must

---

[90] Anton J. Carlson and Victor Johnson, *The Machinery of the Body,* Chicago: The University of Chicago Press, 1953, p. 14.

[91] Thomas M. Rivers, *Viral and Rickettsial Infections of Man,* p. 3; Garrett Hardin, *Biology, Its Human Implications,* San Francisco: W. H. Freeman and Co., 1953, p. 638; Alexander, *General Biology,* New York: T. Y. Crowell, 1956, pp. 30-33.

[92] Anton J. Carlson and Victor Johnson, *The Machinery of the Body,* 4th Edition, p. 4; Cited in R. J. C. Harris, "The Origin of Life," *Journal of the Transaction of the Victoria Institute,* Vol. 81, p. 75.
Referred to in Hideo Moriyama, *The Nature of Viruses and the Origin of Life,* Tokyo: Publishers, Shonan Hygiene Institute, Kamakura: Japan, 1955, p. 141. The book itself is often highly speculative. Outstanding Soviet authorities on viruses view them as being alive, but authorities such as A. I. Oparin view them as "a product of regression." See the quotations in Gustav A. Wetter, *Dialectical Materialism,* pp. 448-449. See his entire discussion.

[93] I. W. Knobloch, "Biology," *Journal of the American Scientific Affiliation,* p. 18. Referring to an article in the *California Monthly* for Jan. 1956.

take into consideration that they have *a limited amount of time in which to work.*

It would be a mistake, however, to assume that with enough time anything and everything can well happen. This mistake was made by George Wald. He wrote: "Time is in fact the hero of the plot. . . . Given so much time, the 'impossible' becomes the possible, the possible probable, and the probable virtually certain. One has only to wait: time itself performs the miracles."[94] With this logic, one can prove that immortality is certain. Given enough time everyone will be resurrected. The author believes in the resurrection, but he does not believe that it is proved by this kind of logic.

Time performs no miracles. Time cannot finish what time cannot start. Things may begin and end in time. But *they are not caused by time.*

"It certainly cannot mean that given enough time, something which is patently impossible becomes possible. For instance, how long would it take to convert an irrational number into a rational one? It just cannot happen; this is completely impossible. The square root of two can never be expressed in terms of a whole number in spite of the fact that there are an infinite amount of numbers to choose from."[95]

Who wants to affirm that given enough time a monkey pounding on a typewriter would pound out all the books in the Library of Congress? Who will calculate this probability? Shall we say that with enough time it is certain to take place? Can a person with "enough time" take the square root of a sonnet?

THE COMMUNISTS ARGUE AGAINST THEMSELVES

The communists' own logic can be turned against them on the question of the spontaneous generation of life. The communists criticize religion because it was in existence before the age of science, and therefore it must be the reflection of nature in man's mind before man had understood that nature is under the reign of law.[96] If the fact that religion existed before the age

---

[94] "The Origin of Life," *Scientific American*, Aug. 1954, p. 48.

[95] Robert Helsten, Personal Communication. Compare Edward Kasner and James Newman, *Mathematics and the Imagination*, New York: Simon and Schuster, 1950, pp. 234-242.

[96] *Capital*, p. 25. Chou En-lai as quoted in C. S. Braden, *War, Communism and the Religions of China*, New York: Harper and Brothers, 1953,

of science discredits religion, the doctrine of the spontaneous generation of life from non-life is discredited for the same reason. Aristotle held to such a doctrine.[97] Lucretius said: "the clear facts, which are known for all to see . . . constrain us to believe that living things are begotten of insensible things. Why, we may see worms come forth alive from noisome dung, when the soaked earth has gotten muddy from immoderate rains."[98] In a note on a similar passage Cyril Bailey said: "A close parallel to this description is found in Empedocles (who died in Sicily about 433 B.C.). . . . The theory that animals, like the plants, were produced from the earth is attributed with certain variations to Anaximander, Anaxagoras, and Democritus."[99]

The communists' own argument is thus turned against them. On their logic the doctrine of spontaneous generation of life cannot be true since the doctrine arose in the pre-scientific age when men had a superstitutious view of nature! Thus the communists must either give up the doctrine, or cease to use such an argument in their effort to discredit religion.

The communist, to be consistent, must explain life's origin by an appeal to the dialectic. Matter called forth its opposite—life. This, of course, attributes to matter a power which cannot be proved to have ever resided in matter. However, to assume that the origin of life must be explained dialectically, does not help the communist but rather leads him to a position which is destructive of his assertion that death ends all. If matter, the thesis, called forth its antithesis, life, then out of the clash between the two *a synthesis, higher than matter and higher than mortal life, must finally arise.* And what could be higher than matter and earth-life? An eternal and heavenly life. Matter is the thesis. Mortality is the antithesis. Immortality is the synthesis!

Some have tried to avoid the problem of the origin of life, by assuming that the physical and chemical elements are alive,

---

p. 66. Frank Wilson Price, "Communist China," *Religion in Life*, Autumn, 1956, p. 515.

[97] *Encyclopedia Britannica*, 1956, Vol. I, p. 48.

[98] Lines 2,870 ff, In *Titi Lucreti Cari De Rerum Natura Libra Sex*, edited with prolegomena, critical apparatus, translation and commentary by Cyril Bailey, Oxford: Clarendon Press, 1947.

[99] Cyril Bailey's comments on lines 783-820. Citations furnished the author by Dr. W. M. Green, University of California, Berkeley. See also Cyril Bailey, Translator, *Lucretius on the Nature of Things*, Oxford: Clarendon Press, 1929, pp. 211-212.

and thus life has always existed. This is not only without scientific evidence, but it enlarges the word "life" so much that it becomes a meaningless term, without boundaries of any kind.[100] How can these individuals find it easy to believe in an *eternal living matter*, and think that it is unreasonable to believe in the *eternal living God*.

THE ATHEIST HAS NOT PROVED HIS POINT

The confirmed atheist lives in the hope that some day man will create life, and that then we shall have positive proof that all can be explained naturally. This, however, would not prove his case. *First*, it is still a matter of hope with him and not a matter of scientific evidence. *Second*, he must believe that "natural forces in the past did with inorganic matter, what modern chemists, with all their apparatus, knowledge, chemicals, X- and other rays, have failed to do even with organic compounds." *Third*, if man creates life in the future all that would be proved is that an *intelligent being* can create life. It would not prove that life was spontaneously generated by matter.[101] *Fourth*, even if nature has the power to create life it could be argued that it had been endowed by God with this power.

Faith in God as the creator of life is in harmony with the evidence which we have concerning life. All the evidence shows that life comes from life. There is no evidence that life comes from non-life. There is also no evidence that human beings brought life to this planet. Since life's origin cannot be found in a natural or a human source, why is it unreasonable to look for it in a superhuman and supernatural source—the living God?

MIND

We are confronted with the fact of mind and with the fact of matter. The realm of mind includes ideas, memories, and the power of reasoning. If it were not for the fact of mind, we would known nothing about the reality of matter. In fact, we would react to matter, but we would be unaware of this reac-

---

[100] Yervant H. Krikorian, *Naturalism and the Human Spirit*, New York: Columbia University Press, p. 247.

[101] Dr. Hans Gaffron, of the University of Chicago, predicted that man would create life in the next 1,000 years, *Science News Letter*, Dec. 5, 1959, p. 380.

tion and of it we would *know* nothing. If one must doubt the
reality of one or the other, why doubt the reality of mind without the existence of which the question of the nature of reality
would never have been raised. But it is not sensible to deny
either.

The communist, however, views mind as but matter in motion.
And yet, such a view is without scientific confirmation. However
intimately mind may function in connection with matter in man,
it is impossible to reduce mind to matter. This is the testimony
of common sense and of scientific investigation.

Although he was an agnostic, Sir Charles Sherrington, Nobel
Laureate, sometimes President of the Royal Society in Britain,
and at the time of his death one of the world's outstanding
physiologists, wrote as follows after having spent well over half
a century in physiological studies: "Mind, for anything perception
can compass, goes therefore in our spatial world more ghostly
than a ghost. Invisible, intangible, it is a thing not even of outline; it is not a 'thing.' It remains without sensual confirmation
and remains without it forever."[102] Although Sherrington leaned
toward viewing mind as a form of energy, he admitted that it is
impossible thus to identify it. Furthermore, in this matter science today has not advanced beyond Aristotle. Says Sherrington,
"Aristotle, 2,000 years ago, was asking how is the mind attached
to the body. We are asking that question still."[103]

Another great physiologist, Dr. E. D. Adrain, Professor of
Physiology at Cambridge University, has pointed out that "The
part of our picture of the brain which may always be missing is,
of course, the part which deals with the mind; the part which
ought to explain how a particular pattern of nerve impulses
can produce an idea; or the other way round, how a thought
can decide which nerve cells are to come into action."[104] Cortical
stimulation may produce reflex action but it cannot touch the
will of man.

"What is the real relationship of this mechanism to the mind?
Can we visualize a spiritual element of different essence capable
of controlling this mechanism? When a patient is asked about
the movement which he carries out as a result of cortical stimu-

[102] *Man on His Nature*, 2nd Edition, p. 256.

[103] Sir Charles Sherrington in Peter Laslett, Editor, *The Physical Basis
of Mind*. Oxford: Basil Blackwell, 1950, pp. 3-4.

[104]E. D. Adrian, O.M., M.D., F.R.S., Nobel Laureate, Professor of
Physiology, Cambridge University, in *The Physical Basis of Mind*, p. 5.

lation, he never is in any doubt about it. He knows he did not will the action. He knows there is a difference between automatic action and voluntary action. He would agree that something else finds its dwelling-place between the sensory complex and the motor mechanism, that there is a switchboard operator as well as a switchboard."[105]

If mind and will be but reactions to physical conditions, why did not the individual imagine that he willed the action?

Let us repeat something which we have previously stated. If the communist view of man is correct, mind and reasoning cannot at all be trustworthy, for they are but reactions to material, economic and class conditions. In fact, their own theories and our theories about mind "could only be nervous disturbances, or perhaps diseases of the liver."[106]

Well did C. S. Lewis say: "Supposing there was no intelligence behind the universe, no creative mind. In that case nobody designed my brain for the purpose of thinking. It is merely that when the atoms inside my skull happen for physical or chemical reasons to arrange themselves in a certain way, this gives me, as a by-product, the sensation I call thought. But if so, how can I trust my own thinking to be true? It's like upsetting a milk jug and hoping that the way the splash arranges itself will give you a map of London. But if I can't trust my own thinking, of course I can't trust the arguments leading to atheism, and therefore have no reason to be an atheist, or anything else. Unless I believe in God, I can't believe in thought; so I can never use thought to disbelieve in God."[107]

Since, however, we are faced with the reality of mind, is it not reasonable to conclude that mind has its source in mind and not in matter? Since man has not existed forever, is it not reasonable to conclude that the fact of mind points to the Divine Mind as its cause?

THE MORAL ARGUMENT

Every individual realizes that there is right and that there is wrong. Men, sooner or later, try to convince themselves that

---

[105] Wilder Penfield, neurosurgeon, and Director of the Neurological Institute, Montreal, in *The Physical Basis of Mind*, p. 64.

[106] William Henry Vincent Reade, *Christian Challenge to Philosophy*, p. 131.

[107] C. S. Lewis, *Broadcast Talks*, London: Geoffrey Bles, Ltd., 1946, pp. 37-38.

they are doing the right thing, and not the wrong thing. They want the approval of their own conscience. All want to feel that they are making some contribution to civilization. Even atheists say that they do this in destroying faith in God. All men have some sense of justice and fairness, and they resent unfairness. Due to ignorance men may not always "draw the line" in the same place. But as A. E. Taylor wrote: "They may draw the line between right and wrong in a different place, but at least they all agree that there is such a line to be drawn."[108]

Men cannot get away from the idea of obligation or duty. In other words, we "cannot escape the fact of conscience." It is a part of man's nature. "Indeed, since the idea of 'ought' has arrived in the mind, it is impossible to escape it, except by using it. For if conscience is invalid, we ought not to be governed by it; that is, we appeal to the 'ought' to overcome the 'ought.' "[109]

If communism is right, man is not a being with moral sensitivity, but simply a material being. Thus to say: "I ought" is no more *morally* significant (for there is no such realm as that of the moral) than to say: "I itch." Both simply express a feeling in man-matter. And yet, the communists themselves speak of duty and maintain that they are on a higher moral level than other people. When they speak of injustice, they are invoking a moral, not a material, concept. When Karl Marx, in *Capital*, implied that capitalism is immoral and unjust, he was admitting the reality of the realm of morality and thus unconsciously admitting the falsity of the materialistic view of man. Some communists become morally indignant when one points out that they continually make judgments and evaluations which imply the existence of a moral realm! They think you are unfairly accusing them!

If there is a moral realm there must also be a realm of freedom. "The moral law is invalid unless man is *free*. As Kant puts it, 'I ought, therefore I can'! If duty is required, freedom is required."[110] If man has no freedom there is no realm of morality, for why "ought" I do something which I cannot do? If man has no freedom we cannot do otherwise than we do; thus it

---

[108] *Does God Exist*, New York: The Macmillan Company, 1947, p. 83. See his Gifford Lectures, *The Faith of a Moralist*. Macmillan and Company, Ltd., 1931, 2 Vols.

[109] W. E. Hocking, *Types of Philosophy*, New York: Charles Scribner's Sons, p. 147-148.

[110] *Ibid.*, p. 149.

could never be said that we *ought* to have acted otherwise than we did.

Furthermore, in this life following the "ought" may result in the loss of friends, fortune, pleasure, happiness, and even of life. But if this is the end of the matter, "no one could quite regard the universe as *just*. If conscience is rooted in reality, and not in illusion, then reality must be a moral order: and it must therefore bring about an agreement between morality and happiness. But the only power capable of doing this would be a power controlling the whole course of experience in this world and the next. That power is what men call God."

In brief Kant argues, "if I accept conscience as a genuine call of the universe to my individual self, and duty begins in this acknowledgment of duty—I must also accept the beliefs in God, freedom, and immortality."[111] Otherwise, one must maintain that the "ought" is an illusion, and that no one is under any kind of obligation to do anything or to refrain from doing anything. Either there is a non-material realm or there is no *moral* realm. But there is a moral realm. No fact is more emphatically borne in on our conscience, or testified to by the actions of men, even of atheists.

Man's moral sensitivity cannot be explained away on the grounds that men differ in their judgment as to whether or not certain actions are right or wrong. This does not do away with the fact that man is *morally sensitive*. Furthermore, the basic moral sense is the same among all men, i.e. all believe that men are obligated to do the right—whatever the right may be. No people believe that they are morally obligated to do the evil and to oppose the good. To be morally binding, the action must contribute to the good. Even the so-called primitive man "does not regard anything as obligatory which is not a part of, or a contribution to, what he believes to be good. The only self-evident intuition which he seems to recognize is that of a necessary connection between value and obligation, between what is on the whole good and what he ought to do; and the only intrinsic good which he seems to recognize is that of doing what he believes to be right or obligatory."[112]

Being confronted with the fact of the concept of duty, with man's moral sensitivity, how are we to explain its origin? Is it

---

[111] *Ibid.*, p. 150.

[112] A. Macbeath, *Experiments in Living*, London: Macmillan and Company, 1952, p. 421. The Gifford Lectures for 1948-1949.

reasonable to conclude that non-moral matter finally created man with his moral sensitivity? Is it more in line with what we know—that it takes a moral being today to produce a moral being—to conclude that moral man's source must be sought in some moral being, God, rather than in non-moral matter?

THE EXISTENCE OF ORDER

In our own experience, order and meaningfulness are marks of intelligence. When we meet with order, even though we do not see the cause of that order, we postulate the existence of an intelligent being as the cause. If we walked by the seaside and found some pebbles on the beach which spelled out the sentence, "man is immortal," we would conclude that an intelligent being was behind the orderly arrangement of the stones.

Regardless of the aspect of reality which we examine, there is order. The fact that there is some disorder does not prove that there is no order. If there were no order at all, disorder could not be recognized as disorder. If disorder were universal, there would be no orderly mind of man in existence to recognize the presence of disorder.

The communists themselves postulate the existence of order both in the material world and in the world of humanity. They accept the fact of order in the material world when they maintain that scientific investigation is possible. If there were no order, it would be impossible to state the relationships in the realm of matter in the form of laws. Communists accept the idea of some order in human history and human life today when they maintain that there is a law at work—the dialectic—which inevitably carries humanity to higher and better forms of social order. While we do not agree with their philosophy of dialectical materialism, we point out that they themselves are in this very philosophy assuming the existence of order and a force making for greater and greater order.

In the material realm, there is much evidence of order. Lawrence J. Henderson, a Professor of Biological Chemistry in Harvard University, observed that "the teleological appearance of nature and the forms of life is a universal fact of human experience. Hence it has been quite impossible for natural science or philosophy permanently to ignore the problem of teleology. Merely to explain away the order of nature is no more satisfactory than to explain away matter itself. We may argue against such ideas ever so ingeniously, but the experiences of daily life steadily oppose the arguments, and gradually overwhelm them. Thus men must always inquire into cause and significance of the teleological appearance of things."[113]

The presence of order is so clear that even agnostics continually find themselves forced to use the language of purpose and design in describing this order. Said the agnostic Sherrington, "We all drop into this mode of thought; we adopt it as we dissect."[114]

It is only when we allow ourselves to be lost in isolated details that we lose sight of the fact that "the cosmos is an ordered entity."[115] Professor Henry Norris Russell, head of the Princeton Observatory, has stated that there are at least ten features of the arrangement of the solar system, which are not the necessary consequences of the law of gravitation and which thus show that "the solar system is clearly no accidental aggregation of bodies."[116]

If there were material differences in the distance of the earth from the sun, the size of the earth, the depth of the ocean, the rotation of the earth or the gases of the atmosphere, life would be impossible. How could it be that these things are the result of the non-directed, non-intelligent motions of matter.[117]

The marvels of order in the animal and insect world are many.[118]

Man is surely as good a sample of reality, as excellent a key

---

[113] *The Order of Nature*, Cambridge: Harvard University Press, 1925, pp. 182-183. Compare p. 193.

[114] *Man on His Nature*, p. 107. See also S. D. Vavilow, *The Eye and the Sun*, Moscow: Foreign Languages Publishing House, 1955, p. 88.

[115] Frederic Wood-Jones, *Design and Purpose*, p. 13. He was Professor of Anatomy in the University of Manchester. That evolution has not destroyed the argument from the existence of order has been admitted by evolutionists from Darwin to our day. T. H. Huxley and Francis Darwin, *Life and Letters of Charles Darwin*, Vol. I, pp. 554-556, Frances Mason, Editor, *The Great Design: Order and Intelligence in Nature*, New York: The Macmillan Company, 1955. H. F. Osborn, *Evolution and Religion in Education*, pp. 12-13, 61-62. Frederic Wood-Jones maintained that "William Paley's *Natural Theology* is one of the greatest expositions of the ordering of Nature that has ever been written," *Design and Purpose*, pp. 36-37.

[116] See *Astronomy: A Revision of Young's Manual of Astronomy*, New York: Ginn and Company, 1926, Vol. 1, pp. 461-462.

[117] A. C. Morrison, *Man Does Not Stand Alone*, New York: Fleming H. Revell Company, 1944, pp. 94-96.

[118] For a popular account of the marvels of the bird, see Alan Devoe, "The Miracle of Birds," *Reader's Digest*, Oct. 1953, pp. 67-70.

to reality, as is an atom.[119] Why is it reasonable to explain everything, including man, in terms of a material atom, instead of
looking at something higher than an atom—man—and looking for
the ultimate reality in terms of the highest that we see in the
universe.

Man is indeed fearfully and wonderfully made. This is impressed on us when we study the various systems which make
up his body and also when we see how these systems are in-
tegrated into one working system, i.e. the human body.

That something can go wrong with the wonderful mechanism
of man's body is no argument against man being fearfully and
wonderfully made. It does prove that man is not made to live
forever on this earth, but it does not prove that it is reasonable
to believe that man is the non-purposed result of the blind motions of matter.

The body is a machine, but it is so much more than a machine that Dr. Walter B. Cannon, then Professor of Physiology
in Harvard Medical School, wrote a book entitled *The Wisdom
of the Body.*

Complicated processes are carried on within the body. As
Professor E. C. Dobbs, of the University of London, wrote: "It
is rather a terrifying thought that the whole of the protein in
the human body is replaced in roughly 160 days, and at the
present time we can only speculate on the mechanism controlling this elaborate re-synthesis, where even a single amino acid
must not be out of place if the hormone is to have its activity or
the antibody its potency."[120] This is only one illustration of
what a complicated organism man is.

The heart is a marvelous mechanism which pumps some five
thousand gallons of blood a day, supplies some 12,000 miles of
circulatory system and which may beat over two and a half
billion times in a lifetime. It can beat twice as fast, put forth
twice as much blood per beat, against an increased arterial
pressure of up to 30 or 40 per cent at a moment's notice.[121]

The unity of the body and of man also passes understanding.
Although man is made up of around thirty million million cells,

---

[119] Ralph S. Lillie, *General Biology and Philosophy of Organism*, Chicago: University of Chicago Press, 1945, pp. 194-195.

[120] *British Medical Journal*, Dec. 2, 1950, p. 1242.

[121] W. B. Cannon, *The Wisdom of the Body*, New York: W. W. Norton
and Company, Inc., 1932, p. 233. See also A. R. Short, *Wonderfully Made*,
London: Paternoster Press, 1951, p. 43.

and several different systems, the body functions as a unit. What is more significant is that man is conscious of himself as one individual and not as an isolated aggregation of cells and systems.

The skin is a protective jacket; it repels and kills some germs; it is an umbrella and sun shade; it is a thermostat and a stockroom. It is self-repairing[122] and contains a complex alarm system. Although full of holes it can close them up with oil glands to keep out the water and it provides a complicated apparatus for each hair.[123]

The eye is such a marvelous mechanism that it gave Darwin cold shudders and he agreed that it did seem "absurd in the highest degree" that it should have arisen by chance and evolution—though he thought that it did.[124]

The wonder of wonder, however, is the *seeing* itself. We do not see the electrical storm, so to speak, which is set up in the nerve fibers and the brain; electrical charges which do not contain brightness, shadow, distance, right-side-upness, etc., but we see things possessing these qualities. Although physics and chemistry can tell us much about the eye and the brain, they offer us not a word concerning the *seeing* itself.[125]

---

[122] A. I. Brown, *God's Masterpiece Man's Body*, pp. 39-41.

[123] Susan Voight, "Amazing Facts about Your Skin," *Coronet*, Feb. 1952, pp. 153-154.

[124] *Origin of Species*, New York: A. L. Burt, From Sixth London Edition, pp. 170-171; *Life and Letters of Charles Darwin*, Vol. II, New York: Basic Books, Inc., p. 67. See also Sir Charles Lyell in the *Life of Sir Charles Lyell*, Vol. II, p. 448.

[125] Sir Charles Sherrington, *Man on His Nature*, 2nd Edition, pp. 114-117, 119, 121-122. There are those who criticize some features of the eye. For example, Professor Helmholtz, criticized it from the standpoint that it was not a perfect optical instrument. Of course, no man made optical instruments *see*. But Professor Helmholtz did not intend to deprecate the eye, but to show that its perfection is not a mechanical one, but one which was adapted to the needs of the organism. See the quotation in C. A. Row, *Christian Theism*, 2nd Edition, London: Hodder and Stoughton, 1890, pp. 144-147. Helmholtz made a criticism on the basis that "the lens system of the eye is uncorrected for colour," but he did not know, as we know now, that the eye does correct for color through a nervous reflex rather than through an optical method. Robert E. D. Clark, *Science and Religion*, 1948, Vol. I, p. 121. H. Hartridge, *Nature*, Vol. 156, 1945, p. 666. See also G. H. Best and N. B. Taylor, *The Human Body and Its Functions*, 1932, p. 305; and Gordon Lynn Wallas, *The Vertebrate Eye and Its Adaptive Radiation*, 1942, p. iv. S. Vavilow said that although the "image on the retina is far from perfectly corrected. . . . It must be noted, however, that so-called spherical aberration is quite well corrected in the

We could also think of the nervous system, the skeletal system, the blood, the process of reproduction, etc. Whatever we study about the human body, or about any system or part of a system, furnishes more material than men can learn in a lifetime. When we think of this we are impressed anew with the conviction that he who can believe that the body was the result of blind force moving matter should find it easy to believe all the fables and fictions ever told. How can he accuse the theist of being unreasonable, when he himself attributes to dead matter such creative power?

Although it is not reasonable to believe that all these evidences of order are the product of the blind workings of the forces of nature, it is reasonable to believe that this order points to an intelligent Creator as the cause and creator of this order. In drawing this conclusion we are acting in line with the evidence which we have, i.e. that order is a mark of intelligence.

THE UNIVERSE IS NOT A SELF-CONTAINED, SELF-EXPLAINED SYSTEM

If atheism is true, the universe must be a self-contained and self-explained system. It must be explained in terms of present day processes. An atheist cannot look beyond the system of nature today in order to explain things, for such would involve a non-natural explanation. However, scientists are more and more coming to the conclusion that the present laws of nature do not explain the universe. Thus they are contending that our present order of things had a beginning at a time not infinitely remote.

One of the best established laws in science is the second law of thermodynamics. This law tells us that the amount of energy available for energizing processes of the world is ever growing less."[126] This is called the law of entropy.

---

human eye. This is mainly due to the fact that the inside layers of the crystalline lens are of greater density than the outside layers." *The Eye and the Sun* (p. 92).

[126] J. A. McWilliams, *Cosmology*, New York: Macmillan Company, 1933, p. 42 as quoted by Elton Trueblood, *The Logic of Belief*, p. 155. For a further discussion of the scientific foundation of this line of thought, see Georges Lemaitre, *The Primeval Atom*, New York: D. Van Nostrand Company, Inc., 1950, pp. 17-18; J. W. N. Sullivan, *Limitations of Science*, New York: New American Library, p. 32; an outstanding British mathe-

In other words, the universe is running down; it is going from a more perfect state of organization to a less perfect state of organization.

This must point back to a beginning at some time in the past not infinitely remote. For if the universe had been running down from all eternity, it would have already run down since eternity is time enough to do anything. But it has not run down as yet; it has not reached a state of complete disorganization—of the equal distribution of energy throughout the universe.

Furthermore, since there is no self-winding system in nature whereby natural processes—those occuring without external interferences—carry energy from a less to a higher state of organization, this highly organized state of energy in the beginning could not have been the result of a process of naturalistic evolution. Some power or force external to the universe itself, some force which was not the result of the laws which now operate, must have originally set the universe in operation in a high state of organization. Such a power could not be matter, for matter has no such self-organizing power. It must have been a supernatural, and superhuman power.

In this connection, Sir James Jeans used the illustration of a clock. The universe is like a clock which is running down. It has not yet run down, so it has not always been running. It is not self-winding, thus it must have been wound up at some time in the past by some power external to the clock. Thus the running clock is not a self-contained, self-explained system.

There are in nature radioactive clocks, so to speak, such as thorium and uranium. One half of each mass of these materials decomposes every so many years, and one half of that in so many more years, and so on. But such radioactive elements still exist, and are still disintegrating. So they have not been disintegrating forever since in an eternity they would have already decomposed. Furthermore, if we trace this backward then so many years ago a particular amount of radioactive material possessed twice the mass that it did before, and so many years before that it possessed twice that much more. And if one reasoned back to infinity each of these would have possessed infinite mass; but this is absurd. So something happened in the

matician and physicist, Sir Edmund Whittaker, *Space and Spirit,* Chicago: Henry Regnery Company, 1948; A. S. Eddington, *The Nature of the Physical World,* Cambridge, 1930, p. 84.

distant past which is not now happening. Thus the present laws of nature do not present us with a self-contained, self-explained system.[127]

The philosophy of the dialectic is in direct opposition to the fact of entropy. If the realm of the material is the only realm, the second law of thermodynamics holds good in all of the manifestations of matter, including matter-man. Thus the course of human history should be downward instead of upward. And yet, the dialectic assumes that there is a power at work in matter and in human history which inevitably carries society onward and upward to higher and to better forms of order. In this the communist contradicts the fact of entropy.

The law of entropy forces us to look beyond nature for an explanation of nature. A supernatural, not a natural, explanation is essential. The present processes of nature do not explain themselves. It is necessary to postulate the existence of the Supreme Being in order to account for the order and organization which exists in the universe.

In view of all these considerations, why should it be thought unreasonable to conclude that God, not matter, is the creator? How, then, can communism be true, since it assumes the doctrine of atheism to be scientifically demonstrable?

Of course, in affirming the existence of God, the Christian is not denying the reality of the material, nor the self-evident fact that man must eat. He who affirms the need for air is not at the same time denying the need for food. He who affirms the reality of God does not deny the fact that various forces, such as the economic, have worked in history.[128] We are affirming, however, that the philosophy of life which leaves out God is leaving out an essential aspect of reality, and strips man of his true humanity.

The communists, however, are not only atheistic materialists, but they are dialectical materialists. This aspect of communism will now be considered.

---

[127] Robert E. D. Clark, *Creation*, London: The Tyndale Press, 1946, pp. 8-11.

[128] Compare Alexander Miller, *The Christian Significance of Karl Marx*, New York: Macmillan Company, p. 77.

CHAPTER FOUR

Dialectical and Historical Materialism

Since the communist is a materialist he believes, as Mao Tse-tung states, that "there is nothing in the world apart from matter in motion."[1] Lenin maintains that everything is derived from matter and is wholly of the nature of matter.[2] Marx agrees that ideas do exist but only as reflections in the material mind of man of the external material world.[3]

The communist, however, is an activist who endeavors to escape from the confines of *mechanistic* materialism. He has accepted instead a philosophy of materialism which is *dialectical.*[4] Today the communist is called on to "master more thoroughly the philosophy of our movement—dialectical materialism."[5]

WHAT IS DIALECTICAL MATERIALISM?

The Greeks used the term "dialectic" to refer to logic, argumentation, and debate. In discussions contradictory viewpoints were presented, and out of the clash of these contradictions a better grasp of truth emerged. Or one might search out the contradictions in an opponent's position and through resolving these contradictions arrive at truth.

Hegel, a German Idealist, maintained that God the Absolute reveals Himself in history in a dialectical process. A movement arises in history. This movement is an inadequate representation

---

[1] *On Contradiction*, New York: International Publishers, 1953, p. 20.

[2] *Materialism and Empiro-Criticism*, New York: International Publishers, p. 14; Frederick Engels, *Socialism: Utopian and Scientific*, New York: International Publishers, "Introduction."

[3] *Capital*, p. 25. Alexander Miller, *The Christian Significance of Karl Marx*, p. 21.

[4] Engels, *Ludwig Feuerbach*, pp. 36, 52-57.

[5] A CP Sub-Committee Report, "On Social Democracy in the U.S." *Political Affairs*, Jan. 1957, p. 8.

of the totality of reality. In opposition to its onesideness, and as a corrective to it, another movement arises. The original movement is called the *thesis*. The opposition movement, which is a reaction movement "born of the limitations of the 'thesis,' " is called the anti-thesis or *antithesis*.[6] After a time the antithesis also manifests its shortcomings and the next stage, the *synthesis*, is in order. The synthesis emerges out of the clash between the thesis and the antithesis. The synthesis catches up within itself that which was valuable, in both the thesis and the antithesis.[7] It is thus a higher stage of the manifestation of the Absolute.

The synthesis itself is inadequate and thus it becomes a thesis which calls forth its own antithesis. The process thus starts all over again, but on a higher level.

Diagrammed, the dialectical process appears as follows:

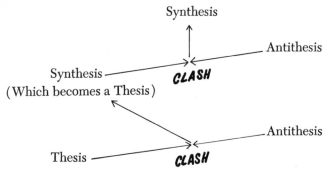

Karl Marx accepted Hegel's idea that reality must be viewed dialectically. He maintained, however, that Hegel was wrong in that he made the Idea instead of matter primary. Marx interpreted reality materialistically and concluded that instead of the Ideal being unfolded in history the Ideal was "nothing else than the material world reflected by the human mind, and translated into forms of thought."[8]

Dialectical materialism is the all-inclusive term which includes the universe, nature, man and society while the term *historical materialism* applies to the history of man and society.[9] Human

6 William Temple, *Nature, Man and God*, New York: St. Martins Press, Inc., p. 58.

7 *Ibid.*, 58-59.

8 *Capital*, p. 25.

9 M. M. Bober, *Karl Marx's Interpretation of History*. 2nd Edition Re-

history, so the communists maintain, has moved according to the laws of the dialectic and will continue so to move. These laws will be discussed shortly.

CHARACTERISTICS OF THE DIALECTICAL METHOD

According to communism, the dialectical method is character-ized by interconnectedness, change and progress. (a) *Intercon-nectedness.* All phenomena is related and conditioned by surrounding circumstances. All are related in the dialectical bond. Thus a movement cannot be understood in isolation, but only in its position in the dialectical process. (b) *Change.* All nature and society are in a process of dissolution and develop-ment, of decay and of birth on a higher level, or destruction and evolution. The "dialectical method regards as important primarily not that which at the given moment seems to be durable and yet is always beginning to die away, but that which is arising and developing, even though at the given mo-ment it may appear not to be durable, for the dialectical method considers invincible only that which is arising and developing." *Change is inevitable,* irresistible and progressive. (c) *Progress.* The antithesis is on a higher quantitative level than the thesis, and the synthesis represents a qualitative step. Thus changes develop from quantitative differences to qualitative differences, "a development in which the qualitative changes occur not gradually, but rapidly and abruptly, taking the form of a leap from one state to another; they occur not accidentally but as the natural result of an accumulation of imperceptible and gradual quantitative changes."[10]

This, then is dialectical materialism. What, according to Marxism, are the dialectical stages in human history?

SIX STAGES

Communists maintain that human society has passed through four stages and that it will pass through two more stages: (1) primitive communism, (2) slavery of antiquity, (3) feudalism,

---

vised, p. 45. Maurice Cornforth, *Materialism and the Dialectical Method* New York: International Publishers, 1953. See also his *Historical Material-ism,* New York: International Publishers, 1954. Howard Selsam, *What is Philosophy?* New York: International Publishers, 1938, pp. 70-71. *History of the Communist Party of the Soviet Union* (*B*), p. 105.

[10] *History of the Communist Party of the Soviet Union,* p. 107.

(4) capitalism, (5) socialism (a transition stage), and (6) communism. How do they explain these stages in the light of thesis, antithesis and synthesis?

Communism maintains that in primitive society men labored in common to produce and the products of their common labor was shared in common. They had to work in common in order to survive. Lands, cattle, women, children, and husbands all belonged to the community. This was primitive communism.[11] However, as time went on development resulted in a division of labor and broke up the system of communal production by the entire tribe.[12] The product then began to be appropriated by the producer, who now was not the entire community. Products began to be exchanged for other products. There was the growth of private property on the one hand and the growth of a dispossessed-non-owning-class on the other hand.[13] Then, too, there was a growth in the productivity of labor. A man began to produce more than he consumed. This surplus made it profitable for certain men to benefit without labor from the labor of others. Thus slavery arose, for it was now profitable to capture and utilize slaves.[14]

Thus private property arose as an antithesis to primitive communism. Out of the clash between these two arose the slavery of antiquity. Slavery was the synthesis, and therefore represented an advancement over primitive communism.

In this connection Engels says, "With slavery, which attained its fullest development under civilization, came the first great cleavage of society into an exploiting and an exploited class. This cleavage persisted during the whole civilized period. Slavery is the first form of exploitation, the form peculiar to the ancient world; it is succeeded by serfdom in the middle ages, and wage-labor in the more recent period. These are the three great forms of servitude, characteristic of the three great epochs of civilization; open, and in recent times disguised, slavery always accompanies them."[15]

After a while, however, slavery became a fetter on production. Although slavery for a time accelerated the "development of the

---

[11] Maurice Cornforth, *Historical Materialism*, p. 55.
[12] *Ibid.*, p. 56.
[13] *Ibid.*, p. 57.
[14] *Ibid.*, p. 57.
[15] *Origin of the Family, Private Property and the State*, New York: International Publishers, 1942, p. 160.

productive forces," "the further development of the productive forces proved incompatible with the slave system. Slavery was replaced by feudalism...."[16] Slave labor began to be unprofitable due to revolts and to the nature of slave labor itself. Free workers rather than slaves were more productive; so slavery declined and feudalism arose. This system was characterized by the feudal landowners, the serfs and peasants who although usually tied to the land yet were not slaves.[17] The communists are not clear in their discussions of the rise of feudalism. In fact, Maurice Cornforth said that the "process of transition from slavery to feudalism has been little studied by Marxist historians. Hence only very tentative observations can be made at present about the factors operating in it."[18]

However, they believe that the dialectic was at work. Thus they believe that the *thesis* (slavery) became a fetter on production and called forth its *antithesis* (the freedman or free workers). Out of the clash between these two systems there emerged the *synthesis* (feudalism). This was a higher stage than any stage of human society which had existed before. Once more production increased for a time, but finally feudalism also became a fetter on production and an antithesis developed.

After a while "within feudalism, manufactories began to arise and with them new classes, the urban bourgeoisie and the wage-earning class." The interests of the manufacturers conflicted with those of the feudalists, while feudalism was further weakened by peasant revolts. Feudalism passed away and capitalism took over.[19]

But how can this be fitted into the dialectical frame work? It was the rise of the industrial age, and not a reaction to feudalism which led to modern industrial capitalism. In no meaningful sense can modern industrial society be said to be the synthesis resulting from a clash between feudalism as the thesis and something else as an antithesis. What is the antithesis to feudalism, which was begotten by feudalism? Individual landholders—landholders who were formerly serfs—would be more of an antithesis to feudalism with its landlords and serfs. And yet, it was machinery which made possible the small manufacturer at

---

[16] Maurice Cornforth, *Historical Materialism*, p. 73.

[17] *Ibid.*, p. 75.

[18] *Ibid.*, p. 75. See Maurice Dobb, *Studies in the Development of Capitalism*, New York: International Publishers.

[19] Maurice Cornforth, *Historical Materialism*, p. 75.

first and later the big manufacturer. And machinery is certainly not an antithesis to feudalism, called forth by inadequacies of feudalism. With the introduction of machinery and mass production, a new factor was introduced which was not at all explainable by the dialectic.

Capitalism, it is maintained, creates its antithesis in that it creates the laboring class in industrial society. This is the proletariat which is made up of wage slaves who have nothing to sell but their labor. These make up the exploited class while the owners make up the exploiting class. These two classes clash until the proletariat, under the leadership of the Communist Party, seize the reigns of government and introduce the dictatorship of the proletariat.[20] This dictatorship is supposed to be a temporary stage which eliminates opposition, introduces socialism and finally gives way to communism. Communism is supposedly the classless society wherein there are no rival classes—no exploiters or exploited. Justice, plenty and peace prevail.

Capitalism is thus viewed as the thesis, the proletariat as the antithesis and communism as the final synthesis.

Diagrammed the course of human history appears as follows:

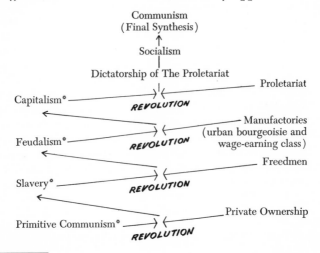

[20] "Why is it that the means of production are concentrated in the hands of the working class, represented by the state, and not in the hands of plants and factories, mines, etc.? In the first place, because largescale socialist production must be planned and run on a nationwide scale; and this function is performed by the proletariat organized in the state. Secondly, the working class can exercise its leadership of the peasantry only

What does all of this mean when viewed in the light of the characteristics of the dialectical method: interconnectedness, change and progress?

(a) *Interconnectedness.* Social systems must be evaluated in the light of the conditions which gave birth to them, and in the light of their position in the dialectical process. They are not to be viewed in the light of some supposedly eternal principles.[21] For example, says Engels, incest was moral under primitive communism.[22] Slavery thus viewed was also good and necessary at one point in human history. It was an advancement over primitive communism. Capitalism also served a necessary historical function and constituted an advance over Feudalism.

(b) *Change.* No system, however, is permanent; and thus as slavery passed away (only in communist theory, of course, since slavery has been revived on a large scale in Russia and Red China) capitalism will pass away. It is not permanent. It is inevitable that it will be destroyed by the antithesis, the proletariat, which is supposedly a higher stage in the dialectical scale. The forces behind change are the internal contradictions which inhere in all things.[23] These changes inevitably produce revolutionary consequences.

(c) *Progress.* Change is progressive. Each stage is higher in the dialectical process than the previous stage; thus it is a better stage. The change is brought on by continuous *quantitative* changes within the society, and then in the revolutionary period a *qualitative* leap is made to the higher form of society. The last leap, which is still in the future, is the leap to communism. This is the leap from the realm of necessity into the realm of freedom. When this stage has arrived, the dialectic will continue to work, but it will not work violently since there will be no classes to clash with one another. Dialectical opposition between man and nature and between interest groups will exist, but it will not break forth in violence. Thus man will continue to make progress in peace and prosperity.[24]

---

when it acts as a single organized force represented by the state both economically and politically" (D. Chesnokov, *World Marxist Review*, July 1959, p. 44).

[21] *History of the Communist Party of the Soviet Union*, pp. 109-110.

[22] Engels, *The Origin of the Family, Private Property and the State*, pp. 31-33.

[23] *History of the Communist Party of the Soviet Union*, p. 109.

[24] Herbert Aptheker, *Class Lectures*, Jefferson School of Social Science, July 1954.

Unless communism is achieved there can be no lasting peace and prosperity, so say the communists. Thus they maintain that "one must be a revolutionary, not a reformist." One must "not try to check the class struggle but carry it to its conclusion."[25]

In order to arrive at a fuller understanding of dialectical materialism, let us examine it from the standpoint of the *dialectical laws*. The most important of these laws are: (a) The universality and the particularity of contradiction, (b) The identity, the unity or interpenetration of opposites in the contradiction, (c) Progress comes through the struggle between the opposites, (d) The transformation of quantity into quality in a revolutionary leap, and (e) The negation of the negation. Some of these laws you will find stated by Engels.[26]

THE UNIVERSALITY AND CONTINUITY OF CONTRADICTIONS

The universality of contradictions teaches that contradictions exist in the development of everything and in the development of each thing from the beginning to the end of the process.[27] Says Engels, "Motion itself is a contradiction: even simple mechanical change of place can only come about through a body at one and the same moment of time being both in one place and in another place, being in one and the same place and also not in it. And the continuous assertion and simultaneous solution of this contradiction is precisely what motion is . . . this is even more true of the higher forms of motion of matter, and especially of organic life and its development . . .

---

[25]*History of the Communist Party of the Soviet Union,* p. 111. In Soviet Russia today the term "dialectic" is often used synonomously with the "dynamic"; or in some cases the "historical" approach in contrast with what they view as a static or metaphysical approach (Gustav A. Wetter, *Dialectical Materialism,* p. 310). Neither Hegel nor Lenin considered the thesis-antithesis-synthesis triad as the basic element of the dialectical approach (*ibid.,* p. 311). It was more the external side than the essence of dialectical materialism. In fact Lenin said: "No other role remains for the triads than as a lid and a skin. . ." (Lenin, *What the "Friends of the People" Are and How They Fight the Social-Democrats,* Moscow: Foreign Languages Publishing House, 1946, p. 50). The *laws* of the dialectic are the most important aspects of dialectical materialism.

[26] *Dialectics of Nature,* Moscow: Foreign Languages Publishing House, 1954, p. 83.

[27] Mao Tse-tung, *On Contradiction,* p. 15.

life consists just precisely in this—that a living thing is at each moment itself and yet something else. Life is therefore also a contradiction which is present in things and processes themselves, and which constantly asserts and solves itself; and as soon as the contradiction ceases, life too comes to an end, and death steps in."[28]

Contradictions not only exist in everything, but in each thing from its beginning to its end. For example, there "has been contradiction between labor and capital ever since they came into being—only at first it was not yet intensified."[29]

Contradictions do not lead to annihilative revolutions unless they are contradictions between classes. Thus the communists maintain that contradictions or differences do exist between the peasants and the workers in the Soviet Union, and between the Party and the people in Red China, but that these will not be intensified into a revolutionary struggle, for according to their theory their own system cannot breed classes and thus cannot result in revolutions. Therefore the revolution in Hungary was very embarrassing to the dialectician. In that revolution the proletariat revolted against the dictatorship of the proletariat!

As applied to the present, the communists believe that contradiction exists between capitalism and proletarianism, and between capitalism and the Communist Party which claims to represent the proletariat. Antagonism is *universal* and *perpetual*. The old antagonism ceases to exist only with the "emergence of a new process." Mao Tse-tung explains that this new process emerges "when the old unity and its constituent opposites yield place to a new unity and its constituent opposites, and the new process then emerges in place of the old. The old process is completed, and the new one emerges."[30]

The basic contradiction in capitalistic society, according to Marx, is "the contradiction between the social character of production and the private character of ownership."[31] This contradiction ceases when private ownership is destroyed, and men not only work together to produce but also own the means of production. However, under communism the state instead of private individuals owns the means of production. State Mo-

---

[28] *Anti-Dühring*, pp. 137-138.
[29] Mao Tse-tung, *On Contradiction*, p. 18.
[30] *Ibid.*, p. 18.
[31] Cited in *On Contradiction*, p. 31.

nopoly Capitalism is inevitable in communism. Economic and political power is concentrated in the hands of the Party leaders and bureaucrats.

THE PARTICULARITY OF CONTRADICTION

The particularity of contradiction is the communist corrective to the dogmatic assumption that because contradiction is universal one can draw up a rigid set of rules as to how one is to act in all contradictory situations. Each contradiction is in a specific situation, and there must be a study of the specific contradiction and its setting in order to know how to resolve the particular contradiction. "The use of different methods to resolve different contradictions is a principle which Marxist-Leninists must strictly observe."[32] Although the basic contradiction of a system exists until the end of the system, yet the conditions of one stage may differ from that of another, and thus they must be dealt with in different ways.[33]

Not only quantitatively different systems, but also qualitatively different situations call for different treatment. In fact, qualitatively different situations call for qualitatively different methods. As Mao-Tse-tung put it: "Qualitatively different contradictions can be resolved by qualitatively different methods. For example: The contradiction between the proletariat and the bourgeoisie is resolved by the method of socialist revolution; the contradiction between the great masses of the people and the feudal system is resolved by the method of democratic revolution; the contradiction between colonies and imperialism is resolved by the method of national revolutionary war; the contradiction between the working class and the peasantry in socialist society is resolved by the method of collectivization and mechanization of agriculture; the contradiction within the Communist Party is resolved by the method of criticism and self-criticism; the contradiction between society and nature is resolved by the method of developing the productive forces."[34]

THE UNITY OF OPPOSITES

What is meant by the unity of opposites? What is meant by the identity of the different aspects of a contradiction? It is not

---

[32] *On Contradiction*, p. 23.
[33] *Ibid.*, p. 26.
[34] *Ibid.*, pp. 22-23.

a denial of the fact of opposition,[35] since contradictions "exclude each other, struggle with each other, and are opposed to each other."[36]

The unity of contradiction means, *first* of all, that the aspects of a contradiction cannot exist in isolation. There can be no antithesis without a thesis. Thus they are united in the sense that for a period of time they coexist in the dialectical bond.

Second, there is identity in that due to certain conditions the contradictory aspects of a situation may be transformed into their opposites. Mao Tse-tung explains it this way: "You see, by means of revolution, the proletariat, once the ruled, transforms itself into the ruler, while the bouregoisie, originally the ruler, is transformed into the ruled, transferred to the position originally occupied by its opposite. This has already taken place in the Soviet Union, and will take place throughout the world. I should like to ask: If there is no interconnection and identity of opposites under certain conditions, can such a change take place?"[37]

To sum it up: "All contradictory things are interconnected, and they not only coexist in an entity under certain conditions, but also transform themselves into each other under certain conditions—this is the whole meaning of the identity of contradictions."[38]

The unity of opposites, however, is temporary. Says Lenin, "The unity (the coincidence, identity, resultant force) of opposites is conditional, temporary, transitory, and relative. The struggle of the mutually exclusive opposites is absolute, as movement and evolution are."[39]

PROGRESS THROUGH CONTRADICTION AND STRUGGLE

"Development is the 'struggle' of opposites," so says Lenin.[40] Echoes Mao Tse-tung, ". . . it is the contradictions inside things that cause their development."[41]

---

[35] Editor's Comment in Lenin, *Materialism and Empirio-Criticism*, p. 323.
[36] Mao Tse-tung, *On Contradiction*, p. 42.
[37] *Ibid.*, p. 44.
[38] *Ibid.*, p. 45.
[39] *Materialism and Empirio-Criticism*, p. 324.
[40] *Ibid.*, p. 323.
[41] *On Contradiction*, p. 11.

The contradictions always struggle with one another, even during their period of relative rest or coexistence. The time comes finally, however, for "conspicuous change." During the period of *relative rest*, quantitative changes take place. When these reach a certain point, a qualitative change takes place.

This means that the period of coexistence between the aspects of a contradiction is "conditional relative." The struggle, however, is "unconditional, absolute."[42]

It is not until conditions are ripe that the contradiction "adopts the form of open antagonism which develops into a revolution." "The time when a bomb has not yet exploded is the time when contradictory things, because of certain conditions, coexist in an entity. It is not until a new condition (ignition) is present that the explosion takes place.... It is very important to know this situation. It enables us to understand that in a class society revolutions and revolutionary wars are inevitable, that apart from them the leap in social development cannot be made, and the reactionary ruling classes cannot be overthrown so that the people will win political power. Communists must expose the deceitful propaganda of the reactionaries that social revolution is unnecessary and impossible, and so on, and firmly uphold the Marxist-Leninist theory of social revolution, so as to help the people understand that social revolution is not only entirely necessary but also entirely possible, and that the whole history of mankind and the triumph of the Soviet Union all confirm this scientific truth."[43]

THE TRANSFORMATION OF QUANTITY INTO QUALITY

When the quantitative changes have accumulated until revolution is possible and inevitable, the old system is destroyed by revolution. Thus the leap is made from the lower form of society to a higher form. The dictatorship of the proletariat is higher than capitalism because this dictatorship is supposed to advance the cause of mankind by bringing into existence socialism and then communism. It is higher because it is higher in the dialectical scale. With the successful revolution something new has been added and society is thus transformed.

---

[42] *Ibid.*, pp. 48-49.
[43] *Ibid.*, pp. 50-51.

THE NEGATION OF THE NEGATION

The proletariat is the antithesis, or negation which negates or destroys capitalism. With the complete destruction of capitalism, by revolution and by the dictatorship of the proletariat, the proletariat has created the conditions of its own negation or cessation. When the proletariat builds a classless society the proletarian class ceases to exist. There can be no classes in a classless society. Thus there is the negation of the proletariat which previously negated the capitalist class.[44]

What influence does the dialectic have on the communists in their day to day struggle to conquer the world? To this our attention is now turned.

---

[44] Supposedly there is a conservation of the better aspects of the negation. Gustav A. Wetter, *Dialectical Materialism*, pp. 356-363.

CHAPTER FIVE

The Dialectic and Conduct

To those who think that the communists do not take their philosophy seriously, it may seem impossible that the dialectical interpretation of reality has any bearing on the conduct of the communists. Those who think thus are in error. For example, the doctrine of peaceful coexistence and the communists' approach to subversion are tied in with dialectic. Their belief in the inevitability of communism is also based on the dialectic.

THE DOCTRINE OF PEACEFUL COEXISTENCE

It is in the light of the dialectic and its laws that we must view the periodic communist emphasis on peaceful coexistence. Peaceful coexistence is embraced in the law of the unity of opposites. It is the period of time during which the thesis and the antithesis coexist in the unity of the dialectical bond. It is also the period during which the antithesis endeavors to bring about the quantitative changes which finally make possible the revolution, the qualitative leap to a new form of society.

The dialectic helps us to realize several things concerning the doctrine of peaceful coexistence. First, *this doctrine is not new in communism.* It has always been implied in the contention that the thesis and the antithesis exist side by side for a period of time. Thus Adam Lapin stated that peaceful coexistence was not a "new look" but an old policy, and that it had been "the cornerstone of the foreign policy of the Soviet Union ever since it came into being in 1917."[1] "From its very first day of existence the Soviet State proclaimed peace, non-interference in the internal affairs of other countries, recognition of the right of all peoples to self-determination and the establishment of the system of their choice as the basic principles of its foreign

---

[1] *Coexistence or No Existence,* New York: New Century Publishers, Mar. 1955, p. 9.

policy."[2] Already in 1920 Lenin said: "Our plans in Asia? The same as in Europe; peaceful coexistence with the peoples [note, he did not say, with the governments, J.D.B.], with the workers and peasants of all nations."[3] Stalin also talked of peaceful coexistence.[4] In 1949 William Z. Foster, National Chairman of the Communist Party in America wrote: "The key to an intelligent internationalism in our day is friendly cooperation between the United States and the Soviet Union. This collaboration is indispensable if world peace is to prevail."[5] This is from the book which he dedicated to his great grandson whom he said would live in a communist United States.

Secondly, the *communists do not believe that coexistence is perpetual.* Khrushchev stated that although historical conditions make coexistence possible now, it will not always continue. "The situation has developed in which two systems exist simultaneously in the world. You, perhaps, will regard this as the way of providence. We consider it a result of historical development. You hold that capitalism is immutable, that the future belongs to the capitalist system. We, on our part, consider that communism is invincible and that the future belongs to the communist system. These are two diametrically opposite views." "As to how long this coexistence can last, the answer is, That that will depend on historical conditions, on historical development."[6]

In a conversation with Sam Watson, General Secretary of the National Union of Mineworkers, Durham Area in England, Khrushchev said concerning their political system: "In this field there can be no coexistence."[7] Watson summed up Khrushchev's views as Khrushchev expressed them in this conversation. "Coexistence in the field of trade—immediately; coexistence militarily and diplomatically—on terms; coexistence ideologically—never."[8] Ilychov said that it was a distortion of the principle of peaceful coexistence to extend it to the ideological sphere.[9]

Furthermore, while communist ideology allows for various

[2] L. Ilychov in the *World Marxist Review*, Nov. 1959, p. 11.

[3] Quoted in *Coexistence or No Existence*, p. 9.

[4] Stalin, *For Peaceful Coexistence. Postwar Interviews*, New York: International Publishers, 1951.

[5] *The Twilight of World Capitalism*, p. 167.

[6] N. S. Khrushchev, N. A. Bulganin and G. K. Zhukov, *We Stand for Peaceful Coexistence*, New York: New Century Publishers, 1955, pp. 9-10.

[7] St. Louis *Post-Dispatch*, Sept. 27, 1954, p. 8b.

[8] Letter to the author, 21st of October, 1954.

[9] *World Marxist Review*, Nov. 1959, p. 8.

forms of coexistence for periods of time, it does not allow for the concept of perpetual coexistence. This is made crystal clear in Mao Tse-tung's statement that peaceful coexistence is the period before the bomb is ignited, but that with the ignition of a bomb a new situation develops.[10]

Thirdly, the period of peaceful coexistence is *the period wherein quantitative changes accumulate until a revolutionary, qualitative leap is possible.* It is the period of dialectical tension between the thesis and the antithesis, in which the thesis is supposed to weaken, the antithesis to become stronger and finally able to end the tension by destroying the thesis.

According to Lenin and Stalin, the changes which the communists endeavor to bring about during the period of coexistence are: (1) to have time to digest their gains, (2) to divide their enemies, (3) to intensify subversion within the free world, (4) to increase their own strength industrially, militarily and otherwise, (5) to capitalize on wars or tensions between colonial people and the country which rules them (in other words, to capitalize on national aspirations and wars for independence),[11] (6) to conduct psychological warfare against their enemies so as to paralyze them with *false fears* or lull them to sleep with *false hopes,* so as to disarm their enemies psychologically and physically,[12] and (7) to try to undermine the non-communist world economically.

Such aims are found in the following quotations from Lenin and Stalin. It should be borne in mind that Lenin is being re-emphasized today. The April 6, 1956 issue of "For a Lasting Peace, for a People's Democracy!" headlined the following claim: "The Communist Party has always been victorious due to its fidelity to Leninism."

Stalin quotes from Lenin and comments on him as follows: " 'The revolutionary parties,' says Lenin, 'must complete their education. They have learned to attack. Now they have to realize that this knowledge must be supplemented with the knowledge how to retreat properly. They have to realize—and the revolutionary class is taught to realize by its own bitter

---

[10] *On Contradiction,* pp. 50-51.

[11] Stalin, *Foundations of Leninism,* New York: International Publishers, 1939, p. 98.

[12] Lord Coleraine's statement in the *Times* in 1954 reporting on his visit to Russia with the British Parliamentary delegation.

experience—that victory is impossible unless they have learned both how to attack and how to retreat properly.'

"The object of this strategy is to gain time, to disrupt the enemy, and to accumulate forces in order later to assume the offensive.

"The signing of the Brest Peace may be taken as a model of this strategy, for it enabled the Party to gain time, to take advantage of the conflicts in the camp of the imperialists, to disrupt the forces of the enemy, to retain the support of the peasantry, and to accumulate forces in preparation for the offensive against Kolchak and Denikin.

" 'In concluding a separate peace,' said Lenin at that time, 'we free ourselves as much *as is possible at the present moment from both hostile imperialist groups*, we take advantage of their mutual enmity and warfare, which hinder them from making a deal against us, and for a certain period have our hands free to advance and to consolidate the socialist revolution.'

" 'Now even the biggest fool,' said Lenin, three years after the Brest Peace, 'can see that the "Brest Peace" was a concession that strengthened us and broke up the forces of international imperialism.'

"Such are the principal conditions which ensure correct strategic leadership."[13]

"Lenin pointed out that at such moments revolutionary parties should perfect their knowledge. During the period of rise of the revolution they learned how to advance; during the period of reaction they should learn how to retreat properly, how to go underground, how to preserve and strengthen the illegal party, how to make use of legal opportunities, of all legally existing, especially mass, organizations in order to strengthen their connection with the masses."[14]

Again Lenin wrote: "To carry on a war for the overthrow of the international bourgeoisie, a war which is a hundred times more difficult, prolonged and complicated than the most stubborn of ordinary wars between states, and to refuse beforehand to maneuver, to utilize the conflict of interests (even though temporary) among one's enemies, to refuse to temporize and compromise with possible (even though transitory, unstable, vacil-

---

[13] Stalin, *Problems of Leninism*, Moscow: Foreign Languages Publishing House, 1954, p. 88. See also P. Rusov, *World Marxist Review*, Dec. 1959, pp. 3, 5.
[14] *History of the Communist Party of the Soviet Union*, p. 132.

lating and conditional) allies—is not this ridiculous in the extreme? Is it not as though, when making a difficult ascent of an unexplored and hitherto inaccessible mountain, we were to refuse beforehand ever to move in zigzags, ever to retrace our steps, ever to abandon the course once selected to try others?"[15]

For such reasons Stalin once said: "We must not forget Lenin's words to the effect that much depends on whether we succeed in delaying the war against the capitalist world, which is inevitable, until the proletarian revolution is ripe, or until the capitalists start fighting among themselves."[16]

Thus it has always been that whenever the communists have needed additional time they have claimed peaceful intentions. This they did in 1918. But A. J. Sacks, Director of the Russian Information Bureau in the United States, warned America that the communists were the enemies of Russia and of the world and that we should not be deceived by their talk "about the necessity for cooperating with the bourgeois elements."[17] They have said this time and time again when they needed more time —as for example, in Korea.[18]

As the Vice President, Chen Cheng, of the Republic of China put it: "From my 30 years of experience in combating the Chinese Communists, I have learned that alternate use of force and negotiation has been their consistent strategy. As pointed out by Lenin, to the Communists negotiation is merely a means of gathering strength, and this tactic is used to ensure the safe withdrawal of their forces whenever they are not strong enough to overcome the enemy in the field. Their purpose is to gain a respite during which they can recover from exhaustion, but once they have regained strength, they will strike again at the very first opportunity."[19]

---

[15] *"Left-Wing" Communism, An Infantile Disorder*, New York: International Publishers, 1940, p. 52.

[16] At the 15th Convention of All-Russian Communist Party in 1928. Quoted in the *Bulletin of the All-Russian Liberation Committee*, pp. 3-4.

[17] A. J. Sacks, *The Birth of the Russian Democracy*, New York: Russian Information Bureau, 1918, p. 513.

[18] For an instructive speech on coexistence see Louis Waldman, "Coexistence, Containment and Liberation," *Vital Speeches*, June 15, 1955. Also Marshal D. Shulman, "Is the Soviet Union Changing," *Problems of Communism*, May-June, 1956.

[19] Chinese News Service, Nov. 18, 1958, p. 1.

THE DIALECTICAL APPROACH TO SUBVERSION

The communists not only have spies but they also take a dialectical approach in endeavoring to undermine a country. The dialectical approach, it will be remembered, includes the searching out of contradictions within the other person's argument and utilizing these contradictions to undermine and to destroy the opponent's argument. The communists apply this approach in an effort to subvert enemy nations, and all nations which are not under their control are viewed as enemy nations. They endeavor to find conflicting interests and divisions within a country and to exploit these. In so doing they further weaken a country, as well as gain a temporary ally who helps them accomplish some immediate goals and which ultimately leads to the subverting and conquest of even the temporary ally. Thus Yevgeni Zhukov wrote: "The dialectical formula of 'alliance and struggle' expresses the essence of the relationship between the Chinese working people and the national bourgeoisie and discloses the latter's dual character. Notwithstanding its vacillations, the national bourgeoisie can be an ally in the anti-imperialist and anti-feudal struggle. Yet, by virtue of its class nature it cannot but resist development along socialist lines. However, the very form of the alliance determines the conditions and the methods of struggle which pave the way to the gradual re-education of the former exploiters into workers, members of socialist society."[20]

As Lenin put it in 1920: "It is possible to defeat a more powerful enemy only by exerting the utmost effort, and by being thorough, careful, attentive and skillful in taking advantage of various kinds of fissures, even the smallest ones, on the part of the enemy, of every conflict of interests among the bourgeoisie of various countries or in one country; by taking advantage of every opportunity, even the smallest one, of gaining an ally."[21]

President Chiang Kai-shek has had to contend with the communists for over thirty years. He knows from first-hand experience how they work to conquer a country. In discussing the dialectic as utilized by the communists he pointed out that: "To create class contractions, the Communists always analyze a

---

[20] "Impact of the Chinese Revolution on the National Liberation Struggle," *World Marxist Review*, Nov. 1958, p. 20.

[21] *Selected Works*, Russian Edition, Vol. 10, as quoted by Chiang Kaishek, *Soviet Russia in China*, New York: Farrar, Straus and Cudahy, 1957, p. 361.

country's social structure before infiltrating it. They not only explore and exploit, but also create professional, regional, and religious contradictions. Then in the midst of confusion, they win the masses over by disseminating propaganda about class struggle and establishing party cells among them."[22] He pointed out that in China they infiltrated the labor movement in order to use it in the political struggle by gaining an ally and by sharpening any differences between labor and capital. They also organized farmers' movements in the country.

Explains Chiang Kai-shek: "After the reorganization of Kuomintang in 1924, we adopted a policy of alignment with Russia and of the admission of Chinese Communists into our party. We did so because of the belief that Soviet Russia was going to help us 'achieve national unity and independence.' But the assistance given by the Russian Communists was actually used to cover up their infiltration and subversive activities against us."[23]

INCITING RACIAL MINORITIES

"The Chinese Communists have also tried to incite racial minorities to rebellion."[24] For a period of time they advocated Lenin's doctrine of so-called "self-determination for all racial groups." This was in order to weaken a nation by promising independence to each racial group within it. Thus for years in America the communists advocated the idea of a black republic in America. This they called "self-determination for the black belt." "Complete right to self-determination includes also the right to governmental separation, but does not necessarily imply that the Negro population should *make use of this* right in all circumstances, that is, that it must actually separate or attempt to separate the Black Belt from the existing governmental federation with the United States. If it desires to separate, it must be free to do so; but if it prefers to remain federated with the United States it must also be free to do that."[25]

---

[22] *Soviet Russia in China*, p. 361.

[23] *Ibid.*, p. 362.

[24] *Ibid.*, p. 362.

[25] Elizabeth Lawson, *The Communist Position on the Negro Question*, p. 50. This is a series of essays, with an introduction by Elizabeth Lawson, and was published by the Communist Party. The date and place of publication is not contained in the pamphlet. This same Party line on the Negro question is presented in James S. Allen, *Negro Liberation*, p. 21.

The Party line has changed so that today instead of advocating a segregated Negro Republic, the communists are endeavoring to use the integration issue as a means of creating dissension within the country. The Party line now is as follows: "This program is designed to enlarge the area of equal rights for the Negro people, extend the bonds of Negro-white working people's unity and alliance, and advance the Negro people's freedom movement to the eve of the struggle for its ultimate form and expression as would then conform to its needs and aspirations, and the leveling of all barriers to the enjoyment of equal rights on the part of individual Negro citizens and minority groups."[26]

The united front movement is being revived. Open and hidden communists are endeavoring to use racial problems as a means of dividing our country and making and using for their own purposes those who are blind enough to form temporary alliances with them. They are not interested in solving these problems but in weakening the country so that it will be easier for them to take over. The communists search out "contradictions" between racial groups not in order to solve them but to intensify them so as to hasten the day of revolution. That they are not interested in solving racial problems is shown by the admission of Khrushchev that Stalin transported entire racial groups from their native lands.[27]

USE OF YOUTH GROUPS

The communists have long been preparing for the intensification of racial problems in America. They also see their opportunity in connection with youth. In March, 1935, Gil Green said: "The vast majority of American young workers and youth generally are organized, but in organizations directly or indirectly controlled or influenced by the ruling class. These organizations are the Y's, Settlement and Community Houses, Church Organizations, Amateur Athletic Union, etc. It is precisely in these organizations where we must work to win the youth for a working class program and leadership—not only the young workers, but also the farming and student youth."[28]

Continues Mr. Green: "While in most districts the major

---

[26] *Political Affairs*, Dec. 1957, p. 18.

[27] Speech of Feb. 25, 1956 before their 20th Congress, *The Congressional Record*, June 4, 1956, p. 8473.

[28] "Full Speed Ahead," *International of Youth*, Mar. 1935, p. 25.

problem is to send the bulk of our members into these organizations of the youth, in some places the problem is to reorganize
the work of our present League so as to give leadership to our
comrades already in these organizations. For example, in the
South we have more than 300 members who are also members
of church youth organizations—especially the Baptist Young
Peoples Union. In this district (Alabama) the problem confront-
ing the leadership is to completely change the organization
structure of the League. Where possible we should build shop
units and everywhere else units in the church youth organizations. Why? Because in the South, especially for the Negro
youth, the church is the center of all cultural and social activity.
It is here that we must work. By building our units in the church
organizations we can also improve our work under the illegal
conditions, as it will be easier to work in the church organizations. In Alabama there are certain places in which we can in a
short while take over the church organizations of youth, under
our leadership, and these can become legal covers for our work
in the South."

"However, our League in the North is not like that in the
South. In most districts the problem of work in the mass organizations will be more difficult. We will have to teach many of
our comrades how to work in these organizations."[29]

This is their dialectical approach to subversion. What the
communists endeavor to do with the race question and in the
youth organizations, they also endeavor to do with the problems
of labor and management and with any other point of tension,
conflict of interests or of misunderstanding in American society.

Further applications of the "laws of the dialectic" are also
pointed out by Chiang Kai-shek. "The Communists' camouflage,
deception and propaganda war are practical manifestations of
their dialectic laws of contradictions and of negation. For instance, their resort to political assault to disguise their military
operations, their assumption of a defensive posture to cover
their offensive action, their use of propaganda war containing

---

[29] *Ibid.*, pp. 25-26. For a discussion of how the communists endeavor to
use the race problem in America to further their conquest of America see
Subversion in Racial Unrest, Parts I and II of the Public Hearings of the
State of Louisiana's Joint Legislative Committee, Baton Rouge, Louisiana,
Mar. 1957. Also two booklets on Communism and the race question published by the Georgia Commission on Education, 19 Hunter St., S. W.,
220 Agriculture Building, Atlanta 3, Georgia.

nothing but casuistry and falsehood, and their combining entice-
ments with intimidation, all these are based on the principle of
'unity of contradictions.' Again, for instance, their use of peace
talks to negate or undermine their opponent's morale and their
use of hostilities at the same time to negate the peace talks with
their opponent, are based on the laws of 'negation of negations.' "[30]   ·

THE DIALECTIC AND SEMANTIC SABOTAGE

An understanding of the dialectic helps one to understand
how the communists use words, and thus how they try to undermine their opposition by lulling them to sleep through using
terms which convey an entirely different meaning to the communists than they do to the non-communist.[31] The dialectic
teaches that progress, peace and prosperity are possible only if
one works for communism. Communists represent the antithesis
which is against the reactionary, war-minded thesis. Thus to
work for peace means to work for the destruction of capitalism,
since capitalism is the cause of war.[32] By crying Peace, Peace,
the communists try to enlist on their side the natural yearning
of man for peace.

Those who are against communism are, therefore, for war, so
say the communists. Resistance to communism during the time
when there is no large-scale hot war is cold war being waged
against communism. This is how they define cold war. " 'Cold
war'—an aggressive political policy, adopted after the end of
World War II towards the USSR and the people's democracies
by the reactionary circles of the imperialistic powers headed by
the United States and Great Britain."[33] "The aggressive imperialist forces have let loose upon the world their horrible offspring—
the cold war."[34] Cold war is any form of resistance to commu-

---

[30] *Soviet Russia in China*, p. 374. See his entire Appendix on "A study
of the Communists' Use of Dialectics," pp. 350-379. All of this is done in
order to "hasten the disintegration of the bourgeois—capitalist society for
the sake of the final consummation of the whole historical process," Karl
Lowith, *Meaning in History*, p. 33.

[31] Stefan T. Possony, *Language as a Communist Weapon*, Washington,
D.C.: Government Printing Office, 1959.

[32] Editorial in *International Affairs*, Moscow: Soviet Society for the
Popularization of Political and Scientific Knowledge, Nov. 1959, pp. 3-5.

[33] *Large Soviet Encyclopedia*, 2nd Edition, Vol. 46, 1957, p. 297.

[34] *International Affairs*, Nov. 1959, p. 3

nism which is short of a hot war. So when the communists ask
for a relaxation of tension and the ending of the cold war, all
communists understand this to mean that the non-communist
world must cease its opposition to communism, and let down its
guard in the midst of the communist struggle for world conquest. For example, the overseas bases of the United States must
be liquidated.[35] It does not mean that the communists cease
their aggression. People of the non-communist world who do not
realize this think that the communists are indicating that they
are renouncing their desires and plans for world conquest when
they speak of ending the cold war.

THE INEVITABILITY OF COMMUNISM

Khrushchev was appealing to the dialectic when he said that
history was on their side and that they would bury us. Communists represent the antithesis which the dialectic has decreed
will destroy us, the thesis. It is this faith which helps keep the
rank and file members at their tasks when the going is difficult.
For not only is time on their side, but also the dialectic! This
The Jeffersonian stated thus: "It is not simply because we 'want'
social progress that we believe it will come, but because we
know there are powerful forces at work which, given a little
shove, will bring about the changes mankind so deeply yearns
for. We, too, see that imperialist reaction is dominant today; but
we also see its clay feet—and we understand why, of necessity,
the developing working class and people's movement for job,
peace and democracy is stronger; why it has the power; first to
frustrate the drive to war and fascism, and then to move on to
greater democratic advances.

"Our confidence rests on that deep understanding of social
forces which only the science of Marxism affords. We seek to
bring such understanding to the masses of working people."[36]
But if socialism is inevitable, if the laws of society are iron laws,
why work for the advent of socialism? What need is there for
a "little shove"? Does one found a party in order to bring about
a lunar eclipse?[37]

---

[35] *Ibid.*, pp. 123-125.

[36] August 2, 1954. A mimeographed publication by the Jefferson School
of Social Science, New York City. This school was dissolved after being
required to register by the Subversive Activities Control Board.

[37] Stammler as cited by Gustav A. Wetter, *Dialectical Materialism*,
p. 398.

However, the dialectical is not the key to reality and the Marxist faith is thus founded on a distorted view of reality. This fact will be discussed in the next chapter.

CHAPTER SIX

The Dialectic Is Not
the Key to Reality

According to Engels the dialectic is supposed to be "the science of the general laws of motion and development of Nature, human society and thought."[1] Thus they call their socialism scientific. If it is the law of nature, or even a law of nature, it should enable a person to prove something or to produce something. And yet, Engels maintained that it is not "a mere instrument through which things can be proved, as in a more limited way formal logic or elementary mathematics can be regarded."[2] Laws of nature tell us what will happen under a given set of circumstances, but the dialectic does not so tell us.[3]

ENGELS ILLUSTRATES DIALECTICS

The communists maintain that natural processes, as well as social processes, are governed by the dialectic. Engels maintained that the cycle of the barley seed illustrates dialectics. The seed is the thesis, the plant is the antithesis which negates the grain. The stalk dies after the grain has ripened and this is the negation of the negation but it has borne the grain which is multiplied over what it was when planted.[4] This is the synthesis. But this is childish. The plant is not an antithesis to the grain. There is no qualitative change, nor a synthesis on a higher level. There is only a quantitative change from one seed into many seeds. One still has barley seed, and the cycle starts all over again but not on a higher qualitative level.

---

[1] *Herr Eugen Dühring's Revolution in Science*, New York: International Publishers, n.d. p. 160.

[2] *Ibid.*, p. 153.

[3] Max Eastman, *Marxism: Is It Science*, New York: W. W. Norton and Company, Inc., 1940, pp. 137-138.

[4] *op. cit.*, p. 154.

This knowledge of the so-called scientific law does not enable a person to produce anything, as Engels admitted. "The mere knowledge that the barley plant and the infinitesimal calculus are both governed by the negation of the negation does not enable me either to grow barley successfully or to use the calculus; just as little as the mere knowledge of the laws of the determination of sound by the thickness of strings enables me to play the violin."[5] It will, however, tell you something about what size strings to put on the violin if you want certain qualities of sounds. But what does the dialectical approach to the barley plant enable one to do?

The fact that the seed must die in order for many seeds to come into being has long been recognized. Jesus referred to it centuries ago.[6] However, to point to this fact does not in itself explain anything. The fact is one thing, the explanation that some people attempt is quite another thing. The acorn becomes the oak, but that does not explain the presence of life within the seed. The acorn derived its life from a living tree, and so on. "In other words, no entity, not even one which possesses what we call 'immanent activity,' adequately accounts for its life or motion. All such beings are endowed with a principle of activity which they have received from another. Consequently, no being which reproduces itself through a process of negation contains within itself an adequate explanation of the vital activity which plays such an essential role in this process. For such an explanation recourse must be had to some being outside itself."[7] One cannot forever trace through a line of dependent beings or things. One cannot explain the tree by the acorn, the acorn by the tree. One must finally get back to something beyond both which is able to explain the origin of the first acorn or of the first oak.

DOES HISTORY PROVE DIALECTICAL MATERIALISM?

Dialectics has not been established by the experimental method. What experiment performed in the laboratory could prove that dialectical materialism is the key to reality? The fact that positives and negatives exist was known long before Karl Marx, but this does not establish dialectical materialism.

---

[5] *Herr Eugen Dühring's Revolution in Science*, p. 161.
[6] John 12:24.
[7] Charles J. McFadden, *The Philosophy of Communism*, p. 194.

The study of history and society does not prove dialectical materialism. To prove that the dialectic is the key to reality one would have to know both the beginning and the end of history. And yet, so far as human knowledge goes, history is a stream concerning whose source and destiny man stands in ignorance. Thus it would be impossible to say that one stage of history is the thesis, another the antithesis and another the synthesis. Of course, if one has sufficient imagination and is sufficiently ignorant of facts, he can make any event a thesis or antithesis or synthesis. "Thus, the Norman Conquest can be represented as a synthesis of Roman and Anglo-Saxon cultures, or as a thesis of which the age of the Plantagenets and that of the Tudors are respectively the anti-thesis and the synthesis. Such irresponsible treatment simply reduces history to a game for which the only qualifications are a lively imagination and much ignorance."[8]

A country may go on for centuries without any change of great significance. For example, consider the history of India. Why was not the dialectic at work in the past centuries in India? Marxism cannot explain the unprogressiveness of many nations.[9]

Progress may vary widely within different aspects of a civilization. Great political changes may take place, without significant change in domestic life. Religious beliefs may remain constant although the economic system may change. " . . . we find great political and military and some economic changes in France in the last third of the eighteenth century, whereas in England there are at the same time the most momentous economic changes but no political changes to speak of, and in the military sphere none whatever. It may even happen that of two insignificant customs, one falls into desuetude after a short time, whereas the other is preserved through a thousand years. The same may be said of institutions, as well as of systems of all kinds."[10]

There is no guarantee that a higher stage will arise out of a conflict between two opposites. The conflict may lead to a stalemate, it may lead to progress, or it may lead to a backward step.

---

[8] R. N. Carew Hunt, *The Theory and Practice of Communism*, pp. 41-42.
[9] Charles J. McFadden, *The Philosophy of Communism*, p. 252.
[10] Karl Federn, *The Materialist Conception of History*, London: Macmillan & Company, Ltd., 1939, p. 211.

Marxism is unable to account for retrogression in history. According to communists the dialectic works in everything, at all times and in all stages. Thus constant progress should always be made. And yet history has many examples of civilizations which have arisen, waxed and then waned and perished. The economic advancement and cultural advancement of a civilization may be lost. Engels admitted that there are at least temporary retrogressions in history, but he asserted that "a progressive development asserts itself in the end."[11] But to admit the fact of retrogression is inconsistent with Marxism, for the movement of the dialectic is always forward, upward, progressive. The antithesis is always higher than the thesis, and it always triumphs and brings about a synthesis. This must be the case if the dialectic works in everything, at all times and in every stage. "As E. I. Watkin remarks, Engel's admission that there has been regress in history but that progress always asserts itself in the end, is a mere optimistic act of faith which not only lacks a basis in Marxian principles but which is actually opposed to them. 'This optimism has no warrant in his materialist philosophy but is a pure act of faith which the founders of Marxism shared with the vast majority of their contemporaries, for whom progress was an unquestioned axiom. But it is an act of faith which can have no foundation apart from belief in Divine Providence.' "[12]

DOES SOCIALISM INEVITABLY FOLLOW CAPITALISM?

The communist assumption that socialism will follow capitalism as a higher stage, is not based on anything in dialectics, even if dialectics were the key to reality. What in the dialectical law says that it is socialism which must follow capitalism? *How by seeing how a law has worked in the past can we predict that in the future this law will produce something which it has never produced at any time in the past?* Even if capitalism is doomed, nothing in the dialectic says that it must be followed by socialism. Communists base this conclusion entirely on the assumption that "socialism is the next higher stage of evolution. And that assumption hangs entirely on the supposition that it is desirable. The thesis of the inevitability of socialism rests in the last

---

[11] *Ludwig Feuerbach*, p. 54.

[12] *Men and Tendencies*, London, 1937, p. 256. Cf. C. Dawson, *Progress and Religion*, New York: Doubleday and Company, Inc., p. 5. In Charles J. McFadden, *The Philosophy of Communism*, pp. 253-254.

analysis on the despised proposition of the despised Utopians that it is desirable."[13] The fact of motion, and of action and reaction, furnishes no ground for the assumption that the motion is upward and that the next stage is socialism. Communists assume first that socialism is higher than capitalism and then they assume that the dialectic's next step will be socialism. And yet, they claim that their position is based on the laws of science and not on assumptions and naive faith.

What a blind faith this is! And the hurtful results that flow from acting on this faith have been demonstrated by what has taken place in Russia. The communists claim that they have built socialism in Russia. In reality what they have in Russia is State Monopoly Capitalism, and this State is a ruthless dictatorship which has built up a new heartless exploiting class— as Djilas, a former associate of Tito, has recognized in his book on *The New Class*.

Even if the dialectic were the key to reality, it would be foolish to try to outline the antithesis or the synthesis in advance. It would be too easy to omit some relevant fact or principle. Unexpected and unforeseen developments constantly occur in history. And these unknown factors and unexpected developments have consequences as surely as do the known factors. We know that a scientific experiment can be upset because one relevant factor was not taken into consideration. How can one know that he has taken into consideration all relevant factors? Who has such an omnipotent grasp of history and society that he knows that there are no factors, or unexpected developments, which will upset his own forecast of the future.[14]

HAS COMMUNISM DISPENSED WITH IDEALS, GOALS, AND PURPOSE?

Marx and Engels seem to have thought that they had gotten away from the assumption of an Ideal Order of existence. Yet the dialectic itself assumes such an order—an ideal order of existence without which the dialectic itself is impossible. The communists assume that the dialectic is headed toward a classless society—the withering away of the dictatorship of the proletariat and the ushering in of an entirely different kind of society

---

[13] John Kenneth Turner, *Challenge to Karl Marx*, New York: Reynal and Hitchcock, 1941, p. 365.

[14] William Temple, *Nature, Man and God*, pp. 59-60.

on a higher level. This higher, and in fact final, level is communism. It is a society which is so superior to our present society that the communists maintain that all which goes before it is not truly human history, but that truly human history starts only with the advent of communism. The classless society is a remote ideal, for even in the so-called classless society in Russia they have more than one class of railway coach and railway waiting rooms! It is also a remote ideal that the dictatorship will wither away without a bloody revolution. It is an ideal even more remote that the dialectic will finally carry man to a social order—communism—where each will so live that he calls forth the best in others, and thus that peace, prosperity and brotherhood will forever prevail. It is certainly a remote ideal that the dialectic will create such a new and higher type of man that men today find it difficult to imagine the high type of man who will then exist.

Without a goal, and an ideal goal, toward which the dialectical movement is progressing, it would be impossible to say that an outcome will be this or that. Either history is progressing towards some goal or there is no reason to affirm that the movement of history is upward at all. The synthesis could as well represent a lower stage of society, instead of a stage higher than either the thesis or antithesis. In fact, one could not affirm that it was higher or lower. He could only affirm that it is different from the thesis and the antithesis, unless there is an ideal goal or standard toward which progress is being made.

James Feibleman put it this way: "Without the existence of a goal, the given thesis or antithesis would be final. There would be no crossing from one extreme to the other, and recrossing, unless there was an approximation of some basic direction. In short, the dialectic would not serve as the approach to a true direction, unless that true direction had first been assumed."[15] "The Marxist dialectic requires some ideal goal in terms of which it can be understood as an approach."[16] "For did it not have a goal, it would not move at all; and did it not endeavor to approach a straight line, it would not waver as it does. Thus the very conception of the dialectic presupposes an ideal, without which it could not be."[17]

---

[15] *Christianity, Communism and the Ideal Society*, New York: International Publishers, p. 205.

[16] *Ibid.*, p. 222.

[17] *Ibid.*, p. 263.

Marx did not get away from a belief in an ideal reality which lies beyond observed reality. His vision of a communist society was not the result of the examination of anything which existed. It was something far in the future. He believed that reality is journeying inevitably toward an ideal, i.e., a classless society in which brotherhood prevails. "Now, to set up ideal conditions and to strive toward them in actuality is equivalent to supposing the existence of an order over and above actuality."[18]

Engels and Lenin had to agree that there are eternal truths. Lenin states: "the relative limits of our approximation to the cognition of the objective, absolute truth are historically conditioned; but the existence of this truth is unconditioned, as well as the fact that we are continually approaching it. . . . In a word, every ideology is historically conditioned, but it is unconditionally true that to every scientific theory (as distinct from religion), there corresponds an objective truth, something absolutely so in nature."[19] The problem, however, Lenin maintained, was that "we must know how to put, and solve dialectically, the question of the correlation between absolute and relative truths."[20]

How can Lenin know that this is the case? If thought is but matter in motion, how does Lenin know that the particular motions of matter in his brain which led him to this position are true representations of reality? If our thoughts are but the reflection in our minds of the material world, of which the economic system is a basis element, how can they know that these reflections are true? This question is especially pertinent when we remember that Marxists maintain that the economic systems of the days of Engels and of Lenin were irrational systems. Thus the reflections in their minds were irrational.

PROGRESS NOT EXPLAINED BY CONTRARIES

Contraries in life do not explain progress. They can as easily produce dissolution of being, or absolute or comparative rest. The communists, however, maintain that the conflict of contraries inevitably results in progress. In other words, a benevolent purpose is being worked out in the universe by means of the dialectic. There is a law making for righteousness or jus-

---

[18] *Ibid.*, p. 261.
[19] Lenin, *Materialism and Empirio-Criticism*, p. 107.
[20] *Ibid.*, p. 104.

tice. Whence this law? How can its origin be in matter? How can one affirm that such a law exists, and then deny the reality of something beyond matter?

Communists are forced to admit the reality of a benevolent purpose in nature, but they maintain that it is not the result of conscious and purposive activity but "lies in the necessity of the thing itself."[21] To say that it lies in the nature of the thing itself does not solve the problem. And right here we point to another contradiction in Marxist thinking. The communists believe that man is the result of the blind working of the forces of nature. A fortunate, undirected by intelligence, concourse of atoms created man. And yet, on the other hand, communism views all things as under the control of a dialectical law which inevitably produces order, harmony and justice. Can these two concepts be harmonized?

To reply that the material organization of a being determines its end does not solve the problem. As Charles J. McFadden states, "The problem which the Marxist has not answered is: What determines the material organization of the being?"[22]

Although Marx maintained that matter in motion is the only reality, he has attributed to matter a purpose which transcended material relationships. Matter in dialectical motion is working for the emancipation of mankind from poverty and war, and man can cooperate with matter to bring about this ideal society! He has arbitrarily filled matter not only with a goal or purpose toward which it must work, but also with a benevolent quality since it is working for man's emancipation.[23]

It is true that there are instances in human history where one extreme has been followed by another, and then in some cases people have sought some golden mean between the extremes. Some people seemingly react in the opposite direction to almost anything. This, however, is far from saying that this is the way that people must act. All people are not reactionists and no one is forced to be a reactionist.

Some may jump from one extreme to another in their thinking, but this is not the way that they *ought* to think or *must* think. Because some have so thought does not prove that this is the way that one must think or travel in order to make prog-

---

[21] Engels, *Anti-Dühring*, p. 79.

[22] *The Philosophy of Communism*, p. 189.

[23] Compare George Gatlin, *The Story of the Political Philosophers*, p. 575.

ress. As James Feiblemann explains, "Logic as an ideal affair is not the description of how thought *has* moved but the study of how it *ought* to move."[24]

To point to what has been does not establish either what ought to be, what can be or what will occur in the future. To assume otherwise is to confuse "history with necessity."[25] For example, past progress in a field of study is not necessarily a reliable indication of what progress may be made in that field in the future.

We can accept the part played in history by conflicting tendencies without accepting such as the universal law which governs all history in all of its aspects.

In fact, "to lean on the dialectic means that because one must detour, it is necessary to make the detour as wide as possible! The dialectic wavering from the true path should be reduced, not exaggerated."[26]

DOES REALITY CORROBORATE DIALECTICAL MATERIALISM?

That dialectics is not the key to reality is proved by the fact that if it were, the communists should have been able to make social predictions on the basis of the dialectical law. And yet, they have failed miserably. According to their interpretation the communist revolution should have taken place first in an advanced industrial and capitalistic country, but it took place in Russia. As we have shown in the chapter on communism and religion, the dialectic has not enabled them to make scientific predictions.

If the dialectical interpretation of reality is scientific, why is it that the great scientific discoveries have been made without any reference to dialectics?[27]

The dialectic does not even diagnose the communist's protest against the private ownership of the means of production and distribution. It cannot be described in terms of the dialectic, for the communist's protest against the private ownership of productive property is not based on an antithesis to private ownership. The idea of the right of private ownership, however, is involved. The theory of surplus value says that capitalism by its

---

[24] *Christianity, Communism and the Ideal Society,* pp. 203-204.
[25] *Ibid.,* p. 204.
[26] *Ibid.,* p. 225.
[27] R. N. Carew Hunt, *The Theory and Practice of Communism,* p. 28.

very nature robs the worker of the product of his labor. In other words, this theory affirms that an individual has the right to the private possession of the fruits of his labor. Why should this concept be limited to physical labor? Why not also include the labor of one's brain. After all, communists must admit that brainwork is important for Marx *did brain work, not brawn work*! And if a man invested what he earned in productive property, why would he not be due something from the investment of his possessions—his investment of the fruit of his labors?

The so-called transition stage, socialism, and the so-called synthesis, communism, are not actually advancements over the private ownership of the means of production and distribution. In fact, socialism and communism maintain the right to private ownership of productive property without maintaining the safeguards of capitalism, and without ownership being as widely distributed as it is under American capitalism. In the so-called socialist Russia the State, the Party really owns the productive property. For, after all, the fundamental aspect of ownership is the right to use and to dispose of property as one sees fit. And under socialism and communism this right is invested in certain individuals or a select group of individuals. There are, however, no safeguards under Russian socialism. The state is not the freely elected representative of the people, accountable to the people. The state is really the top leadership of the Communist Party.

The communists are unwilling to face the fact that the real problem is that of establishing safeguards against unlimited economic and political *power* being placed in the hands of a few individuals—regardless of what this small group of individuals may be called. Under the communist system there is no third party, the State, to whom either employer or employee can appeal as to a referee. Instead, the State is the employer and this employer has all the economic, political and social power under its control in Russia.

There is, furthermore, no assurance within the dialectic itself that a classless society will ever come into existence. The communists assume that under communism there will be no classes, and that the conflict of interests between different interest groups will not reach the stage of violence. How does the communist know this? What in the dialectic says that violent clashes will cease. After all, according to communist theory primitive communism called forth its opposite, a class society. Why cannot this happen again? What proof is there that individuals will not strive for positions of power under communism? Then, too, inefficient bureaucrats could become a fetter on production. Russian communists claim that they have achieved socialism in Russia, and yet they maintain that individuals who have been communists for years may become enemies of the "people." Beria is an example. Furthermore, individuals who have been brought up under communist control in Russia may also become enemies of the "people." The communists admit that they have inefficient bureaucrats. Then, too, in the very nature of the case there will always be some who govern and some who do not, some who are planners and some who are not, some who are executives and some who perform some type of physical labor, some who are in positions of power and some who are not.[28] This dream of so-called classless society wherein there will be no power-lust creates ideal situations for people with lust for power; and as many people have found out in Russia and in Red China, this dream often turns into a nightmare.

Even if the dialectic were working toward communism, it would not mean that man is morally obligated to work for its coming. To say that one has the duty to work for the coming of communism, to work for the good of the "people," is to appeal to a moral realm—and dialectical *materialism* has no grounds on which to make a moral appeal. Sometimes the communists say that they do not work for socialism and communism because they are better but because they are inevitable. But at other times their vocabulary appeals to moral concepts in an effort to get people to work toward these goals.

TWO DAMAGING ADMISSIONS

Communists make two admissions which further undermine their contention that the dialectic is the law of social development and that the social development of man has passed through the forms of primitive communism, slavery, feudalism, and capitalism and that it will pass through socialism into communism. *First*, they admit that historical materialism "by no means implies that the actual economy of every human community *exactly* conforms to one or other of these types. On the contrary, these systems are seldom or never to be met with in a 'pure' form." No slave society existed wherein the entire working

---

[28] Charles J. McFadden, *The Philosophy of Communism*, pp. 252-253.

population was in slavery. In the slave society there were many survivals of primitive communism.[29]

Secondly, it is admitted that every social system or community does not pass through each stage completely before it is able to evolve into the next stage. Furthermore, "the new system does not necessarily appear first in that place where the old one has been most strongly entrenched and most fully developed. Indeed, in those communities where the old system has become most strongly entrenched it may be hardest to get rid of it, so that the break-through of the new system is affected in the first place elsewhere."[30] Thus the revolution and so-called break-through to socialism took place first in Russia which was not one of the more advanced capitalistic countries.

These admissions, which the facts force them to make, destroy their contention that there is a law of dialectical development which is a law of nature and human society. If such a law existed there would be no such break down of the law as implied in these two admissions.

These admissions are out of harmony with Marx's contention that these laws work with the inexorability of laws of nature: "But capitalist production begets, with the inexorability of a law of Nature, its own negation. It is the negation of negation."[31] If such is the case, it must be inevitable that the more highly developed a capitalistic country is the closer it is to the inevitable transformation; while the less developed, the further it is away from the transformation.

Marx further contradicts the above admissions when he wrote: "One nation can and should learn from others. And even when a society has got upon the right track for the discovery of the natural laws of its movements—and it is the ultimate aim of this work, to lay bare the economic law of motion of modern society —it can neither clear by bold leaps, nor remove by legal enactments, the obstacles offered by the successive phases of its normal development. But it can shorten and lessen the birth-pangs."[32] Continues Marx: "My stand-point, from which the evolution of the economic formation of society is viewed as a process of natural history, can less than any other make the individual responsible for relations whose creature he socially

---

[29] Maurice Cornforth, *Historical Materialism*, p. 64.
[30] *Ibid.*, p. 65.
[31] *Capital*, p. 837.
[32] *Ibid.*, pp. 14-15.

remains, however much he may subjectively raise himself above them."[33]

The dialectic is further torn to shreds by the order of events in communist controlled countries. According to the dialectic the old society must develop until it creates the conditions which are ripe for revolution. First capitalism must reach a high stage of development, which includes industrialization as essential to the creation of the proletariat, and then the revolution takes place. But to have a proletarian revolution "first and then to set about creating an industrial society afterwards, makes nonsense of historical materialism."[34] But this is exactly what the communists did in Russia, and this is what they are doing in Red China today. Their own history makes a lie out of the pattern of history prophesied by this philosophy of dialectical materialism.

A FINAL TEST

Max Eastman suggested a scientific test whereby one can determine whether or not the dialectic is the law of thought. Spend a couple of hours with a Marxist and let him point out the process or processes whereby he has reached various conclusions. Then take another Marxist and let him describe, though not in the presence of the previous Marxist, how he reached similar conclusions. This would demonstrate that the dialectical method or *law of thinking* is no law at all. This experiment would disprove the "whole myth about negating negations, and seeking in everything for its opposite, and never resting in an affirmative statement, and studying everything in its logical self-movement, its inner hostility against itself, and remembering that things can be both themselves and their opposites, and that cause and effect merge into each other, and that quantity becomes quality, and that nature makes jumps. . . ."[35] And yet, if the dialectic is *the law* of thought, and if man is wholly material, everyone should think, and would by necessity have to think, not only alike but according to the dialectical *laws*.

Max Eastman further observed that in his discussion of dialectical thinking Lenin sums it up as flexible thinking, and does not hold fundamental the idea of self-contradiction being uni-

---

[33] *Ibid.*, p. 15.

[34] Leonard Schapiro, *The Origin of the Communist Autocracy*, Cambridge: Harvard University Press, 1956, p. vi.

[35] *Marxism: Is It Science*, pp. 140-141.

versal and the idea of the negation of the negation.[36] This is in itself a denial that the dialectic is the law of thought.

Our conclusion is that the dialectic is not the key to reality. Neither materialism nor dialectical materialism constitute the key to reality.

Let us further, however, explore how the dialectic shapes their view of society, man, and progress and morality.

[36] *Ibid.*, pp. 143-145.

CHAPTER SEVEN

The Communist Concept
of Class and Class Struggle

Classes play a basic role in human history, according to communism. Almost the opening sentence of the *Communist Manifesto* asserts that the "history of all hitherto existing society is the history of class struggle."

TWO BASIC CLASSES

What is their doctrine of the nature and function of classes? Although Marx wrote much about class struggle, he did not clearly define what he meant by a class.[1] A summary of his views indicates that a class is made up of a group of individuals who sustain the same relationship to the ownership or the nonownership of the means of production.[2] Lenin has given us the following definition: "Classes are large groups of people which differ from each other by the place they occupy in a historically definite system of social production, by their relation (in most cases fixed and formulated in laws) to the means of production, by their role in the social organization of labour, and, consequently, by the dimensions of the social wealth that they obtain and their method of acquiring their share of it. Classes are groups of people one of which may appropriate the labour of another, owing to the different places they occupy in the definite system of social economy."[3] "What constitutes and distinguishes classes is not primarily differences in income, differences in habits, or differences in mentality, but the places they occupy in social

---

[1] R. N. Carew Hunt, *The Theory and Practice of Communism*, p. 38.

[2] M. M. Bober, *Karl Marx's Interpretation of History*, 2nd Edition, Revised, p. 99. See also Vladimir G. Simkhovitch, *Marxism Versus Socialism*. New York: Henry Holt and Company, 1913, p. 197.

[3] *A Great Beginning*, as quoted in Maurice Cornforth, *Historical Materialism*, p. 60.

production and the relations in which they stand to the means of production, from which their differences in income, habits, mentality and so on arise."[4]

In other words, the relationship which one sustains to the economic system determines one's class in society. If one owns means of production or of distribution he is regarded by the communists as a member of the capitalist class. Those who do not own, but have only their labor to sell, and who work in industrial society, are the proletariat.

Marx did not claim that he discovered the concept of classes, or of class struggle. "Long before the bourgeois historians had described the historical development of this class struggle and bourgeois economists the economic anatomy of the classes. What I did that was new was to prove: (1) that the *existence of classes* is only bound up with *particular, historic phases in the development of production*; (2) that the class struggle necessarily leads to the *dictatorship of the proletariat*; (3) that this dictatorship itself only constitutes the transition to the *abolition of all classes* and to a *classless society.*"[5]

Karl Marx believed that there were more than two classes in society. However, the two most important classes today are the capitalist and the proletariat. In fact, he thought that under capitalism the tendency is toward the creation of two classes since, for example, even the landowners tend to become a part of the capitalist class.[6]

Why is there class struggle? Here again we are confronted with the dialectic. "When dialectics is applied to human history, these two opposing elements become two classes."[7] The capitalist class is the thesis and the proletariat is the antithesis. The owner class needs someone to work in their factories, etc., and this creates the proletariat, the class which has nothing but its labor to sell. Thus the two are in dialectical opposition to one another, and the dialectical interpretation "of history resolves itself into a class-struggle conception of history."[8]

---

[4] Maurice Cornforth, *Historical Materialism*, p. 60.

[5] *Selected Correspondence*, p. 57.

[6] M. M. Bober, *op. cit.*, pp. 104-105; Marx, *The Eighteenth Brumaire of Louis Bonaparte*, New York: International Publishers, n.d., p. 41.

[7] Sherman H. M. Chang, *The Marxian Theory of the State*, p. 38.

[8] *Ibid.*, p. 41.

CLASS STRUGGLE INEVITABLE

Class struggle is inevitable also because according to Marx the ruling class endeavors to squeeze every bit of work possible out of the proletariat, while giving the proletariat just enough to keep them alive. Since there can be no community of interests between the exploited and the exploiters, contradictions and clashes are inevitable.

Says Engels: "Since civilization is founded on the exploitation of one class by another class, its whole development proceeds in a constant contradiction. Every step forward in production is at the same time a step backwards in the position of the oppressed class, that is, of the great majority. Whatever benefits some necessarily injures the other; every fresh emancipation of one class is necessarily a new oppression for another class."[9]

Let us follow Engels' reasoning on this subject. This struggle is intensified when a class becomes conscious of itself as a class. As the capitalistic form of production and exchange becomes more and more inadequate, it becomes more and more a fetter on production. The differences between the exploited and the exploiter grows more and more until it is more and more evident that the interests of the two groups are diametrically opposed to one another. Thus members of the two classes become more and more conscious of themselves as distinct classes with conflicting interests. This continues until the proletariat sees that there is no other way out but to destroy class society and emancipate mankind.[10] Unless all are to perish the class system must perish. Continues Engels: "On this tangible, material fact, which is impressing itself in a more or less clear form, but with invincible necessity, on the minds of the exploited proletarians—it is on this fact, and not on the conceptions of justice and injustice held by any armchair philosopher that modern socialism's confidence of victory is founded."[11] Thus it is that "in the very nature of the case, the working class must be sincerely *revolutionary*," as Marx remarked to Kugelmann.[12]

THE REVOLUTION

The revolution by the proletariat, however, is a different kind

---

[9] *Origin of the Family, Private Property and the State*, p. 161.
[10] *Anti-Dühring*, p. 171.
[11] *Ibid.*, p. 179; Engels, *Socialism: Utopian and Scientific*, pp. 70-84.
[12] *Letters to Dr. Kugelmann*, New York: International Publishers, p. 29.

of revolution. In previous revolutions a new exploiting class, a minority, came into power. "In the socialist revolution, on the other hand," so explains Cornforth, "power passes into the hands of the working class, at the head of all the working people, i.e., into the hands of the vast majority. And this power is used, not to uphold the privileges of an exploiting class, but to destroy all such privileges and to end all class antagonisms."[13] When this has been accomplished the coercive State withers away, since the State according to their definition is but an instrument of a ruling and exploiting class to enable them to hold their position. Lenin tells that "According to Marx, the state is an organ of class *domination*, an organ of *oppression* of one class by another; its aim is the creation of 'order' which legalizes and perpetuates this oppression by moderating the collisions between the classes."[14]

The very "existence of the state proves that the class antagonisms *are* irreconcilable."[15] Thus when class distinctions have been wiped out there is no more need for the State. In fact, so maintains Engels, the State cannot exist, for with the elimination of conflicting classes antagonisms have disappeared, and no organ of repression of one class by another can then exist.[16] As a matter of fact, *the people wither away under the dictatorship of the proletariat.*

The communists believe that although men in the past have always worked in order to be able to exploit their fellowman—for even the revolutions of the past but substituted one exploiting group for another—they, the communists, are the only group in history who wage revolution not to exploit any group but to free all of mankind. History has decreed that they cannot emancipate themselves without emancipating mankind. And since they have such a wonderful goal, and the peculiar view of morality to which they hold, they feel that anything that they do to bring about revolution and the destruction of the capitalist class is a good thing to do.

On the other hand, so the communists assume, anything that hinders the development of the revolution is bad. Thus the communists are not interested in reducing class antagonisms, but in

---

[13] Maurice Cornforth, *Historical Materialism*, p. 84.
[14] *State and Revolution*, New York: International Publishers, p. 9.
[15] *Ibid.*, p. 8.
[16] As quoted in Lenin, *State and Revolution*, pp. 15-16.

sharpening them in order to hasten the day of revolution and thus to hasten the time when all mankind will be free. Therefore the communists insert themselves into any and every sore spot in society into which they can reach, in order to fester the sore, to widen the breaches and to hasten the destruction of capitalist society.

"To accomplish this act of universal emancipation," so says Engels, "is the historical mission of the modern proletariat. To thoroughly comprehend the historical conditions and thus the very nature of this act, to impart to the now oppressed proletarian class a full knowledge of the conditions and of the meaning of the momentous act it is called upon to accomplish, this is the task of the theoretical expression of the proletarian movement, scientific socialism."[17]

So irreconcilable is the conflict between the classes that the communist maintains that there can be no unity of interests. This leads M. J. Olgin to assert, "He who says then that there is unity of interests between employers and employees is committing treason to the working class."[18]

Marx's contention that the capitalist class by its very nature is an exploiting class *is based at least in part on the theory of surplus value*, which he did not originate.[19] The laborer produces more than is absolutely necessary to sustain his own life. Labor is viewed as the sole value-producing agent. Thus the profit which is taken by the capitalist is but a robbing of the working man of that which is rightfully his. As E. Stepanova recently wrote: "Laying bare the mechanism of capitalist exploitation, Marx disclosed the true source of surplus value, the pocketing of the unpaid labour of the workers by the capitalist class. Surplus value is the difference between the value created by the labour of the worker and the value of his labour power, that is, the value of the means of subsistence necessary for the worker and his family. Marx's doctrine of surplus value disclosed the economic basis of the antagonism between the proletariat and

---

[17] *Socialism: Utopian and Scientific,* Chicago: Charles H. Kerr and Company, 1914, p. 139.

[18] *Why Communism?* New York: Workers Library Publishers, Dec. 1933, p. 50.

[19] Engels, Introduction to *Capital,* Vol. II; R. N. Carew Hunt, *The Theory and Practice of Communism,* p. 55; Adam Smith, *The Wealth of Nations,* Chicago: Henry Regnery Company, Book I, Chap. 15; Arnold Lunn, *The Science of World Revolution,* New York: Sheed and Ward, 1938, p. 342.

the bourgeoisie. 'The doctrine of surplus value is the corner-stone of Marx's economic theory.'[20] After the materialist teaching on laws governing the development of human society the doc-trine of surplus value was the second great discovery made by the brilliant theoretician of the proletariat."[21]

THEORY OF REWARD FOR LABOR

On Marx's theory the capitalist does not add anything to value and therefore his profit is a stealing of that which rightfully be-longs to labor.

Since Marx was trying to prove that the manual worker in industrial society is exploited, and thus to galvanize the worker to revolutionary action, he did not include in the term labor the effort put forth by the middleman, the accountant, etc., nor did his theory give proper attention to the influence that scarcity and demand have on value.[22]

Although Marx makes some concession that qualify the labor theory of value, his writings leave the impression that labor is the sole creator of value. This enables him to give "scientific sanction" to the idea that the worker is underpaid. It also capital-izes on his resentment against the system, and intensifies it, by teaching that the system of capitalism by its very nature cheats the worker and is therefore unjust.[23] This concept is not a theory of value at all but a theory of exploitation,[24] and a battle cry for Marxists to use in stirring workers to rebellion.

Labor is involved in the production of value, but it is not the only factor. The scarcity, and the demand for the article, are vital factors also. If nature produced the things which men want, and produced them in the same quantity in which men now produce them, these items would be of the same value which they now have.[25]

As Richard Whately observed long ago, pearls do not bring a good price because men dive for them, but men dive for them because they bring a good price.

---

[20] Lenin, *Marx-Engels-Marxism*, p. 88.
[21] *Karl Marx Short Biography*, Moscow: Foreign Languages Publishing House, 1956, p. 89.
[22] Lunn, *The Science of World Revolution*, pp. 347-348.
[23] *Ibid.*, p. 344.
[24] R. N. Carew Hunt, *op. cit.*, p. 60.
[25] Lunn, *op. cit.*, p. 343.

Labor has not always received its fair share, but there are others also who are entitled to a share. The person who invests capital is investing that which was saved from labor in the past. Why should he be refused the opportunity of making a profit when he invests in a profit and loss situation—and sometimes he sustains a loss rather than receives a profit.

Why exclude from the term "labor" the effort put forth by the middleman, the accountant, etc., Marx had to admit that those who buy and sell do perform useful work in that they free that much labor time for the producer.[26] Why are they not entitled to a share of the profits?

The communists themselves do not promise or give the worker all that he produces. They say that under socialism a man works according to his ability and receives according to his work. And yet this is a far cry from saying that he will receive all that his work produces. Furthermore, they claim that under communism a man will receive according to his needs. This, too, does not say that he will receive all that he produces.

It must also be kept in mind that these communist promises imply a dictatorship which determines what one's ability is, how valuable is his work and how much he needs! This will not be left to the worker to decide but to the totalitarian state. And there is no one to whom the worker can appeal who can remedy the injustices committed by the totalitarian state.

Let us conclude this section with a summary of their doctrine of classes.

"1. Classes are determined by relations to the means of production.

"2. In capitalist society there are two basic classes: the capitalist class and the working class. Their interests are irreconcilable.

"3. The development of capitalist production leads to the sharpening of the class struggle. With the development of industry the working class grows in numbers, strength, and consciousness. The struggle between the two basic classes in modern society becomes more intense.

"The middle classes tend constantly to be ruined by the development of capitalist production and hurled into the ranks of the proletariat. They vacillate between the working class and the capitalist class.

---

[26] *Capital*, Vol. II, p. 149; Vol. III, p. 331.

"The working class is the most revolutionary class. It leads all other exploited sections of the people—farmers, Negro people, etc. Created by capitalism, the work class is the grave-digger of capitalism. Its historical mission is to abolish capitalism and establish socialism."[27]

THE IMPORTANCE OF THEIR CONCEPT OF CLASS

The concepts of class and class struggle are essential parts of Marxism. The law of motion and progress in history, according to "scientific socialism," is the law of class struggle. As Engels put it: "It was precisely Marx who had first discovered the great law of motion of history, the law according to which all historical struggles, whether they proceed in the political, religious, philosophical or some other ideological domain, are in fact only the more or less clear expression of struggles of social classes, and that the existence and thereby the collisions, too, of these classes are in turn conditioned by the degree of development of their economic position, by the mode of their production and by the form of exchange resulting from it. This law, which has the same significance for history as the law of the transformation of energy has for natural science. . . ."[28]

The great impersonal elements of history are found in the productive forces and relationships, but, says Bober the "classes represent the living agents acting in obedience to the impulses propagated by these material realities."[29]

Class struggle is such an essential part of the Marxian philosophy that one cannot abandon it without abandoning Marxism. As Marx and Engels observed: "As for ourselves, in view of our whole past there is only one path open to us. For almost forty years we have stressed the class struggle as the immediate driving force of history, and in particular the class struggle between the bourgeoisie and the proletariat as the great lever of the modern social revolution; it is therefore impossible for us to co-operate with people who wish to expunge this class struggle from the movement. When the International was formed we expressly formulated the battle-cry: the emancipation of the

---

[27] National Education Department, Communist Party, *Theory and Practice of the Communist Party*, New York: New Century Publishers, 1948, p. 10.

[28] In his Preface to Marx, *The Eighteenth Brumaire of Louis Bonaparte*, p. 10.

[29] Bober, *op. cit.*, pp. 111-112.

working class must be achieved by the working class itself. We cannot therefore co-operate with people who say that the workers are too uneducated to emancipate themselves and must first be freed from above by philanthropic bourgeois and petty bourgeois. If the new Party organ adopts a line corresponding to the views of these gentlemen, and is bourgeois and not proletarian, then nothing remains for us, much though we should regret it, but publicly to declare our opposition to it and to dissolve the solidarity with which we have hitherto represented the German Party abroad. But it is to be hoped that things will not come to *that.*"[30]

The editor commented on the letter in which this is contained and said that "Engels wrote this letter in the name of himself and Marx to the members of the leading group of German Social-Democracy. It is among the most important documents in which the revolutionary proletarian line of Marx and Engels is revealed."[31]

Today's communists have not expunged class struggle from the movement. In fact, they maintain that "He who denies the class struggle and does not distinguish his own kind from enemies is by no means a communist, by no means a Marxist-Leninist."[32]

The existence of classes means the existence of conflict. There is conflict unto destruction "between the imperialist camp and the social camp, between the imperialists on the one hand, and all the peoples of the world and all the oppressed nations, on the other, between the bourgeoisie and the proletariat in imperialist countries."[33]

Conflicts among the communists "are partial and short-lived. The conflicts can be corrected." So say the communists. "But in the conflict between imperialism and the people of the world the clashes are becoming more and more acute and there is no doctor who could find a remedy with which to cure this disease."[34]

---

[30] Marx-Engels, *Selected Correspondence*, pp. 376-377.

[31] *Ibid.*, p. 377.

[32] "Political Bureau of the Central Committee of the Communist Party of China." Statement of Dec. 29, 1956, *National Guardian*, Jan. 28, 1957, p. 6. Peaceful Coexistence does not "signify abandoning the class struggle" (L. Ilyichov, *World Marxist Review*, Nov. 1959, p. 10).

[33] *National Guardian*, Jan. 28, 1957, p. 6.

[34] *Ibid.*, p. 6. See also *World Marxist Review*, Nov. 1959, p. 8.

The belief in the existence of classes with irreconcilable interests[35] helps explain why the communist believes that *he is always at war with the non-communist society.* He works against the interest of his own nation in a non-communist country because he views himself as a member of a class with the interest of the class, and its will as expressed through the Communist Party, the object of his supreme loyalty. The cold war started with the call in the *Communist Manifesto* for the forcible overthrow of all existing social institutions. The communist believes that the war for the conquest of the world, whether called World War III or by some other name, has already started. He is now at work to try to bring into existence those conditions which will make possible the seizure of State power in violent revolution.

"Engels pointed out that class struggle was conducted in a threefold way—theoretical, political and the practical-economic. He stressed the importance of the, so to say, concentric attack wherein lay the strength and invincibility of the movement. In his, *What Is To Be Done?*, written in 1902, Lenin emphasized the point that 'Engels recognizes not two forms of the great struggle of Social Democracy (political and economic) . . . , but three, adding to the first two the theoretical struggle.' Lenin regarded this point as being instructive from the standpoint of the problems and controversies of the day."[36]

Because of his concept of classes, the communist will not change his mind because of any improvements in society of the conditions of even the lowest class. For he views these as but an effort to keep the proletariat from accomplishing its historic mission. Thus regardless of how much we do in this country to raise the standard of living for all, the communist discredits our motives and considers all these improvements as but an effort to put off the day of the emancipation of mankind through the dictatorship of the proletariat, socialism and then communism.

THE COMMUNIST CONCEPT OF CLASS UNREALISTIC

Marx assumed, instead of proving, his case. He concluded that socialism is desirable, because he thought that capitalism does

---

[35] "The class interests of the bourgeoisie and proletarians are irreconcilable. . . " (L. Ilyichov, *World Marxist Review*, Nov. 1959, p. 10).

[36] *Ibid.*, Nov. 1959, p. 11.

not justly reward the worker but exploits him, and that the next stage of human society was to be socialism. This was to be a system which more adequately rewarded the worker. As a revolutionist he looked for the group which he thought would overthrow the existing society, and he assumed that the proletariat was the only instrument available.[37]

Marx further assumed that those who own means of production must be exploiters and that if one works for another he is automatically an exploited person. This is based on the doctrine of the labor theory of value, but since this doctrine is false, Marx's conclusion concerning exploitation is false.

Furthermore, exploitation may take place by sabotage and by violence. The so-called dictatorship of the proletariat exploits the worker. Milovan Djilas found out by experience that today's communists have built up a new ruthless exploiting class.[38] "Communism has become for the present rulers of Russia what pan-Slavism was for the czars, with the exception that the Communists of today are much more obedient to the dictators in Moscow than the pan-Slavists were to the czars."[39] Hugh Seton-Watson has pointed out that a new "state bourgeoisie" has arisen in Russia,[40] and W. W. Kulski has discussed the phenomena of "Classes in the 'Classless' State."[41]

Sam Watson, a member of the Labor Party in Britain, visited Russia and raised the question: "How on earth a classless society can afford four classes of railway travel and three classes of waiting rooms would defy even Karl Marx—never mind a simple Methodist like myself."[42]

Liu Shao-Chi, however, maintained that the proletariat does not exploit anyone, but that it liberates mankind. "As the exploited proletariat which we represent does not exploit anybody, it can carry on the revolution to the very end, completely liberate mankind as a whole and eventually make a clean sweep

[37] R. N. Carew Hunt, *op. cit.*, p. 40.

[38] See his book, *The New Class*, New York: Frederick A. Praeger.

[39] Karl Kautsky, *Social Democracy Versus Communism*, New York: The Rand School Press, 1946, p. 137.

[40] "The Soviet Ruling Class," *Problems of Communism*, June, 1956, p. 10.

[41] *Problems of Communism*, Jan.-Feb. 1956, pp. 20-28. Edmund K. Falter-Mayer, *Wall Street Journal*, Aug. 13, 1959, p. 1.

[42] *Reader's Digest*, Apr. 1955, p. 44.

of all forms of corruption, bureaucracy and degeneracy in human society."[43]

This claim is not in harmony with the facts. Consider the experiences of one Chinese youth in a Commune. In China today the property of peasants has been confiscated. The peasants are told that they will be paid "someday." In some of the Communes the people are awakened at 4:30 a.m. Sitting up exercises and military drill take place until 8 a.m. when there is a fifteen minute break for breakfast, after which they work in the fields until noon. There is another fifteen minute break for lunch. Then they work in the fields until 7:20. Fifteen minutes are allowed for supper, and then they work until midnight. When there are political meetings at night, however, they are not required to make up for this loss of time by working after midnight.[44]

In Bucharest in 1958 there were complaints that the Party members in administrative positions were being paid more than the workers. On October 15, 1957, the Bucharest Radio reported that "executives at the Bicaz hydro-electric project had illegally abused the distribution of bonuses in favor of the management, awarding themselves bonuses which in some cases exceeded their annual salaries, at the expense of the workers."[45]

Marx often ignored the fact that a class may be based on another than ownership relation to power. In China over the centuries there was private ownership of property, with some State control, but the ruling class was the class which held the State regulatory power. As Karl A. Wittfogel, in his ground-breaking study of *Oriental Despotism*, wrote: "In hydraulic society the first major division into an order of superior and privileged persons and an order of inferior and under-privileged persons occurs simultaneously with the rise of an inordinately strong state apparatus. The masters and beneficiaries of this state, the rulers, constitute a class different from, and superior to, the mass of the commoners—those who, although personally free, do not share the privileges of power. The men of the apparatus state are a ruling class in the most unequivocal sense of the term; and the rest of the population constitutes the second major class, the ruled."[46] Even the lowest functionaries in such a state ap-

---

[43] *How To Be a Good Communist*, p. 8.

[44] "Misery, Oppression, Fear Inside China's Communes," *Life*, Jan. 5, 1959, pp. 64-74.

[45] As quoted in *The Free Rumanian Press Agency*, Jan. 1, 1958.

[46] *Oriental Despotism: A Comparative Study of Total Power*, New Haven: Yale University Press, 1957, p. 303.

paratus have a privileged position. They can coerce and exploit the masses even though the functionaries own no property.

This same thing is true in a communist state. Party members and bureaucracy constitute the exploiting class because of their relationship to the power of the state.

Dr. Wittfogel has also observed that in situations where total power is held by the state, there is a paralysis of class struggle.[47] The communists view their own system as a classless one, and America as under the domination of monopoly capitalism. And yet, the so-called monopoly capitalism did not prevent the rise of Big Labor, Big Government and of rivals in the field of business. But, the communists do prevent such in their society by monopolizing state power, economic power, education and other aspects of the life of the society. This is monopoly bureaucracy.[48]

In democratic countries, the franchise has given the classes a non-violent means of pursuing their interests, and this fact undermines the dialectical interpretation of class and violent class struggle. And in a democracy *common interests* more and more outweigh so-called class interests. This was recognized by Edward Bernstein, a friend and literary executor of Engels and Marx.[49]

Although class struggle has taken place in history, the facts are against the division of members of a society into classes on the basis of the economic order, and the conclusion that this is the most important division within the society. Individuals may be of the "proletariat" and yet have no class consciousness at all. Far more important to them may be the divisions within society based on religion, race, community of interest and political parties. Other loyalties may far outweigh so-called class loyalties.

The interpretation of history as a history of class conflicts is one-sided and is inadequate to explain the totality of human history. In Marxism the concept of class has its foundation in dialectical materialism. Since dialectical materialism is not the key to reality, an analysis of society based on dialectical materialism as the key to reality is bound to be false.

It is true that class struggle has taken place in history. For example, the revolution in Hungary was a rebellion by the exploited (the people) against the exploiters (the communists).

---

[47] *Ibid.*, p. 328.
[48] *Ibid.*, p. 368.
[49] Vladimir G. Simkhovitch, *Marxism Versus Socialism*, p. 215.

Because some historians may have failed to deal with the fact of class struggle at certain times and places does not justify the sweeping generalization that all history is the history of class struggle.

Power struggles may take place within a class. Certainly the conflict between the popes and the emperors in medieval history was a conflict between groups within what the communists classify as the ruling class.[50]

Classes have cooperated with each other to fight foreign nations. There are far more cases where individuals of different classes have fought as co-nationals against foreign nations than there are of classes fighting classes within a country. Regardless of how the communists may try to explain this, in an effort to save their theory, the facts remain.[51]

Wars may be fought for a number of reasons. Although the motivation and causes may be complex, there have been wars, such as the Crusades, where the religious interest was dominant.[52]

How can all history be the history of class struggle when Marx himself said that there were periods, as in England for example, "in which the class-struggle was as yet undeveloped."[53]

How can class struggle be characteristic of all history, when we find far more cases of class submission, of passivity, than of class warfare? Engels pointed out that "the small freeholders, the feudal tenants, and the agricultural labourers, never troubled their heads much about politics before the Revolution," and that it was quite evident in all modern countries that the agricultural population "never can attempt a successful independent movement; they require the initiatory impulse of the more concentrated, more enlightened, more easily moved people of the towns."[54]

As to the other classes, with the exception of the capitalist class, being swallowed up by the proletariat, such has not taken place. In France Marx spoke of "the aristocracy of finance, the

[50] K. R. Popper, *The Open Society and Its Enemies,* Vol. II, London: Routledge & Kegan Paul Ltd., 1952, p. 116.

[51] Karl Federn, *The Materialist Conception of History,* pp. 191-192. See also "Caste" in James Feibleman, *Christianity, Communism and the Ideal Society,* p. 224.

[52] Charles J. McFadden, *The Philosophy of Communism,* p. 249.

[53] *Capital,* p. 17.

[54] *Germany: Revolution and Counter-Revolution,* New York: International Publishers, 1933, p. 16.

industrial bourgeoisie, the middle class, the petty bourgeois, the army, the *lumpenproletariat* organized as the Mobile Guard, the intellectual lights, the clergy, and the rural population."[55] Have any of these so-called classes been swallowed up by the proletariat?

Marx is wrong in assuming that the proletariat is the revolutionary class. Radicalism may exist among the wealthy, as for example in the case of Corliss Lamont, Frederick Vanderbilt Field, and others. Conservatism may exist among the poor. Mao Tse-tung built his revolutionary movement in the country, not in the cities. He depended at times on the peasants rather than on the small proletariat in China.

If the proletariat is the revolutionary class, how could Marx speak of the "slum proletariat" who could not be relied on.[56]

The Marxist idea that the pressure of events creates the class conscious, revolutionary proletariat is refuted by their constant effort *to convert, through teaching,* the working class so that they will take up their role of the revolutionary class whose historic destiny is to build the classless society.[57] Their theory is further denied by the fact that the leaders of Marxism, including Marx and Engels, have not come from the ranks of the proletariat but from the ranks of the intelligentsia and the bourgeoisie.

The communist concept of classes certainly does not fit America. A man may work himself up from the ranks of labor to the rank of owner and employee. Millions of small businesses as well as many large businesses exist.

And what shall we say about the fact that employees may be stockholders in large corporations. In this ownership of the business may be included many who are not employees of the particular business. In America there are over 12,500,000 stockholders, half of them being in the under $7,500 a year income bracket.[58]

Then, too, a managerial group with considerable influence has arisen and this group belongs neither to the capitalist class nor to the proletariat.

55 *The Eighteenth Brumaire of Louis Bonaparte*, p. 21.
56 *Ibid.*, p. 21.
57 Turner, *Challenge to Karl Marx*, pp. 378-380.
58 *Commercial Appeal*, Jan. 3, 1959. The Conference Board, *Road Maps of Industry*, No. 1229, July 17, 1959.

The workers do not view themselves as a class. There are many different occupations and a wide variety of interests.

The labor unions have also arisen as very influential groups in society.

The facts have disproved the dialectic and the class concept based on it. The living standard of the proletariat has been raised due to the existence of moral principles, invention, industrialization, mass production, competition, government, labor unions, the concern of capitalists for their employees and their recognition of the value of satisfied and well paid employees. Marx was so wedded to the dialectic that he could not see anything but increasing misery for the proletariat. But factors of which he was ignorant, factors to which he closed his eyes, and factors which had not yet developed have all operated to raise the standard of living for the working man in advanced capitalistic and industrialized countries.

History and society do not sustain the communist concept of class. This is a fatal blow to communist philosophy since they claim that communism embraces a scientific understanding of society.

CHAPTER EIGHT

The Communist Doctrine
of Revolution

The *Communist Manifesto* is accepted by communists today as a basic and up-to-date document.[1] The *Manifesto* closes with a call to total revolution: "The Communists disdain to conceal their views and aims. They openly declare that their ends can be attained only by the forcible overthrow of all existing social conditions. Let the ruling classes tremble at a Communistic revolution. The proletarians have nothing to lose but their chains. They have a world to win."

"Workingmen of all countries, unite!"[2]

Engels in 1846 maintained that communists must "recognize no means of carrying out these objects other than a democratic revolution by force."[3] Marx viewed revolutions as "the locomotives of history."[4] "Force is the midwife of every old society pregnant with a new one. It is itself an economic power."[5] Herbert Aptheker said that this was "not advocacy; it is observation."[6] Lenin quoted with approval Marx's statement in his *State and Revolution*.[7]

Why is revolution necessary, beneficial and inevitable: ac-

---

[1] E. Stepanova, *Karl Marx: Short Biography*, pp. 36-37; G. Obichkin, *On The "Manifesto of the Communist Party" of Marx and Engels*, Moscow: Foreign Languages Publishing House, 1955, p. 5; *Political Affairs*, Feb. 1948, pp. 113, 116, 117; William Z. Foster, *History of the Three Internationals*, New York: International Publishers, 1955, p. 27.

[2] *Manifesto of the Communist Party*, New York: International Publishers, 1932, p. 44.

[3] *Selected Correspondence*, p. 2.

[4] Marx, *Klassenkämpfe in Frankreich*, p. 90. Quoted in M. M. Bober, *Karl Marx's Interpretation of History*, p. 111.

[5] Marx, *Capital*, p. 824.

[6] *On the Nature of Revolution*, New York: New Century Publishers, 1959, p. 11.

[7] p. 19.

cording to the philosophy of communism? Why is "revolution on the agenda"?[8]

DIALECTICAL PROGRESS

Revolution is clearly called for by the concept of dialectical progress. The tension between the thesis and antithesis grows until an explosion takes place. Lasting progress comes only in this way. Of course, quantitative progress comes before revolution, but the qualitative leap involves the revolution. "Revolution is the result of the contradictions created between the productive forces of human society and the productive relations within which they operate and develop."[9]

In capitalistic society, Marx argued, one capitalist destroys many capitalists. This trend toward monopoly and centralization continues until "the means of production and socialization of labour at last reach a point where they become incompatible with their capitalist integument. This integument is burst asunder. The knell of capitalist private property sounds, the expropriators are expropriated."

This is interpreted dialectically. Let us hear Marx's interpretation. "The capitalist mode of appropriation, the result of the capitalist mode of production, produces capitalist private property. This is the first negation of individual private property, as founded on the labour of the proprietor. But capitalist production begets, with the inexorability of a law of Nature, its own negation. It is the negation of negation. This does not re-establish private property for the producer, but gives him individual property based on the acquisitions of the capitalist era: i.e., on co-operation and the possession in common of the land and of the means of production."[10]

Capitalism, they assert, in its very nature creates misery and poverty, and results in the concentration of power in the hands of a few. These quantitative changes go on until the people realize that there is no way out of their misery except through the destruction of the capitalistic system. Therefore, the passing away of capitalism and the coming of socialism, and then com-

---

[8] Herbert Aptheker, *On the Nature of Revolution*, p. 3.

[9] V. Adoratsky, *Dialectical Materialism*, New York: International Publishers, 1934, p. 73. See also Herbert Aptheker, *op. cit.*, p. 27.

[10] *Capital*, pp. 836-837. See also M. M. Bober, *Karl Marx's Interpretation of History*, pp. 39-40. The same concept is in *The Theory of the Proletarian Revolution*, New York: International Publishers, 1936, pp. 11-12.

munism, are inevitable. As William Z. Foster said: "Socialism will arrive in this country, not because someone has planned it as a superior type of society; but because, under the accumulating pressures of decaying capitalism, it will have become indispensable for the welfare of the vast masses of the American people.... This robbery [of the producers by the capitalists. J.D.B.] will be brought to a sudden halt by the advent of Socialism, and the country finally will enjoy true democracy"[11]

In 1936 Browder wrote: "History does not show a single example in which state power was transferred from one class to another by peaceful means, whether in the form of voting or some other method of formal democracy." Communists do not want to use violence, but the capitalist will force it on them! "We know that rather than turn over control to the workers they [the capitalists] would first destroy all of civilization."[12]

The destruction of capitalism is inevitable, say the communists, for nothing can stop the working of the dialectic. Thus Khrushchev, at a January 1957 reception for the Premier of Red China, Chou En-lai, discussed our death sentence: "Whether they like it or not they must die. It is like a pregnant woman who is about to give birth. You can't tell her to put it off. She has to give birth. It is a natural phenomenon. It is the same with the death of Capitalism. Of course, we will contribute what we can." At a reception at the Polish Embassy in Moscow November 18, 1956, Khrushchev was equally blunt: "We are Bolsheviks. . . . About the capitalist states, it doesn't depend on you whether or not we exist. If you don't like us, don't accept our invitations and don't invite us to come and see you. Whether you like it or not, history is on our side. We will bury you."[13]

The dialectic, therefore, leads to the conclusion that force has a revolutionary role in history; "that, in the words of Marx, it is the mid-wife of every old society which is pregnant with the new, that it is the instrument by the aid of which social movement forces its way through and shatters the dead, fossilized, political forms. . . ."[14]

---

[11] America's Managed Economy," *Political Affairs,* Aug. 1956, p. 31.
[12] *What Is Communism?*, pp. 127-128. Brackets by J.D.B.
[13] Quoted in *Guardpost for Freedom,* Feb. 1, 1957, published by the Veterans of Foreign Wars of the United States. See the same concept in Georgi Dimitroff, *The United Front Against Fascism,* p. 27.
[14] Engels, *Herr Eugen Dühring's Revolution in Science (Anti-Dühring),*

Although we contend that the dialectical interpretation of history is false, yet we admit that some revolutions have come because of the ruthlessness of a ruling class and the growing misery of the people. In fact, in 1956 such a revolution took place in Hungary. "The Hungarian revolt must have had a devastating effect even on the very orthodox. For here, in a sense, was a classic Marxist revolution: capitalism (of a state type) had so accentuated the material exploitation of the proletariat which it had created through rapid industrialization, that the workers, supported by the population, rose in spontaneous rebellion."[15] How embarrassing to the dialecticians it must have been when the proletariat rose up against the dictatorship of the proletariat!

From a letter of a Moscow student, published in the Austrian Journal *Forum* (Feb. 1957), it is evident that the significance of this strike and rebellion in Hungary was not lost on some students in Russia. Not only did the Party crush the workers, instead of coming to their aid, but, as a student expressed it: "Gradually a question crystallized that is of the utmost significance for a socialist system: Although the party bureaucracy does not possess any formal title to society's means of production, has it not, through its practical control over these means of production, through their ultilization, through the distribution of manpower and through the control which it exercises over wages, already become an exploiting class in the original Marxist sense? And may it not then also become permissible or even necessary to oppose it (the party bureaucracy) by means of the Marxist weapon in the class struggle, the general strike?"[16]

THE CONCEPT OF CLASS

Revolution is implied in Marx's concept of classes, class antagonism, and the increase of class antagonism. This is but

---

p. 209. This is quoted and endorsed by Lenin, *The State and Revolution.* The necessity of violence is still taught. "Naturally, modification of laws is by no means tantamount to their elimination or disappearance, as is claimed by social-reformists and revisionists. The working of the laws of capitalism in a country can be abolished or brought to naught solely by overthrowing bourgeois rule, by the revolutionary breaking up of capitalist relations of production" (*International Affairs,* Moscow, July 1959, p. 10).

[15] Zbigniew Brzezinski, "Ideology and Power: Crisis in the Soviet Block," *Problems of Communism,* Jan.-Feb., 1957, p. 17.

[16] As quoted in *ibid.,* p. 28.

another way of presenting the doctrine of the dialectic. ". . . the antagonism between the proletariat and the bourgeoisie is a struggle of class against class, a struggle which carried to its highest expression is a total revolution. Indeed, is it at all surprising that a society founded on the opposition of classes should culminate in brutal *contradiction*, the shock of body against body, as its final *dénouement*?"

"It is only in an order of things in which there are no more classes and class antagonisms that *social evolutions* will cease to be *political revolutions*. Till then, on the eve of every general reshuffling of society, the last word of social science will always be: 'Combat or death: bloody struggle or extinction. It is thus that the question is inexorably put.' "[17]

In 1932 Foster himself did not hesitate to argue that in "view of the universal lessons to the contrary, it is a crime to teach the workers that they can defeat such a ruthless capitalist class without open struggle." The idea that capitalism could undergo a painless transition to socialism "paralyzes the struggle of the workers," "facilitates the rule of the bourgeoisie" and "is the most insidious [theory J.D.B.] that the workers have to deal with."[18] How could Foster maintain otherwise when the class struggle is viewed as the "immediate driving force of history" without which the proletariat cannot free itself. If class struggle did not take place the working class would remain under "capitalist class domination. . . ."[19]

The class struggle goes on until the time when the executioner, the proletariat, destroys the capitalist states. As Marx said long ago: "To take vengeance for the misdeed of the ruling class there existed in the Middle Ages in Germany a secret tribunal called the *Vehmgericht*. If a red cross was seen marked on a house, people knew that its owner was doomed by the *Vehm*. All the houses of Europe are now marked by the mysterious red cross. History is the judge: its executioner, the proletarian."[20]

To this Lenin agreed: "People always were and always will be the stupid victims of deceit and self-deceit in politics, as

---

[17] Marx, *Poverty of Philosophy*, New York: International Publishers, p. 147. The statement Marx quoted is from George Sand.

[18] *Toward Soviet America*, New York: Coward-McCann, Inc., 1932, p. 218.

[19] *History of the Communist Party of the United States*, 1952, p. 149.

[20] *Selected Correspondence*, p. 91.

long as they have not learned to discover the *interests* of one or another of the classes behind any moral, religious, political and social phrases, declarations and promises. The supporters of reforms and improvements will always be fooled by the defenders of the old, as long as they will not realize that every old institution, however absurd and rotten it may appear, is kept in being by the forces of one or the other of the ruling classes. And there is *only one* way of breaking the resistance of these classes, and that is to find, in the very society which surrounds us, and to enlighten and organize for the struggle, the forces which can, and by their social position, *must* form the power capable of sweeping away the old and of establishing the new."[21]

The communists maintain that they do not "foment" or "export" revolutions but that they "develop in accordance with the sharpening of the class contradictions which engender revolutions."[22]

THE DECREASE OF THE CAPITALIST CLASS AND THE INCREASE IN THE SIZE OF THE PROLETARIAT

Revolution is implied in the communist theory of the decrease of the capitalist class and the increase in the size and the misery of the proletariat. This is one aspect of their doctrine of class conflict.

The misery of the worker will increase because of the law of increasing exploitation. The employer tries to squeeze more and more profits from the worker. He increases the length of the working day, accelerates the intensity of the labor process and cheapens the price he must pay to the laborer by the use of better machines. This brings on increased productivity and "the laborer is cheapened because the commodities comprising his

---

[21] Little Lenin Library, *On the Theory of Marxism*, New York: International Publishers, 1948, p. 9. See also Vice-Admiral Leslie C. Stevens, USN (Ret.), "The Russian Doctrine," *The Atlantic Monthly*, June 1952, pp. 57-59. Vernon Venable, *Human Nature: The Marxian View*, pp. 201-202. Also William Z. Foster's testimony before the Fish Committee. *An Investigation of Un-American Activities and Propaganda*, House Resolution 282, Union Calendar No. 2, House Report No. 2, 1939, p. 19. Stalin's Report to the 1934 Congress, C.P.S.U. in E. Burns, *Handbook of Marxism*, p. 934. L. Trotsky, *The Defence of Terrorism*, London: George Allen and Unwin, Ltd., 1935, p. 52.

[22] L. Ilyichov, *World Marxist Review*, Nov. 1959, p. 12.

means of subsistence are cheapened." Unemployment is increased by technical advances, there is greater competition among employees, whole families will be forced to work in order to have sufficient to live on, and thus the labor market becomes cheaper.[23] For these and other reasons Marx believed that the size and misery of the proletariat will continue to increase. Thus the "accumulation of wealth at one pole, is, therefore, at the same time accumulation of misery, agony of toil, slavery, ignorance, brutality, mental degradation, at the opposite pole, i.e., on the side of the class that produces its own product in the form of capital."[24]

There is no way out of the misery except by the destruction of capitalism by the proletariat. As Browder put it: "The shiftings and changes in the situation and in the consciousness of the working people are proceeding incessantly; their anger, their bitterness, their hatred of the rulers are accumulating, while the solidarity, organization and fighting determination of the oppressed are steadily making headway—until at last quantity will be transformed into quality and the accumulated forces will violently burst to the surface."[25]

Capitalism created its own grave digger, so maintained Engels, in that it tore people loose from the land, where they were content even though in misery and slavery,[26] "liberated [them] from all traditional fetters" and drove them in herds into the towns where their misery would increase and lead them to revolution since they were without any feeling of belongingness in the society, nor did they have their feet on the land, so to speak.[27]

Misery, the sense of dispossession, of alienation, was considered so essential for creating the revolutionary spirit, that Engels thought that the revolutionary spirit would be lost if the workers even owned their own homes. "Give them their own houses, chain them once again to the soil and you break their power of resistance to the wage cutting of the factory owners."[28]

Thus we see that it is through quantitative changes that the

---

[23] Turner, *Challenge to Karl Marx*, p. 123. Turner is anti-Communist.
[24] *Capital*, p. 709.
[25] Earl Browder, "The Working Class Movement and the Imperialist War," *The Communist International*, Dec. 1940, p. 813.
[26] *The Housing Question*, New York: International Publishers, p. 28.
[27] *Ibid.*, p. 29.
[28] *Ibid.*, p. 50.

way is prepared for the qualitative change, i.e., the revolution. Some of the changes are, by way of summary, the decrease in the size of the capitalist class, the abolition of the middle class, the tremendous increase of the proletariat and the increase of misery for the proletariat. These make revolution, the qualitative change, inevitable.

THE CONCEPT OF THE STATE

Revolution is implied in the communist concept of the State. It was Lenin's conviction that "The state, even in a democratic republic, is nothing more nor less than a machine for the suppression of one class by another."[29] It is a class organization of violence for the purpose of holding down some class.[30] It is the coercive instrument of the ruling class by means of which it protects its economic interest. This concept of the "state as the instrument of the ruling class for maintaining its rule" is still held by the communists.[31]

This means that the communist is suspicious of every state, including a democratic one, with the exception of the dictatorship of the proletariat. He blames on the bourgeois state the perpetuation of the evils in society. This state does not belong to the workers, nor is it really friendly to them. It is but the tool of the capitalist. Thus the communist concludes that the way to get rid of the State as an instrument of the capitalist is by the complete conquest of power. This means revolution.[32] It is only the proletarian state which withers away;[33] the capitalist state must be destroyed by force. As Herbert Aptheker put it: "The bourgeoisie takes state power from the feudal lords and then uses the state to further develop an already existing capitalism; the productive masses take state power from the bourgeoisie and then use state power in order to *begin* the establishment of Socialism."[34]

---

[29] *The Proletarian Revolution and the Renegade Kautsky*, New York: International Publishers, 1934, p. 105.

[30] Lenin, *The State and Revolution*, p. 15.

[31] Hyman Lumer, "In Defense of Theory," *Political Affairs*, Feb. 1957, p. 61.

[32] Karl R. Popper, *The Open Society and Its Enemies*, Vol. II, Princeton, N. J.: Princeton University Press, pp. 161-162. Popper is not a Communist.

[33] Lenin, *The State and Revolution*, pp. 15-20.

[34] *On the Nature of Revolution*, 1959, p. 26.

With this view of the state it is not surprising that the communist does not regard his own country as his fatherland. Instead
he looks to Russia as the fatherland of all the workers of the
world.[35] Russia is the homeland of socialism and its flag is the
"worker" flag. As William Z. Foster testified before the Fish
Committee, "the 'red' flag is the flag of the revolutionary class,
and we are part of the revolutionary class." "And all capitalist
flags are flags of the capitalist class, and we owe no allegiance
to them."[36] On being questioned by J. B. Matthews he claimed
that on the flag situation he had changed his mind.[37] This testimony was given in 1939. And yet in a booklet published in June
1939 he stated substantially the same concept in so far as the
Russian flag is concerned. He said that they revered "the American flag because of its democratic and revolutionary significance," but of the Red flag he said much more. "The Red flag
is the international banner of liberty and social advance. . . .
The Communist Party, together with innumerable other workers' parties, trade unions and farmers' organizations in many
countries, honors and supports the Red flag, the historic world
symbol of popular freedom."[38]

In his acceptance speech, as the candidate of the Communist
Party for the Presidency in 1928, Foster spoke on the question
of war between Russia and the so-called imperialist nations.
"When that war begins, the Communist International and the
millions of workers throughout Europe and other countries that
follow its lead will not simply adopt a defensive policy, they
will not merely seek to stop their governments from attacking
the Soviet Union. On the contrary, they will put into effect the
great Leninist strategy. They will turn the imperialist war
against the Soviet Union into a civil war of the workers against
capitalism. They will destroy the capitalist order and begin the
building of the proletarian society [applause]."[39] Foster endorsed

---

[35] Earl Browder, House Committee on Un-American Activities, *Investigation of Un-American Propaganda Activities in the United States*, Vol. 7,
1939, p. 4429.

[36] As quoted in House Committee on Un-American Activities, *Investigation of Un-American Propaganda Activities in the United States*, Vol. IX,
1939, p. 5391.

[37] *Ibid.*, p. 5413.

[38] William Z. Foster, *Your Questions Answered*, New York: Workers'
Library Publishers, June 1939, pp. 115-116.

[39] Quoted in the House Committee on Un-American Activities, *op. cit.*,
Vol. IX, p. 5397.

the resolutions of the Seventh World Congress of 1935 which called for the same type of revolt.[40] He later tried to avoid this by saying that it represented the situation of 1935, but that conditions had changed in 1939.[41]

Earl Browder gave the same sort of testimony.[42]

Browder also wrote that: "So long as the capitalists retain complete control of the armed forces and their deadly weapons, they can defeat the revolt of the masses. . . . But soldiers and sailors come from the ranks of the workers. They can be, and must be, won for the revolution. *All revolutions have been made with weapons which the overthrown rulers had relied on for their protection.*"[43] If this is not a clear statement of their determination to win soldiers and sailors and to bring about mutiny and revolution, just how could such purposes be stated? A well-indoctrinated communist in the armed services is a traitor waiting for the opportunity to destroy the government under whose banner he supposedly marches.

Because the State is the instrument of the oppressing class, Lenin thought that the working class cannot simply take possession of the ready-made state machine, but must smash it.[44] Concerning the bourgeois state, Lenin wrote: "The replacement of the bourgeois by the proletarian state is impossible without a violent revolution. The abolition of the proletarian state, i.e., of all states, is only possible through 'withering away.'"[45]

In light of their current emphasis on Lenin, it is well for us to remember that William Z. Foster views Lenin's concept of the State as one of Lenin's fundamental contributions to Marxism. Lenin freed "marxism from opportunist revisionism" and "restated Marx's basic proposition that the present state is a repressive instrument of capitalism, the 'executive committee of the capitalist class,' thereby theoretically destroying the current Social-Democratic revisionist conception that the modern state under capitalism is a sort of people's state, without specific capitalist class domination." This means that the capitalist state "because of ruling class violent resistance to all democratic advance, would have to be abolished before socialism could be

---

[40] *Ibid.*, pp. 5413-5414.
[41] *Ibid.*, pp. 5413-5414.
[42] Vol. 7, pp. 4428-4431.
[43] Earl Browder, *What Is Communism?*, p. 126.
[44] *The Proletarian Revolution and Renegade Kautsky*, p. 62.
[45] *State and Revolution*, p. 20.

established." Capitalism cannot be transformed gradually into
socialism. Instead the bourgeois democratic revolution will grow
"into the socialist revolution."[46]

CAPITALISM NOT SELF-DEFEATING

Revolution is necessary because capitalism will not collapse of
its own weight. Says Foster: "The implications of all this are
clear: to escape the encroaching capitalist starvation and to
emancipate themselves, the workers of the world, including those
in this country, must and will take the revolutionary way out
of the crisis. That is, they will carry out a militant policy now
in defense of their daily interests and, finally, following the
example of the Russian workers, they will abolish capitalism and
establish socialism."

"By the term, 'abolition' of capitalism we mean its overthrow
in open struggle by the toiling masses, led by the proletariat.
Although the world capitalist system constantly plunges deeper
into crisis we cannot therefore conclude that it will collapse of
its own weight. On the contrary, as Lenin has stated, no matter
how difficult the capitalist crisis becomes, 'there is no complete
absence of a way out' for the bourgeoisie until it faces the
revolutionary proletariat in arms."[47]

As one communist more recently put it: "It is correct that
peace must be imposed upon the monopolists by resolute
struggle . . . if peaceful coexistence is established, will American
monopoly capitalism change its habits? . . . Will it cease being
aggressive and imperialistic (meat-eating) and become more
peaceful (grass-eating)"? "But the establishment of peaceful
coexistence would not mean that U. S. capitalism would cease
to be aggressive, would cease to strive for world domination,
would cease to work for war—the only way to win world domination. The lion would not be turned into a lamb and give up his
carnivorous for a herbaceous diet. Peaceful coexistence must
not be interpreted to mean that monopoly capitalism will become
peaceful."[48]

To this agreed Trotsky: "Consequently, the first condition of
salvation is to tear the weapons of domination out of the hands
of the bourgeoisie. It is hopeless to think of a peaceful arrival

---

[46] *History of the Communist Party of the United States*, 1952, p. 149.
[47] *Toward Soviet America*, p. 212.
[48] William Weinstone, *Political Affairs*, Dec. 1954, pp. 62, 63.

to power while the bourgeoisie retains in its hands all the apparatus of power."[49]

Adoratsky also maintained that, " 'Order' and oppression in class society are maintained by violence, by the organized state power of the exploiters. This 'order' can be destroyed and replaced by a new kind of order only with the aid of the organized violence of the revolutionary class."[50] Since "capitalism will not grow into Socialism," the "great masses of toilers must be in a revolutionary mood; they must have the necessary organization and revolutionary program; they must smash capitalism" under the "general leadership of the only revolutionary party, the Communist Party."[51]

CAPITALISM WILL NOT ABDICATE

Revolution is necessary because the capitalists will not abdicate of their own accord. They will resist "progress" in order to protect their wealth and power. William Z. Foster has written that this was well understood by Marx, Lenin and Stalin. "For as the great Marx has truly said, there is no case in history where a ruling class has yielded up its domination without making a desperate struggle."[52] The ruling class in the United States has a history "of violent resistance to any change on the part of the capitalist class."[53] Although there may be some countries, Khrushchev said, where the communists can take over without a revolution, this cannot be the case in strong capitalist countries. The United States is one of the strong capitalistic countries which will stoop to anything to stop the advance of socialism.[54]

A BLOOD BATH ESSENTIAL FOR PURIFICATION

Revolution is necessary also because the blood bath of the revolution is essential to the purification, education, discipline

---

[49] *The Defence of Terrorism*, p. 35.

[50] *Dialectical Materialism*, p. 75.

[51] William Z. Foster, *Toward Soviet America*, p. 219.

[52] *History of the Communist Party of the United States*, p. 551. *In Defense of the Communist Party and the Indicted Leaders*, New York: New Century Publishers, 1949, p. 23.

[53] Jack Goldring, "The American Road to Socialism," *Political Affairs*, Aug. 1956, p. 51.

[54] Khrushchev, "Report to the 20th Congress," *Political Affairs*, Mar. 1956, pp. 59-60. This is printed in a communist publication in America.

and transformation of the proletariat so that they will be able to transform all society. "Both for the production on a mass scale of this communist consciousness, and for the success of the cause itself, the alteration of men on a mass scale is necessary, an alteration which can only take place in a practical movement, a *revolution*; this revolution is necessary, therefore, not only because the ruling class cannot be overthrown in any other way, but also because the class *overthrowing* it can only in a revolution succeed in ridding itself of all the muck of ages and become fitted to found society anew."[55]

This point of view is not out of date. M. I. Kalinin, a prominent educator in Russia, used the same idea in his book *On Communist Education* in 1950.[56] V. Adoratsky, one of the leading communist theoreticians, presents the same concept when he writes: "In the process of revolution, the proletariat becomes transformed, it becomes trained for the performance of its historic mission. . . . This is one of the fundamental ideas of Marxism. Marx returned to it time and again. . . . Thus, in 1850 in his speech to the Communist League, Marx said, addressing himself to the workers: 'You must pass through fifteen, twenty, perhaps fifty years of civil war and national conflict, not merely in order to change the system, but also to change yourselves and to render yourselves fit for political rule.' And again in 1871, in his pamphlet, *The Civil War in France*, repeating the same thought, Marx said: 'They [the working class] know that in order to work out their own emancipation, and along with it that higher form to which present society is irresistibly tending, by its own economical agencies, they will have to pass through

---

See also *The Communist Conspiracy*, Washington: Government Printing Office, 1956, Part I, Section A, p. xxvii. Mehmet Shehu, "The Unconquerable Ideas of the October Revolution," *International Affairs*, Nov. 1957, p. 60. William Z. Foster, *Political Affairs*, May 1956, pp. 15-17. Herbert Aptheker, *On the Nature of Revolution*, p. 12. Harry Pollett, *Political Affairs*, May 1956, p. 70. See also p. 15. *The Daily Worker*, Nov. 28, 1956, pp. 1, 7. *Political Affairs*, Aug. 1956, p. 62. *History of the Communist Party of the Soviet Union*, p. 21. *The New Leader*, Sept. 17, 1956. Georgi Dimitroff, *The United Front Against Fascism*, p. 98. William Z. Foster, *Toward Soviet America*, pp. 212-214. *History of the Communist Party in the United States*, pp. 550-552. *Political Affairs*, July 1956, p. 62. *Capital*, pp. 31-32.

[55] Marx and Engels, *The German Ideology*, 1939, p. 69. See also pp. 198 and 204.

[56] p. 399.

long struggles, through a series of historic processes, transforming circumstances and men.'

"Here we discern the same unity of opposites, the mutual conflict of these opposites and the inevitable solution of the conflicts by a transition to a new form of society. Without the long and severe training obtained in its struggles, the proletariat cannot fit itself to perform its historical mission."[57]

Part of the struggle which educates the proletariat is going on now in the class warfare which the communists promote. They believe with Lenin that "Only the struggle educates the exploited class."[58] That this, however, is not sufficient by itself is found in the fact that they make strenuous efforts to educate their followers through instruction in Marxism-Leninism.

LIKE THE AMERICAN REVOLUTION?

Communists endeavor to justify their doctrine of revolution by pointing to the American revolution. As Earl Browder put it: "The Declaration of Independence was for that time what *The Communist Manifesto* is for ours. Copy all the most hysterical Hearst editorials of today against Moscow, Lenin, Stalin; substitute the words America, Washington, Jefferson; and the result is an almost verbatim copy of the diatribes of English and European reactionary politicans in the closing years of the eighteenth century against our American founding fathers. Revolution was then 'an alien doctrine imported from America' as now it is 'imported from Moscow.' "[59] John Hardy maintained that the humble masses who fought in the American Revolution were "the forerunners of the working class and its allies of the present period in American history." "The proletariat and its allies have become both the inheritors and the only defenders of the historic American traditions."[60] V. J. Jerome, who is still a leading light in the Communist Party, makes the Communist revolution the extension of the American Revolution. "Communism makes manifest that this nation was cradled in revolution, that the program of the Communist Party is not directed toward some-

---

[57] *Dialectical Materialism*, pp. 33-34.

[58] Quotation from Lenin by Betty Gannett, Assistant Organization Secretary of the Communist Party, U.S.A., *The Communist Party and You*, p. 19.

[59] *What Is Communism?*, pp. 19-20.

[60] *The First American Revolution*, New York: International Publishers, 1937, pp. 127-128.

thing alien to the American people, but that the slogan for the overthrow of capitalism is in genuine American terms the slogan for the fulfillment of what was begun a hundred and sixty years ago."[61] This did not mean, however, that the Communists want to go "Back to 1776"; instead, they want to enlist the revolutionary spirit in "the *new* revolutionary Americanism—the proletarian revolution."[62] This revolution aims at the "dictatorship of the proletariat" and finds its inspiration in the Soviet Union.[63]

The American Revolution, however, bears no resemblance to the Communist doctrine of revolution. *First,* the American Revolution had as its objective the establishment of a reign of law instead of the reign of an arbitrary ruler or rulers—not only a reign of law, but a republic which included "a set of institutions (among them especially general elections, i.e., the right of the people to dismiss their government) which permit public control of the ruler. . . ." The people were given the right to obtain reforms by other than violent means "even against the will of the rulers."[64] The communist revolution, in clear contradiction to this, endeavors to establish a dictatorship of the so-called proletariat whose rule is "unrestricted by law and based on force."[65] They claim, of course, that the dictatorship will finally wither away and that the communist land of peace will arrive. However, we still await proof. Instead we have indications that this is but a day dream which ends in a hellish nightmare. It is the people who wither away.

Secondly, the Revolutionary War did not result in a reign of terror of Americans over Americans. The communist reign of terror in Russia has gone on for more than forty years, and the graves of Siberia are not yet all filled. In the super-purge conducted by Stalin, nine or ten million people were killed. This included "60 to 80 per cent of the top leaders of the Party, the Comsomols, the armed forces, the government, industry, farming and national culture. . . ."[66]

Thirdly, the communist is the subversive agent of a foreign power, i.e., Russia. He works for the overthrow of the govern-

---

[61] "Communism for Americans," *The Communist,* Mar. 1936, p. 274.
[62] *Ibid.,* p. 275.
[63] *Ibid.,* pp. 275-276.
[64] K. R. Popper, *The Open Society and Its Enemies,* Vol. II, p. 151.
[65] Stalin, *Foundations of Leninism,* p. 53.
[66] Victor Kravchenko, *I Chose Freedom,* New York: Charles Scribner's Sons, 1946, p. 236.

ment of his own country and for the enthronement of the rulers in the Kremlin. This is quite different from a revolutionary struggle for freedom within a country which endeavors to set up its own government.

The international nature of the communist conspiracy has always been recognized by the communist government in Russia. Within about five weeks after the Soviet Government was established it issued "An ordinance assigning two million rubles for the need of the revolutionary internationalist movement."[67] In 1919 on November 6, Mr. Chicherin, the people's commissar for foreign affairs declared: "The November revolution, the first act of the world social revolution, at once placed the Russian Soviet Government at the front of the revolutionary movement of the world as the herald and inspiration of the proletarian revolution."[68] Walsh was right when he stated that he thought "that all discussions of the intent of the Soviet Government ought to start with that decree" of November 13, 1917.[69] If the world had heeded his admonition, things could have been much different now. But some are just as deaf today to it as they were then.

The international nature of this conspiracy, under the direction of Russia, was more clearly stated by the Communists in America a number of years ago than it is now. It is not that the communists have changed, but they try to conceal the facts in regard to the conspiracy today in a way they did not conceal them years ago. Over twenty years ago Alex Bittelman wrote: "the revolutionary vanguard of this country can derive deep satisfaction from the fact that it unfailingly received brotherly advice and guidance from the Communist International in the struggle for the revolutionization of the American working class. It was from the outset, and continues to be so, a *mutual collaboration* of the revolutionary proletariat of all countries, organized in a world party, for the victory of the Dictatorship of the Proletariat, for the establishment of a World Soviet Republic. The leading role of the Communist Party of the Soviet Union in the Comintern needs neither explanation nor apology. A party that has opened up the epoch of the world revolution, and that

---

[67] Gazette of the Temporary Workers" and Peasants' Governments, No. 31, Dec. 13, 1917. Quoted by Edmund A. Walsh, *Investigation of Communist Propaganda*, 1930, Part I, Vol. I, pp. 10-11.

[68] *Ibid.*, p. 14.

[69] *Ibid.*, p. 11.

is successfully building a classless society on one sixth of the
earth, is cheerfully recognized and followed as the leading party
of the world communist movement. And by the same token,
the leaders of that party—first Lenin and now Stalin—are proudly
followed as the leaders of the proletariat and of all oppressed
in every country of the world."[70]

It was this allegiance to Russia which lead Earl Browder,
under questions by J. B. Matthews, to admit that he would start
civil war in America if we went to war against Russia.[71] Even
the "naive" communist, if such exists today, who has his head in
the clouds and thinks that he is helping emancipate the world,
is still but the tool of international conspirators.

The communists have always believed that revolution must
not be limited to one country, but must take place in every
country throughout the world. In the *Communist Manifesto*
they called on workers of *all* lands to *unite*.[72]

Today the 1917 revolution in Russia is held up as an example
to the rest of the world. "There is not a single Marxist-Leninist
party which can ensure the victory of socialism in its own country without basing itself upon the fundamental lessons to be
drawn from the experience of the C.P.S.U."[73]

"By their deeds the Bolsheviks showed the workers of the
whole world that it is possible to overthrow the rule of the
bourgeoisie and establish their own. They showed how to overthrow the bourgeoisie and how the proletariat should take power
into its own hands."[74]

Because world wide revolution is deemed essential to the success of world communism, the communists have schools in which
revolutionaries are trained, and from whose halls they are sent

---

[70] "Milestones of Comintern Leadership," *The Communist*, Mar. 1934,
p. 235.

[71] The House Committee on Un-American Activities, *op. cit.*, Vol. VII,
pp. 4428-4431. Foster, in Vol. IX, pp. 5397, 5413-5414.

[72] Compare William Z. Foster, *Toward Soviet America*, p. 258. *For a
Lasting Peace, For a People's Democracy!*, Apr. 17, 1961. Stalin, *The
October Revolution*, Moscow: Co-operative Publishing Society of Foreign
Workers in the USSR, 1934, p. 62. International Publishers, *The Theory
of the Proletarian Revolution*, 1936, p. 22 (no author is listed). Lenin,
The Proletarian Revolution and the Renegade Kautsky, pp. 66-67.

[73] Mehmet Shehu, "The Unconquerable Ideas of the October Revolution," *International Affairs*, Nov. 1957, p. 57.

[74] *Ibid.*, Nov. 1957, p. 56.

into all parts of the world to capitalize on existing trouble or to create trouble.[75]

Fourthly, the American Revolution and the communist revolution differ in that the communists not only work for revolution in non-democratic countries, but also in democratic countries. Thus they are not only trying to overthrow oppressive governments under which some of them have lived, but all governments except those patterned on Russia and subservient to Russia. Russia, as again demonstrated by her action in Hungary in 1956, is against any revolution which aims at freedom from Russia.

Fifthly, the communist revolution was a counter-revolution. The communist revolution in Russia did not overthrow the Czarist government, but the Kerensky government which was not a dictatorship. On March 16, 1917, Nicholas II abdicated and the power of government went to the Duma, and a provisional government, the Kerensky government, was set up and immediately recognized by the United States.[76] This proves that the United States was not opposed to the right of a people to revolt.

The revolution of November 7, 1917, however, was a counter revolution by a very small minority to destroy a democracy and to establish a "brutalitarian" dictatorship.[77]

Sixthly, why should the revolution take so long: As Kravchenko said: How long does revolution last? How long does it take to destroy the previous regime? "The French Terror was over in five years." But it has been over forty years since the 1917 revolution in Russia.[78]

Seventhly, the communist revolution is not only a revolution in government, but also in everything else. It is a revolt against God, religion, morality and humanity. ". . . it seeks to create a new arch-type of humanity entirely of the type called a collective man, as opposed to the individual soul-encumbered man,

---

[75] Montgomery M. Green, "Russia's Universities of Revolution," *Facts Forum News,* Sept. 1955, p. 2.

[76] Edmund A. Walsh, in Hamilton Fish, Jr., Chairman, *Investigation of Communist Propaganda,* Part I, Vol. No. 1, June 9, 13, 1930. Washington, D.C.: Government Printing Office, 1930, pp. 2-3.

[77] The Communists claim that they then had a party of 240,000. See *History of the Communist Party of the Soviet Union,* p. 196. It is probable, however, that they did not number even 40,000. Edmund A. Walsh, *op. cit.,* p. 5. Compare *History,* p. 183.

[78] *I Chose Justice,* New York: Charles Scribner's Sons, 1950, p. 137.

as they describe it, the human individual."[79] The life of the bee
in the beehive seems to be their ideal.[80]

These considerations make it clear that the communist revolution is not a revolution which seeks the "reallocation of sover-
eignty, the transfer of the supreme power in a state from one
group to another," but the suppression of all states to the rule
of one state—Russia.[81]

It is important that these points be stressed. The communist
revolution is a threefold revolution. *First,* the seizure of the power
of the state. *Secondly,* the use of the power of the state to seize
economic, cultural, educational, etc., power and to wipe out all
opposition. In other words, the total centralization of power
in the hands of the ruling group. As Aptheker put it: "the productive masses take state power from the bourgeoisie and then
use state power in order to *begin* the establishment of Socialism."[82]

In speaking of Red China, Yevgeni Zhukov said: "In 1955 and
1956 the Chinese Socialist revolution registered a decisive victory on the economic front (in abolishing private ownership of
the basic means of production). Thanks to the rectification campaign and the struggle against the Rights, a decisive victory was
also won on the political and ideological fronts of the Socialist
revolution."[83]

That the Communist Revolution is more than a revolution
which results in the seizure of state power, is also clearly stated
in an article by Yang Shang-Kun which dealt with the two so-
called historic documents issued in Moscow, November 19, 1957,
at the 40th Anniversary of the October Revolution. The working
class under the guidance of the Communist Party must carry
through "the proletarian revolution in one form or another,"
with the purpose of setting up a dictatorship of the proletariat
and "in using it to effect the Socialist Revolution in the economic,
political and ideological spheres, the general laws operate in
every country advancing along the Socialist road."[84]

---

[79] Walsh, *op. cit.,* p. 6.

[80] See I. Khalifman, *Bees,* Moscow: Foreign Languages Publishing
House, 1955, also the review of this book in *New World Review,* Apr.
1956, p. 65.

[81] Walsh, *op. cit.,* p. 6.

[82] *On the Nature of Revolution,* p. 26.

[83] "The Impact of the Chinese Revolution on the National Liberation
Struggle," *World Marxist Review,* Nov. 1958, p. 21.

[84] "Historic Meetings and Documents," *World Marxist Review,* Nov.

Thirdly, the remaking of society and of man. *The Communist Manifesto* stated that they would forcibly overthrow *all existing social institutions.* " . . . in the Socialist revolution, the working masses, having achieved state power, must start from scratch in remaking the whole character and nature of the social order."[85] This change in the social order, they believe, will result in the change of human nature. There is no permanent human nature, but the nature of man differs in different epochs. " 'Humanity' and 'humanism' are not immutable concepts. They have changed and are still changing their content and form with the march of time."[86] Red China has tried to combine the economic revolution and the revolutionary remaking of human nature. Thus the Communes are not only an effort to strengthen their economic control of the nation, but also to destroy the family and to remake human nature.

Those who understand communism know that the goal for revolution does not stop with the seizure of state power. Instead, this is only the first step in the communist doctrine of total revolution.

THE REVOLUTION IS JUSTIFIED BY THEIR GOAL

The communists not only appeal to the American Revolution to justify their revolution, but they also justify it by their goal. Since revolution is necessary in order to achieve power for the proletariat, and thus ultimately to achieve communism, they consider it irrelevant to criticize the doctrine of revolution.[87] Furthermore, since violence and destruction are inevitable in a revolution, if the objective of the revolution be communism, the communists believe that no cost is too great. People die anyhow, (pestilences sweep the earth), so why worry about the death of millions if communism is thereby achieved.[88] As a recent defector, who was brought up under the communists, said: "If

---

1958, p. 11. See also Premier Cho En-lai, "Report on the 1959 Economic Plan," *Peking Review*, Sept. 1, 1959, p. 15.

[85] Herbert Aptheker, *op. cit.*, p. 26.

[86] Ladislav Shtoll, "The Class Struggle and Humanism," *World Marxist Review*, Nov. 1958, p. 26.

[87] See Sidney Hook, "Why I Am a Communist," *Modern Monthly*, Apr. 1934, p. 145. Sidney Hook gave up communism. See, among other writings, his *Reason, Social Myths and Democracy*, New York: The Humanities Press, 1940, Reprint 1950.

[88] Statement of a communist to Dr. Fred Schwarz. Personal interview.

the Communist Party is willing to sacrifice millions of people for collectivization, would it not sacrifice more for world domination?"[89]

"Blood and iron"[90] are necessary, the laws of history cannot be repealed, so why shrink from revolution.[91] In fact, in view of the goal, and the necessity of terrorism to accomplish it, in "the revolution the highest degree of energy is the highest degree of humanity."[92]

Any so-called excesses and anti-democratic methods during and after the revolution are explained as temporary and necessary expedients to thwart a counter-revolution.[93] "Revolutions are never gentle,"[94] and "far from opposing so-called excesses, instances of popular revenge against hated individuals or public buildings that are only associated with hateful recollections, such instances must not only be tolerated but the leadership of them must be taken in hand."[95]

The revolution, therefore, instead of something to be dreaded, is something to which one looked forward. In fact, in speaking of a revolution which he thought would arise in Russia, Marx wrote: "If Mother Nature is not particularly unfavourable towards us we shall still live to see the fun!"[96]

Not only is the doctrine of the revolution essential to Marxism, but the communist glories in it. "According to Marx and Lenin, revolutions are the most vital and decisive factors in the history of human society. 'Revolutions are the locomotives of history,' Marx said. This aphorism was quoted by Lenin in his pamphlet, *Two Tactics of the Social-Democrats in the Democratic Revolution*, in which he also referred to revolution as 'the festival of the oppressed and exploited.' "[97]

---

[89] External Research Staff, Office of Intelligence Research, Department of State, "The Soviet Union As Reported by Former Soviet Citizens," *Interview Report* No. 17, June 1956, p. 22.

[90] Trotsky, *The Defence of Terrorism*, pp. 59-60.

[91] *Witness Whittaker Chambers*, p. 14.

[92] Trotsky, *The Defence of Terrorism*, p. 70.

[93] William Reswick, *I Dreamt Revolution*, Chicago: Henry Regnery Company, 1952, p. 48. Karl Marx, *Selected Works*, Vol. II, p. 163.

[94] Bruhat in Victor Kravchenko, *I Chose Justice*, p. 137.

[95] Marx, *Selected Works*, Vol. II, p. 163.

[96] *Ibid.*, p. 668.

[97] V. Adoratsky, *Dialectial Materialism*, p. 75.

ARE THESE THINGS RELEVANT TODAY?

It might be thought by some that the preceding discussion of the place of revolution in the philosophy of communism is irrelevant to the current scene. After all Marx and Engels died long ago, and Lenin also departed this world some time ago. To think, however, that these things are irrelevant is to forget the importance of theory in communist thinking. Khrushchev emphasized recently that they are still Marxists. Lenin is being emphasized today as the great teacher of Marxism. Walter Lippmann tells us that "in the Soviet Union the authority of Lenin is treated as infallible and more than human."[98]

The last issue of *For a Lasting Peace, for a People's Democracy*, dated April 17, 1956, carried the following proofs of the present day loyalty to Marxism-Leninism. *First*, Lenin's works have been and are being circulated by the millions. "Between 1917 and April 1, 1956, 289,700,000 copies of Lenin's books have been published in the Soviet Union in 82 languages. His work *The State and Revolution* has appeared in 179 editions during this period, the total number of copies in circulation being 6,-399,000; *Imperialism, the Highest Stage of Capitalism*, in 192 editions of 6,994,000 copies; *Tasks of the Youth Leagues*, in 364 editions of 13,948,000 copies, and so forth. . . . Huge editions of Lenin's works have been published in the Chinese People's Republic, in other countries of people's democracy and in capitalist countries."

Secondly, it is expressly stated that Lenin is the great teacher of the workers of the world and that success will come to them if they follow Lenin's *immortal* ideas. We continue to quote: "Working people the world over sacredly honour the bright memory of their great teacher. The Communist and Workers' Parties are raising still higher the triumphant Leninist banner. Fidelity to Leninism is the guarantee of all the successes of the fraternal parties.

"The ideas of Leninism inspire progressive mankind to struggle for peace, democracy and socialism. To an ever increasing extent life confirms the all-triumphant power of the immortal Leninist idea."

In speaking of the efforts, even though the dissolution of the Cominform was announced in this issue, further to develop and to strengthen international proletarianism or communism, they

---

[98] "The Soviet Challenge," *Commercial Appeal*, Nov. 13, 1958, p. 6.

claimed that "the Communist and Workers' Parties will find new forms of relations and contacts, which are suitable to the present situation. This will strengthen their spirit of mutual co-operation, on the basis of the principles of proletarian internationalism, and further unite and rally them in the common struggle for the cause of peace, democracy, and socialism.

"The Communist and Worker's Parties, which have some 30 million members, are growing stronger and better steeled with every passing year; they look confidently to the future, which belongs to Communism. Their successes and victories spring from fidelity to the great Leninist teaching. Inspired and guided by Marxism-Leninism, the Communist and Worker's Parties will continue boldly and creatively to solve all the tasks facing them, they will constantly strengthen their ties with the broad masses, exchange their accumulated experience and confidently advance along the path of struggle for the triumph of the cause of the working class and the entire labouring people."

It was also stressed that Lenin emphasized that morality is that which serves the interest of the Party in its struggle to emancipate mankind. That is right which furthers class interest. In one of the leading articles in this last issue of *For a Lasting Peace, for a People's Democracy!* we read:

"The Twentieth Congress on the need to combat bureaucratic and stereotyped methods of work and schematism are a mighty stimulus for developing the creative initiative of the masses. The Twentieth Congress are permeated with the Leninist spirit: deep humanism, genuine concern for man, for the high moral sense of the Party member and the Soviet citizen. Speaking of the morality of the Communist, of communist ethics, Lenin always emphasized that they served the struggle for the unity of the working masses against all exploitation, that they served the cause of raising human society a stage higher."

Communist morality, of course, is born in the struggle against the old society. Lenin wrote: "It is the beginning of a revolution that is much more difficult, more material, more radical and more decisive than the overthrow of the bourgeoisie, for it is a victory over personal conservativeness, indiscipline, petty-bourgeois egoism, a victory over the habits that accursed capitalism left as a heritage to the worker and peasant.

"It is communist morality which, in the struggle against the old and obsolescent, is becoming firmly established in the land of victorious socialism."[99]

Khrushchev made it clear that his attack on Stalin was not an attack on Lenin. The closing words of his 1956 speech attacking Stalin were: "Long live the victorious banner of our party—Leninism! [Tumultuous, prolonged applause ending in ovation. All rise.]"

ADVOCACY TO ACTION OR JUST TO BELIEF?

In view of the teaching of the communists concerning the essentiality and the inevitability of revolution, is it reasonable to contend that they advocate that violence be used to overthrow our government when they consider that the time is ripe? Or do they, as some maintain, advocate that a person *merely believe* in something rather than urging an individual to *do* something.[100]

As has been shown previously, the communists do not advocate belief for the sake of belief, but belief for the sake of action. Action without theory is blind and theory without action is dead. They claim that they do not want simply to understand the world, but to change the world. As Khrushchev put it: "Revolutionary theory is not a collection of petrified dogmas and forumulae, but a militant guide to action in transforming the world, in building communism. Marxism-Leninism teaches us that a theory isolated from practice is dead, and practice which is not illumined by revolutionary theory is blind."[101] "The Marxist-Leninist theory provides the scientific basis for a revolutionary policy."[102]

"The principle of peaceful coexistence does not mean or assume that the nations of the socialist countries will renounce

---

[99] *For a Lasting Peace, For a People's Democracy!*, Apr. 17, 1956, p. 3.

[100] Compare the Supreme Court of the United States' decisions No. 6, 7 and 8 of the October Term, 1956, pp. 25-26. This decision was delivered on June 17, 1957.

[101] Khrushchev, *Report of the Central Committee, CPSU to the 20th Congress*, New York: New Century Publishers, 1956, p. 116.

[102] *World Marxist Review*, Dec. 1959, p. 35. This is from an article on "Scientific Foundations of a Revolutionary Policy" which is filled with quotations from the new textbook *Foundations of Marxism-Leninism*. The book was authorized by the Central Committee of the CPSU. The quotation is from the book. Thus "The Communist Party is a Party of Actions." Title of an article by Leon Bohr in the *World Marxist Review*, Oct. 1959, p. 45.

their revolutionary views, and in the same way it does not mean or assume that in the capitalist countries the ruling classes will renounce their ideology."[103]

During the period of peaceful coexistence their efforts, their actions, are directed toward softening up the country for revolution. With this intent they endeavor to divide their enemies, conduct psychological warfare and carry on espionage work. Thus M. J. Olgin wrote: "The overthrow of the State power, and with it, of the capitalist system, grows out of the everyday struggles of the workers."[104] Class struggle must continue because the "objective grounds for revolutionary struggle" cannot disappear as long as capitalism exists.[105]

What happens when the time is ripe? Revolution! As M. J. Olgin puts it: "Armed workers and soldiers and marines seize the principal governmental offices, invade the residences of the President and his Cabinet members, arrest them, declare the old regime abolished, establish their own power, the power of the workers and farmers."[106]

The communist understanding of their doctrine of revolution is that they are called on not merely to believe but also to act. Their own understanding of their doctrine of revolution is quite different from the understanding held by some influential Americans.

VIOLENCE AFTER THE COMMUNISTS GAIN POWER

After the communists have gained state power they will use the power of the state to set up the dictatorship of the proletariat and to crush violently those who oppose them. This is uniformly taught by all communist leaders, past and present.

Karl Marx taught that "Every real revolution is a social one, in that it brings a new class to power and allows it to remodel society in its own image."[107] Elsewhere he wrote that after "every

---

[103] K. Vladin, "American 'Research' In Soviet Foreign Policy," *International Affairs*, Nov. 1957, p. 168.

[104] *Why Communism? Plain Talks on Vital Problems.* p. 74. This pamphlet was published in New York by the Workers' Library Publishers. It speaks of the leadership of the Communist Party in this fight, and contains on p. 95 the emblem of the Communist Party, the hammer and sickle.

[105] See *World Marxist Review*, Oct. 1959, p. 45.

[106] See the entire discussion of revolution, from which the quotation is taken, in *Why Communism? Plain Talks on Vital Problems*, pp. 74-79.

[107] *Selected Works*, Vol. II, p. 677.

revolution marking a progressive phase in the class struggle, the purely repressive character of the State power stands out in bolder and bolder relief."[108]

Engels' concept of the state and the dictatorship of the proletariat is stated so clearly that it cannot be misunderstood: "As the State is only a transitional phenomenon which must be made use of in the revolutionary struggle in order forcibly to crush our antagonists, it is pure absurdity to speak of a Free People's State. As long as the proletariat *needs* the State, *it needs it not in the interests of freedom, but for the purpose of crushing its antagonists; and as soon as it becomes possible to speak of freedom, then the State, as such,* ceases to exist."[109]

Lenin is in line with Marx and Engels. He makes it crystal clear that they will establish a ruthless dictatorship instead of a democracy. "The state is a special organization of force; it is the organization of violence for the suppression of some class. What class must the proletariat suppress? Naturally, the exploiting class only, i.e., the bourgeoisie."[110]

"Kautsky talked about everything, about everything that is acceptable to liberals and bourgeois democrats, and does not go beyond their system of ideas, but he did not talk about the main thing, namely, that the proletariat cannot achieve victory *without breaking the resistance* of the bourgeoisie, *without forcibly suppressing its enemies,* and that, where there is 'forcible suppressing,' where there is no 'freedom,' there of course, is no democracy. This Kautsky did not understand."[111]

Elsewhere Lenin said, "The dictatorship of the proletariat is the most determined and the most ruthless war waged by the new class against the *more powerful* enemy, against the bourgeoisie . . . the dictatorship of the proletariat is necessary, and victory over the bourgeoisie is impossible without a long, stubborn and desperate war of life and death, a war which requires perseverance, discipline, firmness, indomitableness and unity of will . . . absolute centralization and the strictest discipline of the

---

[108] *Civil War in France,* 1933, p. 38.

[109] Lenin viewed this as a most important passage. The quotation is from Engel's letter to Bebel in 1875. Quoted in Appendix II, Marx, *Critique of the Gotha Programme,* 1933, pp. 79-80. It is found on pp. 47-48 in the 1938 edition.

[110] *The State and Revolution,* 1932, p. 22.

[111] Lenin, *The Proletarian Revolution and Renegade Kautsky,* p. 38.

proletariat are one of the basic conditions for victory over the bourgeoisie."[112]

Stalin described the role of the proletariat thus: Its rule is "unrestricted by law and based on force."[113] Stalin acted on this principle to destroy all opposition, and the Communist Party in America endorsed rather than condemned such action. So we read: "The turn in policy of the Communist Party of the Soviet Union from the policy of limitation and squeezing out of the capitalist elements to the policy of the complete liquidation of the kulaks as a class, is thus destroying the last remnants of capitalist exploitation in the country, is removing the last inner class basis for the imperialist intervention and abolishing the last inner basis of restoring capitalism in the Soviet Union."[114]

The communists have not changed their goal or proposed method of procedure. They still teach that the dictatorship of the proletariat must destroy the capitalist or imperialist class. A December 29, 1956 statement, issued by the political Bureau of the Central Committee of China's Communist Party and summarized by the Soviet news agency Tass, makes this clear: "Even after destruction of the exploiting class, democratic methods of administration can grow, laws can be 'normalized,' bureaucratic tendencies overcome. . . . Even then, 'socialist democracy' is not to be confused with 'bourgeois democracy.' Socialist democracy aims only to strengthen socialism, cannot be used to weaken, attack or subvert the dictatorship of the proletariat. It cannot be extended to enemies of socialism. Lenin called the dictatorship of the proletariat the 'most essential part of Marxism.' The preservation of proletarian rule may require discipline, stern measures, even violence."[115]

This concept is still considered basic. Although the communists want the United States to allow their Party freedom, they are clear that when they are in power there will be no freedom for a party which engages "in efforts to overthrow the government by force and violence."[116] Not only is this true, but they will use the power of the state to dictate to and destroy all other

---

[112] *"Left-Wing" Communism An Infantile Disorder*, Moscow: Co-operative Publishing Society, 1935, pp. 16-17.

[113] *Foundations of Leninism*, p. 53.

[114] *Central Committee Plenum, Thesis and Resolutions for the Seventh National Convention of the Communist Party of U.S.A.*, Mar. 31-Apr. 4, 1930, New York: Workers' Library Publishers, 1930, p. 5.

[115] *National Guardian*, Jan. 28, 1957, p. 6.

[116] *Political Affairs*, Apr. 1956, p. 38.

classes. The Marxist conceives of the state as "the instrument of the ruling class for maintaining its rule—as the dictatorship of the ruling class. And from this, in turn, arises the concept of the dictatorship of the proletariat as the instrument of the working class, having achieved political power, for establishing socialism and abolishing classes altogether."[117]

Communism, so its founders and adherents have stated and restated, holds as inevitable and beneficial the coming of communist revolution throughout the world. When the non-communist world comprehends and believes what the communists say, they will know how to deal with the communists in their midst as well as with communists in other countries.

What is the attitude of the communists toward religion? When they seize power are they friendly to religion? To this attention will now be turned.

---

[117] Hyman Lumer, "In Defense of Theory," *Political Affairs*, Feb. 1957, p. 61.

CHAPTER NINE

The Communist Attitude toward Religion

Is permanent peaceful coexistence possible between communism and religion? From time to time the communists have tried to leave the impression that such is possible. While trying to recruit a church member to the Communist Party, it was explained to him that the Communist Party is a nonsectarian organization which respects the various religions, and is even related to Christianity.[1] It has been argued that there is no incompatibility between the two, and that communism has been anti-religious only where an oppressive church has existed. When religion is not on the side of the exploiters, so some contend, communism is not anti-religious. The headquarters of the Communist Party in Japan told the author in November 1955, that they were not engaged in an anti-religious campaign. In fact, the Soviet "regime currently is going to considerable trouble to create an impression of religious toleration. . . ."[2]

To come to the conclusion, however, that communism is not basically anti-religious is to fall for the Party line which endeavors to lull us to sleep. It is but a part of their coexistence propaganda and is carried on "for the sake of the effect on foreigners."[3] Those who fall for their propaganda are ignorant of the communist view of the nature and function of religion.

WHY COMMUNISM IS AGAINST RELIGION

We will not repeat here what was said in Chapter 3. We will cite the several reasons why communism is basically opposed to

---

[1] J. Edgar Hoover, "God or Chaos?" *Redbook Magazine*, Feb. 1949. Howard Fast, once a communist author, claimed that one of his sources of "socialism" is the Bible. "A Letter from Howard Fast," *The New Leader*, July 30, 1956, p. 17.

[2] *Notes: Soviet Affairs*, March 28, 1956, p. 5.

[3] *Ibid.*, p. 5. Bela Fabian, "Red Clerics Visit United States," *New*

religion. These reasons have not been affected in any way by the current coexistence propaganda.

a. Communism is *militant atheism.* Therefore by its very nature it is antagonistic to theism. It is not content to accept the continued existence of a world committed to theism, for from the beginning the communists have said that they are not interested simply in *interpreting* the world, but that their goal is "to change it."[4] This statement of Marx was but enlarged on by Khrushchev when he said to the 20th Congress in 1956 that "Revolutionary theory is not a collection of petrified dogmas and formulae, but a militant guide to action in transforming the world, in building communism. Marxism-Leninism teaches us that a theory isolated from practice is dead, and practice which is not illumined by revolutionary theory is blind."[5] In line with this the great soviet encyclopedia, published in Moscow in 1950 and translated into German in 1955, called on the Party actively to oppose religion and "to fight for the 'full victory' of atheism."[6]

b. Communism is a *totalitarian system which demands the complete loyalty of its subjects.* It demands control of the inner and the outer life of man. Thus, by its nature it must oppose religion which says there is a higher will and law than that of the state or Party. In the booklet on *How To Be A Good Communist* by Liu Shao-chi, three principles were emphasized. First, thorough and continual *indoctrination* in Marxism-Leninism. Second, whole-hearted *dedication* to the Party. One must denounce any personal life which would in any way interfere with communistic objectives. Third, continued *participation* in any phase of the revolutionary struggle to which he might be assigned by the Party. The claim of this totalitarian system on the whole life of its adherents is summed up in Lenin's statement that the Party is the mind, the honor and the conscience of this epoch.[7] Since communism embraces a world view to which the communist is called on to be totally committed, com-

Leader, July 26, 1954. Reprinted in the *Congressional Record,* July 26, 1954, A5383.

[4] Marx's Eleventh Thesis on Feuerbach in Frederick Engels, *Ludwig Feuerbach,* p. 75.

[5] *Report of the Central Committee, CPSU to the 20th Congress of the Communist Party of the Soviet Union,* p. 116.

[6] Quoted in *The Christian Century,* 1956, p. 85.

[7] *For a Lasting Peace, For a People's Democracy!,* Apr. 1956. Notice that this is a current emphasis.

munism cannot perpetually coexist with any religion which has
a different world view.

c. Communism is antagonistic to religion because it claims to
be the *scientific world view* which must oppose religion because
religion represents an unscientific and prescientific world view
which is opposed to scientific progress. He who is for scientific
progress, according to the communists, must oppose religion.
Said Stalin, "The Party cannot be neutral towards religion, and
it does conduct anti-religious propaganda against all and every
religious prejudice because it stands for science, while religious
prejudices run counter to science, because all religion is something opposite to science."[8]

d. Communism maintains that religion is a *tool of the ruling
class* for the perpetuation of its power and the control of the
masses. Religion is but a bourgeois prejudice behind which lurks
in ambush bourgeois interest.[9] To Lenin the clergy meant reaction, therefore he hated religion and the clergy.[10]

Marx had more personal reasons for the hatred of clergymen.
Theologians had blocked Bauer's appointment to a professorship
and had brought about, because of his atheism, his discharge as
an instructor. This kept Bauer from bringing young Marx into
the university as his protege.[11]

Lenin looked upon religion as a tool in the hands of the
"oppressing classes." Said he: "All oppressing classes need two
social functions to safeguard their rule: the function of the
hangman and the function of the priest. The hangman is required to quell the protests and the indignation of the oppressed;
the priest is required to console the oppressed, to paint for
them the prospects of mitigation of their sufferings and sacrifices
(this is particularly easy to do without guaranteeing that these
prospects will be "achieved"), while preserving class rule, and
thereby to reconcile them to class rule, wean them from revolu-

---

[8] *Leninism*, Vol. I, p. 386. Communism is full of contradictions. It is
not scientific. See Subcommittee of the Senate on Internal Security, *Contradictions of Communism*, Washington, D.C.: Government Printing Office,
1959.

[9] The *Communist Manifesto*, New York: International Publishers, 1932,
p. 20.

[10] George Catlin, *The Story of the Political Philosophers*, p. 572.

[11] Leopold Schwartzchild, *Karl Marx, the Red Prussian*, New York:
Grosset & Dunlap, 1947, pp. 44-45.

tionary action, undermine their revolutionary spirit and destroy their revolutionary determination."[12]

This view of religion has not changed since Lenin's day. As late as 1951 V. J. Jerome wrote: "The present manufactured rage of religionism among bourgeois intellectuals has its direct services to çapitalism. It is designed to paralyze the will to struggle against the imperialist enemies of mankind, by implanting a 'guilt feeling' in the common man, disposing him to self-abnegation and self-humiliation, and leading him to fatalistic acceptance of suffering and destruction."[13]

In the light of this view of religion, it is easy to understand that communists maintain that in order to represent the proletariat and to overthrow capitalism it is necessary to oppose all religion.

e. Communism is anti-religious because, as a corollary to the above, it claims that religion is *the opiate of the masses*, which leads them to be submissive to their masters and more or less content with their lot. It helps deaden the pain of existence for the exploited, so claim the communists. This keeps them from participating in the struggle for world revolution.[14] By looking to the "other world" they endure the miseries of this world, without fighting for rewards in the here and now. A humorous side light may be found in a case in Bulgaria where "the concerns of church and synagogue were assigned, with an almost comical honesty, to the Ministry of Foreign Affairs!"[15]

Lenin put it this way: "Marx said 'Religion is the opium of the people'—and this postulate is the cornerstone of the whole philosophy of Marxism with regard to religion. Marxism always regarded all modern religions and churches, and every kind of religious organization as instruments of that bourgeois reaction whose aim is to defend exploitation by stupefying the working-class."[16] Trotsky wrote: "But as a whole, Christianity, like all

---

[12] *The Collapse of the Second International*, Moscow: Foreign Languages Publishing House, 1952, p. 46.

[13] V. J. Jerome, "Let Us Grasp the Weapon of Culture," *Political Affairs*, Feb. 1951, p. 206.

[14] Earl Browder, *Communism in The United States*, p. 334; *What Is Communism?*, p. 146.

[15] Robert E. Fitch, *Commentary*, July 1954, p. 84.

[16] Lenin, *Religion*, p. 12. Lenin, *Marx-Engels Marxism*, p. 193. On Sept. 22, 1955 Khrushchev "told the president of the French National Assembly during a visit by French notables to Moscow: 'Communism has not changed its attitude of opposition to religion. We are doing everything

other religions, became a method of deadening the consciousness of the oppressed masses."[17]

f. Communism is anti-religious because *it regards religion as a symbol of mans' alienation from himself.* Religion, as man's reaction to mystery and to misery, leads man to look outside of himself for help, and thus keeps him from bringing about his own emancipation.

In a system in which there is private ownership of the means of production, so reason the communists, the worker is alienated from the machine, for he does not own it. He is also alienated from the system, for it denies him the right of personal identification with the means of production. It is something outside of himself. It is also something which he does not understand, since being separated from the ownership of the means of production and distribution the worker views the whole economic process as a mysterious process. Although religion may vary in different systems, since it is but a reflex of the world, it exists as long as man does not socially own the means of production and distribution.[18] This alienation is symbolized by man looking to God, someone outside himself, for aid instead of looking to himself and the dialectic—which, of course, is outside of man.

g. Communism is *against any religion which teaches the reality of moral law.* The communist views morality as but a means of furthering class interests. Therefore, any religion which teaches the reality of moral law is endeavoring to bind on the exploited class the means of protecting the class interests of the ruling class. To achieve the values of the proletariat the non-proletarian morality must be repudiated. Therefore, religion must be repudiated.

h. Communism is against any religion *which teaches love, since class hatred is the way of progress.* In 1929 Emilian Yarovslavsky, the head of the Society of the Godless, told Pierre Van Passen that they intended utterly to destroy Christianity because "communism is an irreconcilable opponent of the morality of Christ, which is based on love." Communists must be "as hard as steel." They must not "know what pity, mercy, or com-

---

we can to eliminate the bewitching power of the opium of religion' " (U.S. Information Agency, *A Primer on Communism,* Washington, D.C., Apr. 1956, Third Printing, p. 39).

[17] *The Defence of Terrorism,* p. 38.

[18] Compare Karl Lowith, *Meaning in History,* pp. 49-50.

passion is."[19] The Czechoslovak poet, Jiri Wolker, expressed the same concept under the idea of class hatred. "Let us assume that class hatred could disappear in a class society. Nothing could be more harmful to the working class than that. They would be degraded to the position of oxen under an eternal yoke, for it is only hate that helps to maintain the worker's human dignity—class hate which one day will abolish all classes."[20] If hate, not love, is the way of true progress, communists must of necessity hate any religion which advocates love.

This rejection of mercy is reflected in a *Bulletin of the Cheka*, September 1918, on "Why Are You Soft?" In a revolution one cannot be soft. Instead use, when necessary, refined torture "the mere description of which would" instill "cold terror into the counter-revolutionists." Of one it was said: "Get out of him what you can and send him to the other world."[21]

i. Since communism may be aptly described as the *Communist Crime Syndicate*, an international organization of criminals directed by cunning and ruthless thugs in the Kremlin, it must be antagonistic to *any religion which stands for any measure of truth, holiness and justice.*

It was for such reasons as some of the above that Earl Browder said that we "Communists do not distinguish between good and bad religions, because we think they are all bad for the masses."[22] These considerations also account for Rudas' vigorous attack on those who tried to water down Engel's onslaught against religion.[23]

These elements of the communist world view justify the conclusion that communism is basically anti-religious.

The opposition of communism to religion does not mean that atheism has been a formal requirement for party membership.[24]

---

[19] "Closed Are the Gates of Mercy," *Family Circle*, June 1956, p. 34.

[20] As quoted in Ladislav Shtoll, "The Class Struggle and Humanism," *World Marxist Review*, Nov. 1958, p. 28.

[21] This blast was called forth by the release of Lockhart—whom they called a British agent. The entire article is reprinted in the May 29, 1956 release of the House Committee on Un-American Activities on *The Communist Conspiracy*, Part I, Section B, pp. 27-28.

[22] *What Is Communism?*, p. 149.

[23] L. Rudas in the Introduction to Engel's *Ludwig Feuerbach and the Outcome of Classical German Philosophy*, New York: International Publishers, n.d., p. 11. In this chapter we have not endeavored to refute the communist attack on religion. It is our intention to critically evaluate their attack in *Two Worlds: Christianity and Communism.*

[24] Earl Browder, *What Is Communism?*, p. 147.

But the process of the liquidation of one's religious beliefs, or
their complete liquidation as in the case of William Z. Foster,[25]
is going on in anyone who becomes a member of the party. And
since religious beliefs have never been considered a "private
matter insofar as it concerns members in our revolutionary
Party," it is expected that under Party education and discipline
the new member will soon get rid of all of his religious beliefs.[26]

In what way or ways does communism express its basic antagonism to religion?

HOW THEIR ANTAGONISM TO RELIGION IS
EXPRESSED[27]

The fact that communism is in irreconcilable opposition to
religion does not mean that it must express its antagonism in
one inflexible manner. The kind of opposition may vary at different times and places. Communists, it must be kept in mind,
do not regard Marxism as a dogmatic blueprint which must be
inflexibly followed even when conditions change. It is a guide
to action, and as a guide to action it takes into consideration
existing circumstances in order to act so as to make the most
possible progress toward their unchanging goal. It is in this
manner that their current line is explained by V. J. Jerome,
editor of the Communist Publication, *Political Affairs*, in a Preface to an article by William Z. Foster, until recently National
Chairman of the Communist Party. "Capitalist apologists are
now also saying that Khrushchev, in enunciating the possibility
of achieving Socialism by parliamentary action, has discarded
Marxism-Leninism. This is ridiculous. As Foster makes clear in
his article, all the greatest Communist leaders, proceeding upon
the basic principle that Marxism is a guide to action, not a
dogma, have upon various occasions during the past century
restated their perspective of the road to Socialism in accordance

---

[25] *The Twilight of World Capitalism*, p. 158.

[26] Earl Browder, *What Is Communism?*, p. 147. See also Stalin, *Leninism*, Vol. I, p. 386 and William Z. Foster's statement before the Fish
Committee, *Investigation of Un-American Activities and Propaganda*,
House Resolution 282, Union Calendar No. 2, House Report No. 2, 1939,
p. 18; Lenin, *Religion*, pp. 9-10.

[27] The author is devoting an entire book to *The Pattern of The Communist Attack on Religion*.

with changing economic and political conditions. This is what Khrushchev has done."[28]

Lenin well emphasized the desirability of this adaptability when he wrote: "It is necessary to combine the strictest loyalty to the ideas of communism with the ability to make all the necessary practical compromises, to 'tack,' to make agreements, zig-zags, retreats and so on. . . ."[29] " . . . the revolutionary class, in order to fulfill its task, must be able to master *all* forms or sides of social activity without exception. . . . *Second*, that the revolutionary class must be ready to pass from one form to another in the quickest and most unexpected manner."[30] For "revolutionaries who are unable to combine illegal forms of struggle with *every* form of legal struggle are very poor revolutionaries."[31]

In August, 1935, Georgi Dimitroff, General Secretary of the Communist International, told the Seventh World Congress of the International that "We would not be revolutionary Marxists, Leninists, worthy pupils of Marx, Engels, Lenin and Stalin, if we did not suitably *reconstruct* our policies and tactics in accordance with the changing situation and the changes occurring in the world labor movement."

"*We are enemies of all cut-and-dried schemes.* We want to take into account the concrete situation at each moment, in each place, and not act *according to a fixed, stereotyped form* anywhere and everywhere; not to forget that in *varying* circumstances the position of the Communists cannot be *identical.*

"We want soberly to take into account *all* stages in the development of the class struggle and in the growth of the class-consciousness of the masses themselves, to be able to locate and solve at each state the *concrete* problems of the revolutionary movement *corresponding* to this stage."[32]

This makes crystal clear a lesson which some civilized people have found almost impossible to learn, i.e., that a change of tactics by communists in reference to religion, *does not signify a change of heart*. Thus well did a Church of England Council

---

[28] *Political Affairs*, Apr. 1956, p. 4.

[29] Lenin, *"Left-Wing" Communism, An Infantile Disorder*, Moscow: Co-operative Publishing Society, 1953, p. 94. See page 76 in the 1940 International Publishers edition.

[30] *Ibid.*, p. 95.

[31] *Ibid.*, p. 96.

[32] Georgi Dimitroff, *The United Front*, New York: International Publishers, 1938, pp. 91, 92.

say: "Conditions in Communist countries vary but the Communist objectives remain constant, namely to undermine and destroy the Christian Faith and the Christian Church in the most effective possible way."[33]

The fact that some refuse to learn this lesson does not mean that the communists have not learned and applied this principle of flexibility. Thus Earl Browder, who views all religions as bad, once said: "We can well say that the cessation of ineffective, rude and vulgar attacks upon religion is a positive improvement in our work."[34] This change made it possible to establish a united front with some religious people on some questions, and thus care needed to be exercised unless some offensive remark about religion might close the ears of some religious people to their attack on capitalism. Lenin cautioned against doing that which "only leads to the strengthening of religious fanaticism."[35]

What have been some of the ways in which the opposition of communism to religion has been expressed?

ANTI-RELIGIOUS PROPAGANDA

Anti-religious propaganda, including propaganda for atheism, has been one way in which the communists have expressed their opposition to religion.[36] This work is carried on before they come to power, and it is continued after they come to power. The intensity of their anti-religious propaganda may vary from time to time, as seen for example in the appeal in *Pravda*, July 1954, for an intensification of the attack on religion.[37]

Stalin said: "The Party cannot be neutral towards the bearers of religious prejudices, towards the reactionary clergy who poison the minds of the toiling masses. Have we suppressed the

---

[33] Council on Foreign Relations, *The Churches of Europe under Communist Governments*, London: Church Information Board, Church House, Westminster, S.W.I., 1954, p. 2.

[34] *What Is Communism?*, p. 148.

[35] *Religion*, p. 6. Mao Tse-tung is endeavoring to follow in China this principle of Lenin. See *China Youth*, Feb. 1, 1955 as quoted by Hollington K. Tong, *What Is Ahead For China?*, Washington D.C.: Chinese Embassy, 1957, p. 164. See also *Religion in Communist China*, Hong Kong: China Viewpoints, 1957.

[36] Lenin, *Religion*, pp. 5, 15.

[37] *New York Journal-American*, July 28, 1954. *New York Times*, August 10, 1954.

reactionary clergy? Yes, we have. The unfortunate thing is that it has not been completely liquidated. Anti-religious propaganda is a means by which the complete liquidation of the reactionary clergy must be brought about. Cases occur when certain members of the Party hamper the complete development of anti-religious propaganda. If such members are expelled it is a good thing because there is no room for such 'Communists' in the ranks of the Party."[38]

PHYSICAL PERSECUTION

One aspect of the liquidation process is *physical persecution*. In fact, in China today public "trials" and executions are used as a part of the process of "educating" the masses.[39]

Thus when the communists take over a country they search out as possible reactionaries the clergymen and build a file on them for later use. Thus we find the following Order issued on November 28, 1940 by the Peoples Commissar of NKVD of the U.S.S.R. "Into the alphabetic files must be entered all those persons who, because of their social and political past, their nationalistic-chauvinistic inclinations, religious beliefs, moral and political instability, are hostile to the socialistic form of state and consequently might be exploited by foreign intelligence services and counter-revolutionary centers for anti-Soviet purposes. Among such elements are to be counted. . . . The clergy of religious communities, orthodox priests, Roman Catholic priests, sectarians, and active members of religious congregations."[40]

In Russia after the revolution thousands of clergymen were killed, pauperized, imprisoned or exiled to Siberia.[41]

In North Korea, especially after 1950 which marked the beginning of the war of aggression against South Korea, in "some areas 60 to 80 per cent of the Christian leaders were killed off."[42]

In 1954-1955 in North Viet Nam, Lieutenant Thomas Dooley came face to face with examples of people being persecuted

---

[38] *Leninism*, Vol. I, p. 387.

[39] "Triumph of Terror in China," *Reader's Digest*, June 1956, p. 49.

[40] Joseph Zack Kornfeder, *Communist Deception in the Churches*, pp. 4-6. Kornfeder has seen the original order.

[41] Robert E. Stripling, *The Red Plot against America*, pp. 178-179.

[42] Pedro Vazquez Lopez, *A Christian's Handbook on Communism*, Revised edition, p. 39.

because of their religious beliefs. To make a mock crown of thorns, communists drove nails into a priest's skull. A teacher had taught seven children the Lord's prayer. The communists sawed off his tongue with a bayonet. They drove chopsticks into each ear of the children and tore the ear drums.[43]

Communists make it clear that persecution is conducted on political pretext and not on religious grounds,[44] and that communists try to keep from carrying persecution to the point where it increases what they call religious fanaticism.[45]

EFFORTS TO CONTROL RELIGION

In addition to open persecution of religion, *religious organizations are harassed in one way or another.* Lands, institutions, education and social services are nationalized; church activities are restricted to "actual services of worship inside the church building"; active anti-religious propaganda is carried on while the church is not permitted to oppose it; spies invade the churches and create suspicions and fears; an effort is made to turn religious people against one another; non-cooperative church leaders are gotten rid of on some charges other than religious, or they are "re-educated"; and church ties with other lands are severed,[46] at least until they have leaders whom they can trust to conduct themselves "properly" in these contacts.[47]

When they take over a country the communists endeavor to curb and destroy religion through various restrictions. Basically they endeavor to do two things: (1) to control the total educational experiences of the children, and (2) to leave people little or no

---

[43] *Deliver Us from Evil*, New York: A Signet Book, 1961, pp. 114-122. See also *Reader's Digest*, Apr. 1956, pp. 44, 160, 161. Personal interview, Nov. 1958.

[44] Earl Browder, *Communism in the United States*, p. 345.

[45] Marx and Engels, *On Religion*, p. 10.

[46] Pedro Vazquez Lopez, *A Christian's Handbook on Communism*, pp. 42-45.

[47] For additional accounts of Communist persecution of religion see Geoffrey T. Bull, *When Iron Gates Yield*, London: Hodder and Stoughton, 1955. Compare Douglas Hyde, "Faith ... Stumbling Block for Reds," *Our Sunday Visitor*, Oct. 25, 1953; "Russian Jehovah's Witnesses Sent to Slave Camps," *Christian Century*, May 30, 1956, p. 672; Maurice S. Sheehy, "Communism Still Wars on Religion," *U.S. News and World Report*, Apr. 6, 1956, pp. 144-147; Dr. Richard F. Staar "The Church of Silence in Communist Poland," *The Catholic Historical Review*, Oct. 1956, pp. 296-321.

time for their souls to breathe. What happened in Russia well illustrates this.

The entire educational system was placed under the control of the communists. There are no private schools maintained by churches. Thus Article 122 of the RSFSR, Criminal Code, enacted in 1926 stated that: "Instruction of the under-aged or minors in religious doctrines in state or private educational institutions and schools or the violation of the rules established for this is punishable by corrective labor for a period of one year."[48]

Theological training for religious leaders is under communist control. The law of April 1929 said: "Theological courses may be opened with the permission of the NKVD, or in Autonomous Republics, of the appropriate Central Executive Committee."[49]

Not only does the communist government control the educational system, but it endeavors to keep the children from being taught religion in the home. Thus as they themselves put it: "The basic work in Communist education and the overcoming of the survivals of religiousness must be carried out by the school teachers in the process of teaching the foundations of the sciences . . . the basic task of Communist education and overcoming the survivals of religiousness in our present condition is to prove to the pupils the complete contrast and complete irreconcilability between science—the real and correct reflection of the objectively existing world in the consciousness of the people—and religion as a fantastic, distorted and, consequently, harmful reflection of the world in the consciousness of the people . . . the school must pose the question before parents who are believers as to the extreme harmfulness . . . and inadmissibility of imposing religious influence on children. . . . Parents who are religious believers in the great majority of cases realize that they have no right and that it is not in their interest to maim their children morally and to place them in a dual situation by bringing them up at home on religious prejudices which are in radical contradiction with the true scientific instruction and education of the school."[50]

---

[48] Quoted in *Notes: Soviet Affairs*, Mar. 1956, p. 3. In East Germany today the Communists are the only ones with any say so about the schools, *The Christian Century*, 1956, p. 85.

[49] *Ibid.*, p. 4.

[50] *Narodnoye Obrazovaniè*—Popular Education—"Some Aspects of Education," Apr. 1949. Quoted in *Notes: Soviet Affairs*, Mar. 28, 1956, p. 3.

"U.S. Protestant churchmen visiting Moscow in March 1956 were told by Russian priests that religious instruction by priests is now permitted. The truth of this statement is open to question. The law specifically prohibiting such instruction is still on the statute books. Furthermore, the Metropolitan Pitirim of Minsk and Belorussia made a similar statement in England in 1955. He blandly added that there were no anti-religious museums in the USSR. But the Soviet journal *Science and Life* in its issue for June 1955 announced proudly that the Museum of Atheism housed in the former Kazan Cathedral in Leningrad was being improved and expanded and had been visited by 225,000 people in 1954, and the *Baku Worker* on October 12, 1955, described a travelling anti-religious exhibit then at the local museum. There has also been no let up in the intensive propaganda drive, both among school teachers and parents, for the atheist education of children."[51]

Churches are forbidden to "organize special prayer or other gatherings for children, youths, or women" or any other special meetings for religious instruction.[52]

Religious organizations cannot carry on benevolent work.[53]

THE CHURCHES AND RELIGION IN RUSSIA TODAY

What have the attacks on religion done to the Churches in Russia? What are the conditions today?

In Moscow there are a few large congregations, but they are predominately composed of older people and women. Constant atheistic indoctrination over a period of years has set the face of millions toward atheism.

Some church buildings have been repaired since the war, a few have been rebuilt, and some of these have been taken over for other purposes. Church property is used only at the mercy of the government.

There is no religious education, except in some homes and that which takes place with the occasional visit of a preacher. There are no Sunday Schools or church schools.[54] From kinder-

---

[51] *Notes: Soviet Affairs*, p. 5.

[52] *Ibid.*, p. 3.

[53] *Ibid.*, p. 3.

[54] American Friends Service Committee, *Meeting the Russians*, Philadelphia, 1956, p. 77. William Z. Foster years ago emphasized that when they take over America "religious schools will be abolished and organized religious training for minors prohibited" (*Toward Soviet America*, 1932, p. 316).

garten on the children are taught that religion is bad. The universities do not have organized religious groups operating on their campuses.

The press has an anti-religious slant, anti-religious propaganda abounds and counter propaganda is not allowed. Religious literature can only be printed if the State approves, and most of material printed consists of books used in worship. No member of the Communist Party is supposed to be a church member. Religion is regarded as an emotional hangover from a pre-scientific stage.[55]

It is demanded of the churches that they support the home and the foreign policy of the Kremlin. They must not criticize communism and its political apparatus. For example, religious leaders support the so-called peace offensive of the communists, especially through the World Peace Council.[56]

In fact, "the Orthodox Church in Russia is chained hand and

---

[55] American Friends Service Committee, *Meeting the Russians*, p. 78.

[56] *Notes: Soviet Affairs*, Mar. 28, 1956, p. 5. In an account of the visit of some Moslem, who lived in the Soviet Union, to Mecca, their leader K. Salikhov told how "we explained to our foreign coreligionists that the Soviet government does not interfere in religious matters." "We all felt and it made us very happy, that the truth about life and religious freedom in the Soviet Union is becoming known to more and more people in the Moslem Countries." He represented the "Soviet people to be their [Egypt's] disinterested friends." "And today we are with the Egyptians heart and soul in their manful resistance to the colonialist attempts to pressure them in connection with the nationalization of the Suez Canal" ("Mecca, 1956," *News: A Soviet Review of the World Events*, Oct. 1, 1956, p. 22). In the same issue is printed an Australian clergyman's impression of his visit to Russia. Victor James, obviously pro-Communist, told nothing of the religious conditions in Russia but argued that "Here were demonstrated the practical results of a planned society." The Soviet Union is foremost among those striving for peace, and "If scriptural warrant is needed to bear out the reality of the socialist way of life it can be found in the words: 'By their fruits ye shall know them'" (p. 26). Obviously he has closed his eyes to the fruits of the crimes of the Stalin era, and of the crimes which are now going on as Russian communists and Russian-trained communists work for the subverting of the nations. For earlier illustrations see the Church of Scotland, *The Church under Communism*, Student Christian Movement Press, 1952.

In a statement by the delegation of the National Council of the Churches of Christ in the U.S.A. to Church leaders in the Soviet Union, issued on arrival in New York, Mar. 23, 1956. Dr. Barnes spoke of the sameness of statement on the status of religion as made by religious leaders and by the chairmen of the two councils of the Soviet Government dealing with religious affairs" (*U.S. News and World Report*, Apr. 6, 1956, p. 139). William O. Douglas, "Religion in the Godless State," *Look*, Jan. 10, 1956.

foot by the state."[57] Dr. Wilhelm Starlinger, who was for six
years a doctor imprisoned with Russian political prisoners, tells
us that the Orthodox Church in Russia is "a manipulated instrument in the grip of the political system, rigidly directed from
the top."[58] For example, we know that Major General G. G.
Karpov, an NKVD officer, was minister of cults and religious
affairs in 1951, and may still be.[59]

There are millions of atheists in Russia.[60] This is evident from
the fact that millions are members of the Party which is avow-
edly atheistic. Furthermore, an educational system which is
atheistic, and a general environment in which atheism is taught,
is bound to result in some people believing the atheism which
they have been taught from infancy.

In spite of these things, however, Communists have been unable to abolish religion. Some of the young people, who have
been brought up on atheism, are religious. In 1948 there were
forty-nine people expelled from the Communist Party in Georgia (Russia) because they had participated in religious rites. In
speaking of these individuals, a Communist publication, *Dawn
of the East*, said on January 28, 1949: "The facts again and again
remind us of the necessity of strengthening the anti-religious
propaganda among the population."[61] The renewed drives, from
time to time, against religion testifies to the fact that atheistic
education has not killed religion in Russia. And this has baffled
some of the Russian Communists.[62]

"Church statistics in the Soviet Union are not published, but
a Soviet spokesman has given out these figures for the number
of churches functioning in the USSR today:

   20,000 Orthodox
    5,400 Baptist
    1,500 Roman Catholic (including 1,000 Old Believers)
     800 Lutheran or Reformed
     500 Seventh Day Adventist
     500 Jewish Synagogues

---

[57] *The Christian Century*, Mar. 14, 1956, p. 324.

[58] *U.S. News and World Report*, Nov. 4, 1955, p. 145.

[59] Vladimir Petrov, *Empire of Fear*, Reference in a press release of
July 1, 1956, by the Internal Security Subcommittee.

[60] William O. Douglas, "Religion in the Godless State," *Look*, Jan.
10, 1956.

[61] *Notes: Soviet Affairs*, Mar. 28, 1956, p. 3.

[62] According to Mr. Conniff in *U.S. News and World Report*, Mar.
11, p. 91.

100 Armenian

50 Buddhist

He did not give the number of mosques currently in operation."[63]

What the communists have done in Poland furnishes us with another illustration of the way in which they treat the churches once they conquer a country. First they maintained that they were friendly to religion; their only request was that the clergy keep out of politics. Soon, however, clergymen were arrested; some were tried, others just disappeared. The clergy was infiltrated, with some clergymen being bought, some re-educated and some blackmailed. Religious schools were closed. Orphans were brought under the authority of the state. Atheistic literature was published. Two theological schools, under the control of the communists, were established. It is made difficult for an individual to carry on church affairs, and files are kept on clergymen. The "progressive" parish priests plug the Party line, and more and more Moscow works toward setting up a church under her domination.[64]

Communists, however, have realized that they cannot destroy religion simply through persecution, restrictions and laws. Thus they have tried to use religion, in one way or another, until they can completely eradicate it. In fact, to use it is one of the ways in which they destroy it. In *A Christian's Handbook on Communism*, the current policy of the communists toward religion

---

[63] *Notes: Soviet Affairs*, Mar. 28, 1956, p. 4; Billy Graham, "Impressions of Moscow," *Christianity Today*, July 20, 1959, p. 16. For three pro-communist accounts of religion in Russia see Corliss Lamont, *Soviet Civilization*, pp. 121-155; G. Spasov, *Freedom of Religion in the USSR*, London: Soviet News, 1951; William Howard Melish, *Religion Today in the USSR. Problems of Communism*, May-June, 1955, pp. 19-28; Ivan Bilibin, "Religion in the USSR Today," *The Listener*, Sept. 2, 1954, pp. 352-353.

[64] See Ann Su Cardwell, "Communist Attack on Polish Church," *The Christian Century*, Feb. 22, 1956, pp. 232-233. Dr. Richard F. Staar, "The Church of Silence," *The Catholic Historical Review*, Oct. 1956. Although the pattern may vary some from country to country, due to different conditions, the above is in the main the pattern of their attack on religion when they come to power. See Robert E. Fitch, "Communism's Attack on Religion," *Commentary*, July, 1945, pp. 84-85. A review of George N. Shuster, *Religion Behind the Iron Curtain*, New York: Macmillan and Company. "Soviet Campaign to Destroy Poland's Catholic Church," *Facts Forum News*, Mar. 1956, pp. 18-19. For a pro-communist account see Monica Whately, "What Every American Catholic Should Know," *National Guardian*, June 4, 1956, p. 7.

is summed up as follows: "Religion will inevitably disappear, therefore all-out efforts to destroy it are not necessary, and are not desirable since they only increase the fanaticism of its followers. Accordingly, it is best to make religion, while it exists, the servant of the totalitarian state, providing constant mass participation in all the programs of the government."[65]

THE UNITED FRONT MOVEMENT AND ITS USE OF RELIGION

When they have thought that it was to their advantage, the communists have endeavored to form working coalitions with other movements and organizations. In the united front movement people who were not communists *consciously* united with communists in the pursuit of some goal which they assumed to be common to both. Particularly the decade from around 1928 to around 1938[66] was the period of the united front. There was a time in America when the communists were successful in getting some religious people to unite with them in various movements. The facts show us that we should not dismiss as an empty claim the following statements from the pen of Earl Browder:

"It is significant that the Communist Party, more than any other labor group, has been able to achieve successful united fronts with church groups on the most important issues of the day. This is not due to any compromise with religion as such, on our part. In fact, by going among the religious masses, we are for the first time able to bring our anti-religious ideas to them. We have been able to unite with them because we have been able to convince many church leaders, and especially their followers, of the necessity for unity if we are to protect our rights, among them religious freedom, which are endangered by the rise of fascism. They have found that it is the anti-religious Communists who fight for freedom of religious belief. They have seen that it is the fascists, who supposedly march

---

[65] Revised edition, Apr. 1955, pp. 41-42. Circulated by the Committee on World Literacy and Christian Literature, National Council of the Churches of Christ in the USA.

[66] J. B. Matthews, "The What and How of Communist Fronts," *The American Mercury*, Aug. 1955. Martin Ebon, *World Communism Today*, New York: McGraw-Hill Book Company, Inc., 1948. pp. 22, 284, 285 dates the period of the united front from 1935-1938.

under the flag of religion, as in Germany, who destroy all freedom including religious freedom. Hence, many church organizations have joined in the broad united front against war and fascism, and are glad to find the anti-religious communists fighting along side of them, shoulder to shoulder.

"It is true that we have learned to be much more careful about the quality of our mass work in this field. We take pains not to offend any religious belief. We don't want to close the minds of religious people to what we have to tell them about capitalism, because of some remark or action offensive to their religion. We can well say that the cessation of ineffective, rude and vulgar attacks upon religion is a positive improvement in our work.

"Our aim is to remove all obstacles that stand in the way of mobilizing the religious masses of this country into a movement against fascism and war. This is especially important work because the greatest organized section of our population is in or around church groups. Only a 'Leftist' simpleton would suggest that we communists should keep ourselves 'pure' and uncontaminated by association with the millions of church-goers in this country; only a reactionary will advise the church followers to keep themselves uncontaminated by the united front with the Communists."[67]

"We will do everything possible to draw them into the common struggle against a common foe—the capitalist system."[68]

From Browder's statements we can draw the following conclusions concerning their attack on religion in the united front. *First*, this close contact gave them opportunities to inject their anti-religious propaganda in one form or another. *Secondly*, by using religious people and organizations to help them accomplish their objectives they were endeavoring to hasten the day when they could take full control. When this objective is

---

[67] *What Is Communism?*, pp. 147-148.

[68] *Ibid.*, p. 150. For Browder's directive to the members of the Party to try to "influence the integration of the Catholic community into the democratic front" see *The Communist*, Vol. XVIII, No. 1, Jan. 1939, pp. 18-19. For a discussion of the united front, and some of the fronts, see J. B. Matthews, *Odyssey of a Fellow Traveler*, pp. 91-201. In the entire discussion of Communism and its efforts to use religion, keep in mind the statement of Professor Emile Cailliet that "The danger that the ministry could in some ways be influenced by Marxism may become greater than that of its falling victim to the enticement of Capitalism. . . . This is why it is so important for the Christian to view Marxism aright" (*The Christian Approach to Culture*, p. 233).

achieved in any country, all manner of persecutions against religious people are then set in motion. So by uniting with communists in a united front, religious people are helping bring about the day when, if it arrives, will result in strenuous methods on the part of the communists to liquidate religious people.

Religious people should be alerted to the fact that the communists are once more endeavoring to establish the united front.[69] Such was one of the objectives of their denunciation of Stalin. Such is an objective of their peaceful coexistence campaign. They would like, for example, to have various religious bodies and leaders to unite with them in an effort to get the free world to disarm and to ban the thermo-nuclear weapons. Thermo-nuclear weapons wipe out whatever advantages the communists may have in manpower, and thus she does not want such weapons used. Therefore, the World Peace Council meeting in Stockholm from April 5-9, 1956, called on religious people to unite with them in achieving these goals. They passed a declaration to the effect that: "This action requires an effective liaison between our peace movement and all pacifist organizations, political parties, trade unions, churches, religious organizations and movements, all moral forces and leading figures representative of the most diverse points of view.

"Years of cold war have until now made such a liaison with some of them impossible; today the relaxation of tension opens up the prospect of joint actions.

"The World Peace Council instructs its Presidium to make the necessary contacts, so that the action of all on a basis of equality and mutual respect at last brings the world confidence, disarmament and international co-operation."[70]

This was also the one of religious leaders in Russia during the visit, early in 1956, of some American clergymen.[71]

These things no more indicate a change in communism than did Stalin's references to God in his appeal to the churches in the war against Hitler.[72]

---

[69] Dmitry Monin, "Time to Act in Common," *News: A Soviet Review of World Events*, May, 1956, pp. 13-14.

[70] *For a Lasting Peace, For a People's Democracy*, Apr. 1956, p. 1.

[71] "Church Talks Hit Wrangle in Moscow," *Arkansas Democrat*, Mar. 13, 1956, AP dispatch.

[72] Robert E. Stripling, *The Red Plot against America*, p. 181.

USING RELIGIOUS LEADERS IN COMMUNIST FRONT ORGANIZATIONS

The communists have endeavored to use religion as a tool, by duping religious persons into joining or contributing to communist front organizations. In some cases, these organizations are sponsored, or petitions are signed, by the few communist sympathizers in the clergy who are veteran communist-fronters. Some fronts have "operated under the guise of some church commission or religious body."[73]

In the united front people knowingly worked with the communists for some assumed common object. In contrast with this a communist front is an organization which is supposedly not related to the communist conspiracy; it is a "deceptive facade." It is a means of promoting communism, in one way or another, while not appearing to do so in the eyes of the general public. It is, therefore, considered by the communists to be an essential aspect of their conspiracy against civilization.[74]

This aspect of the communist conspiracy, and its use of religion and religious people as a tool, was launched by Georgi Dimitroff, then General Secretary of the Communist International. In August 1935, at the Seventh World Congress of the Communist International he announced this Trojan-horse tactic. "Comrades, you remember the ancient tale of the capture of Troy. Troy was inaccessible to the armies attacking her, thanks to her impregnable walls. And the attacking army, after suffering many sacrifices, was unable to achieve victory until with the aid of the famous Trojan horse it managed to penetrate to the very heart of the enemy's camp.

"We revolutionary workers, it appears to me, should not be shy about using the same tactics with regard to our fascist foe,

---

[73] J. Edgar Hoover, "God or Chaos?" *Redbook Magazine*, Feb. 1949,
[74] See J. B. Matthews, "The What and How of Communist Fronts," *The American Mercury*, Aug. 1955. For a brief description of the nature and function of a "front" see J. Edgar Hoover, "The Communists Are After Our Minds," *The American Magazine*, Oct. 1954. For a list of some of the fronts see *Guide to Subversive Organizations and Publications* (And Appendix), Revised, Washington, D. C.: Government Printing Office. Also *The Communist Party of the United States of America*, Washington, D.C.: Government Printing Office, 1956, pp. 90-96. As to their importance the last publication stated "Without the aid of its numerous front organizations, the Communist Party would be an isolated, insignificant sect" (p. 90).

who is defending himself against the people with the help of a living wall of his cutthroats.

"He who fails to understand the necessity of using such tactics in the case of fascism, he who regards such an approach as 'humiliating,' may be a most excellent comrade, but if you will allow me to say so, he is a windbag and not a revolutionary, he will be unable to lead the masses to the overthrow of the fascist dictatorship."[75] Dimitroff indicated that such tactics were necessary in order to overcome "the *isolation of the revolutionary vanguard* from the masses of the proletariat and all other toilers"; the revolutionary vanguard, of course, being the Communist Party.[76]

Of what value are the communist fronts to the communists? (1) Financially they have raised as much as $10,000,000 in a single year, much of which would be spent as the hidden communists desired. (2) Fronts have enabled the communists to spread some points of their propaganda among millions of people, without being hampered by being openly tied to the Party. (3) Through them contact was formed with individuals some of whom were recruited later to the Party and even into espionage work. *Herbert A. Philbrick* first came into contact with the communists while in the Cambridge Youth Council.[77] (4) Jobs and experience were thus provided for hundreds of members of the Party, people who were not known to be Party members. (5) They were sometimes means of creating or extending division within the country; or of neutralizing people on some important issue, or of creating distrust in our form of government and our economic system, or of getting some specific job done. (6) The fronts helped create a psychological atmosphere which works against some vigorous anti-communists. When it is shown that certain clergymen were on one or more fronts, instead of acknowledging that they were duped, it is not unusual for them and their friends to speak out vigorously and vehemently against the anti-communists who pointed out that they had been duped into joining a communist front organization. But these same men are usually silent about those

---

[75] *The United Front*, pp. 52-53.

[76] *Ibid.*, p. 92. Compare p. 56.

[77] *I Led Three Lives*, pp. 10-15. Philbrick never accepted communism. He did splendid work for his country in his work as a counter-spy for the FBI.

who duped them into joining the organization or signing the petition.[78]

COMMUNISTS IN RELIGIOUS ORGANIZATION

J. Edgar Hoover has pointed out that in "the ranks of the concealed Communists today are labor leaders, educators, publicists, doctors, lawyers, businessmen, and even clergymen."[79] This is a part of their effort to be where the masses are and to influence them. In communist countries such concealed communists are carrying out the objective of making "religion, while it exists, the servant of the totalitarian state."[80]

Joseph Stalin, once a student in a seminary, seems to have been the one who conceived the idea of thus invading this ideological fortress of their enemies.[81] Some think that Metropolitan Nikolas also suggested to Stalin that he turn religious organizations into a tool. From the time of his being made a bishop in 1922 he began a campaign to "deify Stalin" and thus to undermine religion.[82]

Regardless of who conceived of the idea, the Young Communists were instructed to infiltrate religious organizations in a Resolution of the Report of Wilhelm Pieck, August 1, 1935 at the Seventh World Congress of the Communist International. The Executive Committee of the Young Communist International was instructed "to take effective measures to overcome the sectarian secludedness of a number of Young Communist organizations, to make it the duty of the Young Communist League members to join all mass organizations of the toiling youth (trade union, cultural, sports organizations) formed by bourgeois-democratic, reformist and fascist parties, as well as by religious associations; to wage a systematic struggle in these

---

[78] J. B. Matthews, "Some Facts about the Communist Apparatus," pp. 11-12. "The What and How of Communist Fronts," *The American Mercury*, Aug. 1955. The above functions of the fronts, as well as an exceedingly able discussion of the entire question of the fronts, are discussed in any essay by America's foremost authority on the fronts, J. B. Matthews. See 'Triumph of the Trojan Horse," House Committee on Un-American Activities, *Soviet Total War*, Sept. 23, 1956, Vol. I, pp. 110-136.

[79] "The Communists Are After Our Minds," *The American Magazine*, Oct. 1954.

[80] Pedro Vazquez Lopez, *A Christian's Handbook on Communism*, p. 42.

[81] Joseph Kornfeder, personal interview. Kornfeder knew Stalin.

[82] *Newsweek*, Mar. 22, 1954, p. 62.

organizations to gain influence over the broad masses of the youth, mobilizing it for the struggle against militarization and forced labor camps, and for the improvement of its material conditions, for the rights of the young generation of toilers, while striving to establish for these purposes a broad united front of all non-fascist youth mass organizations."[83]

So well has this been done in Russia itself that Yuri Rastvorov, a former M.V.D. agent who defected in 1954, testified before the Senate Subcommittee to Investigate the Administration of the Internal Security Act and Other Internal Security Laws, on April 12, 1956, "that 'the church in the Soviet Union is not independent!' " The Orthodox Church in the Soviet Union has been "penetrated by M.V.D. agents" who were sent "to the seminaries and later they became bishops in many churches in the Soviet Union." This agrees with the statement in *Notes: Soviet Affairs* that "The state is in full control of the Orthodox church. . . ."[84]

The extent to which the leaders of some of the churches in Russia have become the tools of the Kremlin is well illustrated by some of the speeches delivered May 9-12, 1952, at a conference which was held at the Troitse-Sergiyeva Monastery, Zagorsky. The report of it is entitled: *Conference in Defense of Peace of All Churches and Religious Associations in the USSR.*[85] Alexis, Patriarch of Moscow and all Russia, said: "The unjust war in Korea, the employment of the bacteriological weapon in Korea as well as in China, the preparation for another world war—these are the facts which cannot be qualified otherwise than crimes against love and truth, and there can be no doubt that the struggle against these crimes must be the obligatory and sacred duty of every religious person precisely because of his faith."[86]

Metropolitan Nicholas, Member of the World Peace Council, charged: "In contrast to the imperialist policy of war, the Soviet State, from the very first days of its existence, has striven for peace, for friendship and cooperation among nations."[87] "Later, at all stages of its development, the Soviet State continued to pursue a consistent peace policy, being guided by the doctrine

---

[83] Committee on Un-American Activities, *The Communist Conspiracy*, Part I, Section C., May 29, 1956, pp. 346-347.

[84] Mar. 28, 1956, p. 5.

[85] Published by the Moscow Patriarchate.

[86] p. 30.

[87] p. 37.

taught by V. I. Lenin and J. V. Stalin that the peaceful co-existence, co-operation and competition between the two social and economic systems is possible."[88] "In all parts of the globe, the name of J. V. Stalin became the banner of the fight for peace [Applause]."[89] "The Chinese people threw off the yoke of a corrupt, reactionary regime, took their fate into their own hands, and joined the common peace front that is headed by the Soviet Union."[90] In one place he set forth Stalin as "the first sentinel of peace," with an "all-embracing heart," and concluded: "Glory to the great Stalin!"[91] Thus spoke Metropolitan Nicholas of the Orthodox Church in the Soviet Union! There was, however, no such reference to Jesus Christ.

The same sort of infiltration of religious organizations is evident in Communist China. A Christian Manifesto was issued in China in September 1950, by the National Christian Council which the communists organized. There were 400,222 signers. They had to sign or be viewed as enemies of the "people." The Manifesto says: "The Church must expose the evils of past imperialism, purge itself of the influence of imperialism, especially American imperialism which is plotting to use the Church for its own ends. The Church should oppose war and uphold peace, and support the Government's land reform policy.

"Through self-criticism, austerity measures, and through reform of itself, the church should instill a patriotic and democratic spirit among its members and aim at self-reliance."[92]

This invasion of religious organizations is not confined to countries which have been captured by the communists; it is also carried on at any time and place where it is possible. In 1935 Earl Browder said: "You may be interested in knowing that we have preachers, preachers active in churches, who are members of the Communist Party. There are churches in the United States where the preachers preach communism from the pulpits, in a very primitive form, of course."[93] There are, as Reinhold Niebuhr said, a few Stalinists in the Churches.[94]

---

[88] p. 38.

[89] p. 40.

[90] p. 41.

[91] p. 86.

[92] As quoted in Hollington K. Tong, *What Is Ahead for China?*, p. 79.

[93] *Communism in the United States*, New York: International Publishers, 1935, p. 335.

[94] "Communism and the Clergy," *The Christian Century*, Aug. 19, 1953, pp. 936-937. Although he disagreed with much or most of J. B. Matthews'

What do they hope to accomplish in their infiltration of religious organizations? *First,* insofar as possible they hope to keep the churches from teaching anything which would hinder the increasing control of the communists over the minds of the peoples in conquered countries. *Secondly,* they want to use the names of religious leaders to give prestige to communist front organizations.[95] *Thirdly,* they desire to circulate the idea that capitalism is an immoral system and that the sympathies of the believer should be with a society in which there is the so-called community ownership of the means of production and distribution; and to lead believers to be antagonistic to capitalism or at least neutral. *Fourthly,* they could, if nothing more, give, as Douglas Hyde did, a so-called "social slant" to sermons.[96] *Fifthly,* they would like to capture the positions of leadership and turn the churches into a tool of the Kremlin. *Sixthly,* they would like to have the churches oppose anti-communists.

THE FINAL DESTRUCTION OF RELIGION

The communists believe that religion is just one of the reflections in man's mind of the disorders of the economic system. Therefore, when the economic system has been changed from private ownership to social ownership, religion will disappear, for there will be no basic disorder in the economic system to be reflected in man's mind the form of religion.

Engels put it this way: "The actual basis of religious reflex action therefore continues to exist, and with it is the religious reflex itself . . . when society, by taking possession of all means of production and using them on a planned basis, has freed itself and all its members from the bondage in which they are now held by these means of production which they themselves have produced but which now confront them as an irresistible extraneous force; when therefore man no longer merely proposes, but also disposes—only then will the last extraneous force

---

article on the "Reds and Our Churches," he said Matthews had "named all the real Stalinists in the Church." See also J. Edgar Hoover, "The Communists Are After Our Minds," *The American Magazine,* Oct. 1954.

[95] For the names of some veteran fronters see Herbert A. Philbrick, "Clergymen Still Fall for Party Propaganda," *New York Herald Tribune,* July 11, 1954. Also the press release on the petition which protested the placing of the Jefferson School of Social Science on the subversive list.

[96] *I Believed,* p. 45. He renounced Communism.

which is still reflected in religion vanish; and with it will also vanish the religious reflection itself, for the simple reason that then there will be nothing left to reflect."[97] Note that according to the communists man does not think! He merely reflects the economic system. Strict determination is set forth; man is in bondage to the economic system and his mind automatically changes, reflects something else, when the system is changed.

This idea, of course, is also *reflected* by Marx. Says he, "The religious reflex of the real world can, in any case, only then finally vanish, when the practical relations of everyday life offer to man none but perfectly intelligible and reasonable relations with regard to his fellowmen and to nature."[98] In this way "religion dies this natural death."[99]

Thus in attacking capitalism, and endeavoring to bring in socialism and then communism, the communists believe that they are also waging war against religion.[100] When they have changed the economic system they will change that which man's mind reflects. By removing what they call irrationalism in the economic system, they automatically eliminate such irrational reflections as religion. They make religion unnecessary.

Contributing also to this final attack and complete destruction of religion is the advancement in the realm of science. Since religion is also viewed as man's reaction to mystery, an effort to fill the "gaps of human knowledge,"[101] it will vanish when science has dispelled the mystery of life and nature and enlightenment floods the world!

The communists maintain that *they have already established socialism in Russia*, so that there a planned society already exists under the control of the people. They are now engaged in the "big job of building communism."[102] Thus Khrushchev said that a "major historical gain of our Party is the fact that under the socialist system new people, active and conscious builders

---

[97] *Anti-Dühring*, pp. 354-355. See also p. 353.

[98] *Capital*, pp. 91-92.

[99] *Anti-Dühring*, p. 355.

[100] Compare Lenin, *Religion*, pp. 11, 14, 15.

[101] Ivan Levisky, "Communism and Religion" in John Lewis, *Christianity and the Social Revolution*, p. 263.

[102] *Khrushchev, Report of the Central Committee, CPSU to the 20th Congress of the Communist Party of the Soviet Union.* New York: New Century Publishers, 1956, p. 97.

of communism, have developed."[103] Russia, he claimed, "is gradually moving on from socialism to Communism."[104]

Since capitalism has ceased in Russia, according to the communists' own theory religion should have ceased to be reflected in the minds of the people. The roots of religion having been destroyed, religion should have vanished. They claim to have cut the roots of religion, according to a resolution passed on November 10, 1954 by the Central Committee. "Thanks to the victory of socialism, the social roots of religion are pulled up and the foundation on which the church rested is destroyed."[105]

We may well ask, if such is the case, why has religion survived in Russia? Why have some individuals who have been brought up in the theory and practice of Marxism become religious? How can this be if man's mind but reflects the economic system? If its consciousness is determined by the social system, how can it reflect a social system which has ceased to exist, and which, in the case of those brought up under communism, it never saw? Is it ignorance? But how can such ignorance be reflected in the minds of those who have been educated in Marxism? and who now live in a socialist society?

Is it the result of capitalistic encirclement? How can Russian minds reflect the so-called disorders of a capitalistic society which they do not see, and about which they hear but little except the distortions of their own propaganda. Well did Andre Pierre write: "'Survivals of the past,' 'capitalist encirclement'— these are the convenient scapegoats for all the sundry 'scourges' that have afflicted Soviet society. It is clear that such terms have little to do with reality. The Soviet people have been denied contact with other countries for several decades, and no foreign religious 'propaganda' is allowed to penetrate to them. 'Capitalist encirclement,' then, can hardly explain the continuing strength of religion—or, for that matter, superstition—among the masses. And if religious influences are merely 'survivals of the past' among the old, what is to explain the revival of interest among young people, Komsomol members, and other groups of the population?"[106]

As in so many other cases, life and human experience refute

---

[103] *Ibid.,* p. 98. He added that all the survivals of capitalism had not been done away with in the minds of all the people.

[104] *Ibid.,* p. 117.

[105] Quoted in *Problems of Communism,* May-June, 1955, p. 28.

[106] *Problems of Communism,* May-June, 1955, p. 28.

the philosophy of communism for all who have eyes to see, ears to hear and minds to understand. Those, of course, who have surrendered their mind to the Party, and have been drugged by the opiate of Marxism, merely mirror the ideas of their masters.

COMMUNISM THE LEADING OPIATE OF THE WORLD

As is often the case, communism is guilty of that which it accuses others. It is likely the greatest opiate that the world has ever known, and the Kremlin is the center of the most extensive dope peddling racket which has ever existed.[107]

Communism is a powerful drug which *kills the compassion and the conscience of man.* Pierre Van Passen was told years ago by a communist that communism eliminates love, pity and sentimentality and makes men, men of steel.[108]

They justify their brutality by saying that the ends justify the means. Antoni Ekart tells of his conversations, while in the Kotlas labor camp, with G. K. Roginsky, who had been State Prosecutor in the Moscow trials of 1937, as Vyshinsky's deputy. Roginsky defended the system as a necessary stage in the historical progress of humanity. "What does slavery or even the annihilation of one or two generations mean, if by that sacrifice new permanent values can be created for the benefit of humanity and countless generations to come?"

"Justifying the colonization of the Soviet North by slave labor, Roginsky argued: 'In the future, millions of people will live and work up here. What does it matter, then, if today a couple of million people suffer and die a little earlier than they would have done otherwise? Their work will live on. Our government knows that, and is not so timid as to consider the welfare and satisfaction of this one generation only.' Roginsky advised that one must 'try to adapt oneself to the new reality which communism has created for the benefit of humanity,' without 'exaggerating one's own importance' or thinking too much about 'so-called justice in relation to the individual.' "[109]

Communism so deadens one's conscience that if he becomes an ideal communist he is willing to do anything that the Party demands, *without qualm of conscience.* General Wilhelm Zais-

---

[107] Compare Martin Dies, *The Trojan Horse in America,* p. 247.
[108] "Closed Are the Gates of Mercy," *Family Circle,* June 1956.
[109] *Problems of Communism,* No. 3, 1955, p. 44.

ser, Minister of State Security for East Germany, emphasized
that he would not have a man in an important position "who is
not capable of whipping a prisoner to death if need be—himself, and without a qualm."[110]

Communism so deadens the conscience that it leads individuals to betray their own country, and in peace and in war
to work for the Kremlin and against their own country. As Sorge,
one of the most successful spies for Russia said, concerning the
enlistment of qualified Japanese assistants in the work which
he was doing in spying on Japan, "the Soviet Union enjoys an
advantage because, through communism, it can recruit on an
ideological basis, while other world powers must attract agents
with promises of monetary reward, political advancement,
etc."[111] This has been the case in America and in other nations
of the world. Communism has been the dope which has made
the dupes of Russian Imperialism pliable and willing tools of
the leaders of the Party. Thus Ethel and Julius Rosenberg went
to their death June 19, 1953, and as obedient tools of the Party
they would not tell what they knew although silence meant death.

Communism *deadens man's conscience* by teaching him that
morality and the concept of duty are not based on anything absolute and truly moral, but are expressions of class interest. A
thing is right if it promotes the interest of one's class, which
interest for the communist is determined not by any idea of right
or wrong which he may have, or any decision he may personally
have reached, but by the leaders of the Party.

Communism is a dope which *destroys or perverts the religious
and spiritual aspirations of man.* Communism teaches man that
there is no God, that there is no soul, that man is just an intelligent animal and that death ends all. But it is hard for man
to deny his own nature. He is incurably religious. And thus
communism has become for some a new faith, a new religion or
religion-substitute. To be sure, it is an idolatrous religion, for
to become totally committed to other than God is idolatry. Yet
communism endeavors to furnish man with "a reason to live and
a reason to die."[112] It is a "fighting creed"[113] which calls on its

---

[110] Richard Hanser and Frederic Sondern, Jr., "Wilhelm Zaisser—The
Red Himmler," *Reader's Digest*, Jan., 1953, p. 74.

[111] From his autobiographical sketch in Charles A. Willoughby, *Shang-
hai Conspiracy*, New York: E. P. Dutton & Company, Inc., 1952, p. 66.

[112] *Witness Whittaker Chambers*, p. 11.

[113] John C. Bennett, *Christianity and Communism*, New York: The
Women's Press, 1948, p. 22.

adherents to give their all to the Party in order to create a new world.

Communism has its sacred writings, the works of Marx and Engels and their official interpreters. During his lifetime, Stalin was regarded as the infallible voice through which the Party learned the truth. Communists constitute a "new fraternity in a new spiritual climate"[114] with its system of contrition and confession.[115] The proletariat has a messianic mission to free the world from bondage to poverty and to ignorance.[116] The proletarian class is pure, we have the word of the communist for it, since except "for the working class, all other classes which have aspired to take the leadership of society have been exploiting classes."[117] The communist earthly paradise is the heaven for which they work.[118]

Communists maintain that Christians are singing about pie in the sky by and by when they sing the song about "The Sweet By and By." In *The Young Comrade* we read: "In your religious training you are told that even if things are bad on this earth, everything will be wonderful when you die and go to Heaven, for there you will be in Paradise. . . . That is all a lie. When you die, you are dead and that is all there is to it. We want our Paradise right here and now."[119]

What happens if you cease singing about pie in the sky by and by, and start to get your pie now? The Communist Party leaders tell you: "Stop, don't cut yourself a piece of the economic pie now. You must sacrifice your pie and even die, in order that some future generation may have enough pie for everyone. Sing about pie on earth by and by in the communist future paradise where some coming generation will have peace and plenty." In fact you must take the pie from others and sacrifice them also. As Roginsky told Ekart: "What does slavery

[114] Arthur Koestler, *The Yogi and the Commissar*, p. 217.

[115] Gregory Klimov, "The Terror Machine," *Reader's Digest*, Sept. 1953.

[116] Gedeone Peterffy, *The Philosophy of Communism*, New York: Fordham University Press, 1952, pp. 226-228.

[117] Maurice Cornforth, *Dialectical Materialism*, p. 10.

[118] Ernest J. Simmons, "Some Thoughts on the Soviet Concept of Authority and Freedom" in Lyman Bryson, Editor, *Freedom and Authority in Our Times*, New York: Harper and Brothers, 1953, p. 152.

[119] *The Young Comrade*, Vol. I, No. 3, Jan. 1924, p. 1. The Official organ of the Junior Section, Young Workers League of America. From a facsimile in R. M. Whitney, *Reds in America*, New York: The Beckwith Press, Inc. 1924, p. 98.

or even the annihilation of one or two generations mean, if by that sacrifice new permanent values can be created for the benefit of humanity and countless generations to come?"[120]

A statement of Lenin's made it clear that he did not believe that his generation of communists would live to enjoy the pie which communism promises to bring down from the sky to earth. Speaking to the Young Communist Leagues on Oct. 2, 1920, Lenin said that his own generation would not live to see communism, however, the young communists would live in a communist Russia within ten or twenty years.[121] In view of this they were called on to sacrifice for the building of a communist Russia. However, what was the situation in 1940 in Russia? Stalin the dictator was on the throne. Even Khrushchev, in his famous speech in February 1956 admitted that Stalin did some cruel things. In fact, as a result of Stalin's purges some of the very young people, to whom Lenin spoke, were in their graves. They had found peace—the peace of the cemetery. Even in 1961 the communists do not maintain that communism has been established in Russia. They are still in the transition stage —the stage of socialism, they say. And Red China does not expect to live in a communist China for several decades. This makes it obvious that communism is the opiate which they administer to their followers to so dope them that they can make dupes out of them—slaves who give their all·including their lives, at the bidding of their communist masters.

They are asked to be insensible to present sufferings and sacrifices because some day the future will be bright and the classless society will arrive for someone else. As Gregory Klimov came to realize—"we had only continually made sacrifices for the sake of the future. And now our faith in that future was shattered. All our lives we had been chasing after shadows."[122]

Not only is this appeal to live for something supposedly ideal, to live for the sake of others in an oncoming generation, contradictory to the communist criticism of living for "pie in the sky" in the future, but the very fact that man can respond to such an appeal is itself a refutation of their idea that man is simply an economic animal.

---

[120] Quoted in *Problems of Communism*, May-June, 1955, p. 44.

[121] *The Tasks of the Youth Leagues*, Moscow: Foreign Languages Publishing House, 1953, pp. 37-38.

[122] "The Terror Machine," *Reader's Digest*, Sept. 1953, p. 165.

The communists are asked to die for the cause of communism, and for the future happiness of mankind, in spite of the fact that they maintain that death is final and that it is the heaviest blow man can suffer. As one of their leading educational officials said: "We do not look upon death as an end in itself, as something lofty, superhuman in itself. From our point of view death is the heaviest blow that can strike a man."[123]

Having denied that man is immortal, they yet have such a hunger for immortality and such a devotion to communism, that they are promised a synthetic immortality. "Perhaps nowhere is the desire to live as great as in the Land of Soviets. And it is precisely this love of life in the Land of Soviets, in the midst of the Soviet people, that, when this life is endangered, when a life-and-death struggle is being waged to preserve it, causes the citizen of the land of Soviets to lose his fear of death [to die and leave the land of the Soviets! J.D.B.]; his desire to preserve the life of the Soviet people and thereby preserve his own life forever, as it were, overpower his fear. It is no accident that the Communist goes to the scaffold with proudly uplifted head and hurls at the enemy the words, arising from a profound faith: 'I shall die, but our cause will live on forever.' At such a time the individual merges completely with the collective, whose interests he holds higher than anything else and considers stronger than death."[124]

If there is no by and by for me, there is no pie by and by for me. If I must have my heaven now, if I must eat my pie now, I must get it now and I must avoid death at all cause, for my pie eating days are over when I die. Why should one labor so that other animals, if we are but animals, in the future may have pie. Why give up pie for them and delude oneself with this promise of a so-called collective immortality.

That the communist leaders persuade millions of their followers to go without pie, while the leaders enjoy their pie and that of their followers also, is proof positive that communism is a powerful opiate. The Kremlin is the center of this worldwide opium racket.

That it is possible to make appeals to man to put someone or something else higher than himself, to live and die for a cause, is also proof that man is not the economic and class ani-

---

[123] M. I. Kalinin, *On Communist Education*, p. 434.
[124] *Ibid.*, p. 434.

mal which the communists view him to be. In their very appeals
to their followers, such as Kalinin made, they must appeal to
something in man which, if communism is right in its view of
man's nature, *does not exist.* Their own appeals are a powerful
testimony against the truth of their philosophy of life.

Communism is the opiate which drugs its addicts to the extent that they acknowledge the absolute *right* of their rulers to
position, to wealth and to unlimited power.[125] Thus a handful
of party leaders control around 40,000,000 members of the
Party, who in turn help them control around 900,000,000 people
today. Communism is the opiate which leads its addicts to accept their duty to unquestionably obey the rulers. It leads its
adherents to be so passive that they no longer call their soul
their own. It strips their "personality of all freedom of thought
and action. Thus, a man becomes under Communism a mere tool
in the hands of the ruling Party leaders—and what is more passive than a tool?"[126]

Communism itself is not only a mental and moral narcotic,
but communism uses opiates, such as heroin, in its fight against
the freedom of men. As Harry Anslinger, the U.S. Narcotics
Commissioner, told a Senate subcommittee, communist China
was shipping dope to the free world in order to accomplish two
aims: (a) To get money to finance communism. (b) To de-
moralize the free world and thus contribute to its ultimate
destruction.[127]

Anyway you look at it, communism is an opiate. This is underscored by their view of morality, which is presented in the
next chapter.

"It is impossible to understand the tactics and the statements
of Communists and their fellow travelers unless their very special code of ethics be kept constantly in mind."[128]

---

[125] See Stalin's statement that the dictatorship must exercise power unlimited by law, *Foundations of Leninism,* p. 53.

[126] Charles J. McFadden, *The Philosophy of Communism,* p. 290.

[127] *U.S. News and World Report,* July 30, 1954, p. 14. See also *New
York Sunday News,* June 26, 1955, p. 66 for a reference to the testimony of
James C. Ryan, Supervisor of the U.S. Bureau of Narcotics in New York
before a Senate Judiciary subcommittee. They encourage the use of alcohol
also as a means of demoralizing people. See Upton Sinclair, *The Cup of
Fury,* Chapter 11, quoted in *Facts Forum News,* Sept. 1956, p. 62.

[128] Martin Dies, *The Trojan Horse in America,* p. 240.

CHAPTER TEN

The Communist Doctrine
of Morality

What is the communist's concept of morality? Does he believe in the reality of moral law? Does he accept a moral code which is similar to the one which is generally accepted in the United States? How does he view the moral values taught by Judaism and by Christianity? Does he consider himself bound by these moral values?[1]

The communist repudiates the moral values of Christianity and of Judaism. He repudiates the moral values of the so-called bourgeois society. Morality cannot be the expression of the will of God, because the communist denies the existence of God. Morality to him is but a means of achieving class interests. A thing is right if it enables a class to justify, to enlarge and to perpetuate its class interests.

This concept of morality was stated in the *Communist Manifesto.* Speaking of the proletarian, Marx wrote: "Law, morality, religion, are to him so many bourgeois prejudices, behind which lurk in ambush just so many bourgeois interests." Frederick Engels claimed that morality has always been "a class morality; it has either justified the domination and the interests of the ruling class, or, as soon as the oppressed class has become powerful enough, it has represented the revolt against this domination and the future interests of the oppressed."[2]

Lenin set forth more fully their view of morality in 1920. "The whole object of the training, education and teaching of the youth of today should be to imbue them with Communist ethics.

"But is there such a thing as Communist ethics? Is there such a thing as Communist morality? Of course, there is. It is often made to appear that we have no ethics of our own; and very

[1] The author plans to do a book on *Marxism and Morality.*
[2] *Anti-Dühring,* p. 109.

195

often the bourgeoisie accuse us Communists of repudiating all ethics. This is a method of shuffling concepts, of throwing dust in the eyes of the workers and peasants.

"In what sense do we repudiate ethics and morality?

"In the sense in which it is preached by the bourgeoisie, who derive ethics from God's commandments. We, of course, say that we do not believe in God, and that we know perfectly well that the clergy, the landlords and the bourgeoisie spoke in the name of God in pursuit of the interests of their own exploiters. Or instead of deriving ethics from the commandments of morality, from the commandments of God, they derived it from idealist or semi-idealist phrases, which always amounted to something very similar to God's commandments.

"We repudiate all morality taken apart from human society and classes. We say that it is deception, a fraud, a befogging of the minds of the workers and peasants in the interests of the landlords and capitalists.

"We say that our morality is entirely subordinated to the interests of the class struggle of the proletariat. Our morality is derived from the interests of the class struggle of the proletariat."[3]

"That is why we say that for us there is no such thing as morality apart from human society; it is a fraud. Morality for us is subordinated to the interests of the class struggle of the proletariat.

"What does this class struggle mean? It means overthrowing the tsar, overthrowing the capitalists, abolishing the capitalist class."[4]

Then Lenin continues: "The class struggle is still continuing; it has merely changed its forms. It is the class struggle of the proletariat to prevent the return of the old exploiters, to unite the scattered masses of unenlightened peasants into one union. The class struggle is continuing and it is our task to subordinate all interests to this struggle. And we subordinate our communist morality to this task. We say: morality is what serves to destroy the old exploiting society and to unite all the toilers around

---

[3] *The Tasks of the Youth Leagues,* pp. 19-21. See also Third All-Russian Young Communist League, Oct. 2, 1960. Reprinted in House Document No. 619, *The Strategy and Tactics of World Communism,* p. 71. Also in Lenin *On Religion,* p. 47.

[4] Lenin, *The Tasks of the Youth Leagues,* p. 22.

the proletariat, which is building up a new, communist society."[5]

We must turn to the dialectic to understand fully what this means. The communist, it must be recalled, maintains that he represents not only a different class in society, but also a class which is in *opposition* to the *interests* and therefore to the *values* of the "capitalist" class. Thus he does not consider himself to be bound by the same values which we acknowledge. To his way of thinking, to be bound by our moral code would be to be bound by our interests and this would mean that one was a traitor to the interests of the proletariat. Because of this the *Communist Manifesto* says: "But don't wrangle with us so long as you apply, to our intended abolition of bourgeois property, the standard of your bourgeois notions of freedom, culture, law, etc. Your very ideas are but the outgrowth of the conditions of your bourgeois production and bourgeois property, just as your jurisprudence is but the will of your class made into a law for all, a will whose essential character and direction are determined by the economic conditions of existence of your class."

Howard Selsam, one of their leading philosophers in America, pointed out that the values of two classes are *not only different but in opposition to one another* when these classes are opposite in their interests.[6] In the dialectical view of things, be it remembered, the proletariat is the antithesis of the capitalist class. It follows, therefore, that the morality of the communist will be in opposition to the morality of the bourgeois society, and the communist includes in this the ethical outlook and teaching of Judaism and Christianity. The needs and interests of their class, which needs and interests are determined by the Communist Party, are the foundation on which the communist's morality rests.[7]

What this means can be seen by considering three moral principles. *First*, "Thou shalt not steal." The communist maintains that this is the law of a property-holding class whereby they protect their property. It is thus subordinated to class in-

---

[5] *Ibid.*, p. 24.

[6] *Philosophy in Revolution*, New York: International Publishers, 1957, p. 136. "The class interests of the bourgeoisie and proletarians are irreconcilable . . ." (L. Ilyichov, *World Marxist Review*, Nov. 1959, p. 10).

[7] David Guest, *A Textbook of Dialectical Materialism*, p. 99. See also Liu Shao-chi, *How to be a Good Communist*, pp. 55-56. M. J. Olgin, *Why Communism?*, New York: Workers Library Publishers, 1935, p. 62. *International Affairs*, Moscow, July 1959, pp. 8-9.

terest.[8] If theft be wrong, the institution of private property must be right although it may be abused. The communist maintains that the institution of private property is wrong, therefore, the law "Thou shalt not steal" is but a way the property-holding class maintains its hold on its ill-gotten gain. Since the communist represents a class with interests which oppose that of the property-holding class, he believes that it is right to steal if stealing will help the Party. The revolution in Russia was financed in part by bank robberies.[9] The communist in America, whether he is from Russia or an American citizen, will steal information for Russia if so directed by the Party. During World War II, Anastas Mikoyan was the real head of the Soviet Purchasing Commission which was in the United States. He gave orders to all actual Party members of the commission to get all the information possible on industry in America, especially war industries. And thus tons and tons of blueprints, parts of special machines, photographs, etc., went to Russia by airplane and lend-lease ships.[10]

Secondly, there is a commandment which says: "Thou shalt not commit adultery." Communism maintains that this moral law is based on the idea of private property, i.e., that a woman is the private property of a man. Therefore, to protect his private property from being used by another man he teaches that it is wrong to commit adultery. Communism, on the other hand, repudiates the morality of non-communist societies. Therefore, when it is to the interest of the Party the communists believe that it is right to commit adultery. They belong to the Party both body and soul.[11]

Thirdly, another commandment tells children to honor their father and their mother. Communism maintains that this is based on the idea that the children are the private property of the parents, and that therefore they owe them obedience. Children, according to communism, must honor the state (the

---

[8] *Anti-Dühring,* p. 109.

[9] Bertram D. Wolfe, *Three Who Made a Revolution,* New York: The Dial Press, 1948, pp. 389-398.

[10] David J. Dallin, *Soviet Espionage,* New Haven: Yale University Press, 1955. See the testimony of Victor Kravchenko, who once was a high ranking official in the Purchasing Commission, before the House Committee on Un-American Activities. Also his book, *I Chose Freedom,* pp. 465-466.

[11] Elizabeth Bentley, *Out of Bondage,* New York: The Devin-Adair Company, 1951, pp. 198-199. Compare Victor Kravchenko, *I Chose Freedom,* p. 461.

Party) regardless of how much they may have to dishonor their parents. The *Communist Manifesto* acknowledged that the communist will destroy the bourgeois family and the present relationship of parent and child[12] Although communists in Russia have had to retreat from the effort to destroy the family, they are endeavoring through their educational system, including the nurseries, to build loyalty to the Party rather than to the home. Children are taught to report to the authorities any deviationism on the part of their parents. The people's Communes in Red China sometimes segregate husbands from wives and children from parents. Husbands and wives are permitted to be together for only a few minutes each week. The slaves in the Communes are taught that they are against the community if they show much desire to be with their wives and families.[13] True to the "ideals" of communism the Chinese communists are trying to destroy the family and to make the party the supreme object of loyalty.

After taking the position that morality is class morality the communist somewhat reverses himself and claims that his morality is a higher type of morality than that of the capitalist, for his morality is that of the historically progressive class, the proletariat. Since this class is higher in the dialectical scale it is better than all that has gone before it.[14] Furthermore, it is higher because it is supposed to represent a class which is not struggling to exploit others, but to end all exploitation.[15] It is but a small thing to them that they are endeavoring to kill the bourgeoisie! Of course, it is pure assumption which enables them to insert any genuine moral content into the materialistic and dialectical process.

As a matter of fact, there is no proof that the communists represent the so-called coming society. And even if they did it would not prove that it will be a better society than the one in which we now live. Yet they maintain that they are higher in the scale of dialectical development than are others, and therefore they represent a higher moral code. But what right do these materialists have to introduce an ethical content into the dia-

---

[12] See the section on "Proletarians and Communists."

[13] *Life*, Jan. 5, 1959, pp. 44, 69, 72.

[14] A. L. Morton, "Communism and Morality," in John Lewis, Editor, *Christianity and the Social Revolution*, pp. 330-335. Trotsky, *The Defence of Terrorism*, p. 56.

[15] Maurice Cornforth, *Dialectical Materialism*, p. 10.

lectical movement? Then, too, they are only higher in view of
their own philosophy of life, which is a false philosophy of life.
In reality, they are guilty of that which they accuse others, i.e.,
they have used their philosophy to justify their lusts for power,
their selfish interests and their destructive impulses. Even according to their own philosophy, they are not really talking
about being morally better than others; instead, their morality
is but an effort to promote their class interests and to try to
justify their class interests.

It is most amazing that after denying God's existence the
communist affirms faith in a dialectical process which is supposed to be inevitably working for the freedom and ethical development of mankind. He denies God, and yet affirms that a
benevolent power—the dialectic—is at work; that this power
cannot be defeated and that it is using the Communist Party as
its instrument! The dialectic is thus clothed with deity by the
communist.

If morality is but the reflection of class interest many questions are left unanswered. *First,* how is it that man, an economic
animal—according to Marxism—developed a conscience? How
did he become *morally* sensitive? Why did he seek *moral* sanction for his conduct? *Secondly,* why did Marx make a moral
condemnation of capitalism? It is condemned as unjust, immoral
and hypocritical. Why do they say that "hatred of the fascist
fiends is a sacred hatred?"[16] *Thirdly,* why does man have a duty
to the Communist Party and to the people. They assume such
an obligation.[17] Even if the coming of communism were inevitable, it would not mean that man has a moral obligation to work
for it. Death is certain to come, but we are not morally obligated
to hasten its arrival. And yet, the Communist Party constantly
calls on its members to do their duty and to sacrifice their all, if
need be, for the Party. *Fourthly,* to explain morality as a rationalization of class interest explains away morality. If this is
all that morality is, how can those who are conscious of this—as
the communists claim that *they* are—feel any moral obligation
to work for class interest. Why is one not obligated to work
simply for his own interest? In fact, if such a view of morality
is right, there is no *moral* obligation. *Fifthly,* how can one say
that one class is further advanced morally than another? Communists believe that they are closer to truly human morality

---

[16] M. I. Kalinin, *On Communist Education*, p. 441.
[17] Ibid., p. 444-445.

than are capitalists.[18] One group can be better than another group only in the light of some standard. What is this standard? How does one arrive at it? Furthermore, it has to be a standard by which both the communist and the non-communist can be measured. And yet, how can there be a universal standard if morality is but the reflection of *class* interests.

If it be difficult for some people to believe the truth about the ethical code of communism, let them remember that a *communist is a communist* and not a Christian, a Jew or a theist. Why should anyone deceive himself into thinking that, in spite of their express repudiation of God and morality, the communists still cling to the moral code of the civilized world? Communists are taught *to live down to their unbelief.* The dictates of the Party, and its interests, and whether these interests will be advanced by a certain course of conduct, are the only problems in ethics for the consistent communist. Thus we should not expect him to act according to our moral code, but according to his moral code. When we understand this, we shall not carry on negotiations, nor plan our actions in other matters, as if the communist viewed himself under moral law emanating from God.

---

[18] Engels in Burns, *Handbook of Marxism,* pp. 247-249; M. I. Kalinin, *On Communist Education,* p. 399; William Z. Foster, *The Twilight of World Capitalism,* p. 148; Liu Shao-chi, *How To Be a Good Communist,* p. 29.

CHAPTER ELEVEN

The Communist Party

The philosophy of communism is not merely embodied in communists, but in communists who are organized into the Communist Party. The Party is not merely a political party but an organization which has as its aim the subjection of the world to its rule and the remaking of man and all human institutions so as to conform to the communist distortion of reality.

In studying the nature of the Communist Party one is justified in examining Lenin's teachings, for communists still learn from him. Stalin tells us that ". . . Lenin, for the first time in the history of Marxism, elaborated the *doctrine of the Party* as the leading *organization* of the proletariat, as the principal *weapon* of the proletariat, without which the struggle for the dictatorship of the proletariat cannot be won."[1] Says G. Obichkin, "Lenin's teaching on the Party of a new type was an invaluable contribution to the theory and practice of the world Communist movement. It is of tremendous international importance, and the experience of the subsequent decades justified Lenin's words: 'Bolshevism *can serve as a model of tactics for all.*'"[2]

COMBAT PARTY

The organization itself is considered to be a weapon,[3] thus the Communist Party is a *combat* party. This combat party takes at least some of its principles and rules for fighting from Lenin. "The logic of life is driving more and more people to the conclusion that the solution is to be found in the ideas of the man who paved the way to a new world. *That world is called the socialist world, and the man's name is Lenin. The heritage he*

---

[1] *History of the Communist Party of the Soviet Union* (*B*), p. 51. Herbert A. Philbrick tells us that while he was in the party he studied revolution from the pages of this book, *I Led Three Lives*, p. 110.
[2] "Lenin and the Party," *World Marxist Review*, May 1960, p. 24.
[3] *Ibid.*, p. 26.

left is known as Leninism—the living teaching which the Communists are developing."[4] Communists in America state that in 1903 in Russia success crowned "the long struggle waged by V. I. Lenin for the creation of a revolutionary Marxist Party of the working class, a party of a new type, that would differ in principle from the reformist parties of the Second International."[5]

Is the Communist Party a genuine political party? No! The Supreme Court had ample grounds when it decided on June 5, 1961 that the Party was in effect directed by Moscow.

SUPREME LOYALTY

What genuine political party puts loyalty to the political party above loyalty to God, to moral law, to family and to the nation? Georgi Dimitroff, who was General Secretary of the Communist International, of which the Party in America was a part, said: "The Party is above everything else! To guard the Bolshevik unity of the Party as the apple of one's eye is the first and highest law of Bolshevism!"[6] Liu Shao-chi stated that one must unconditionally subordinate his life to the will of the Party and, if necessary, gladly die for it.[7] Communists subscribe to Lenin's statement that the Party is the "mind, honour and conscience of our epoch."[8] Khrushchev stated the same idea when he said: "Never to deviate a single step in anything from the Party interests—this is the bedrock principle by which the Communists are guided in the struggle for the unity in their ranks."[9] Even the writer, to write well, must have "party-mindedness."[10] Thus Victor Kravchenko said he was accused "of forming my impres-

---

[4] Editorial, "Leninism Lives On and Is Triumphing," *World Marxist Review*, April 1960, p. 3.

[5] "Publisher's Note," *The 50th Anniversary of the Communist Party of the Soviet Union* (1903-1953), New York: New Century Publishers, 1953, p. 2.

[6] *The United Front against Fascism*, p. 138.

[7] *How To Be a Good Communist*, pp. 49-60.

[8] Quoted by Communists in *For a Lasting Peace, For a People's Democracy!*, Apr. 6, 1956, p. 2. This was the official journal of the Communist Information Bureau.

[9] "Report to the 20th Congress," *Political Affairs*, Mar. 1956, p. 62. Page 103 in the New Century Publisher's edition.

[10] Valentin Katayev as quoted in Gleb Struve, "The Second Congress of Soviet Writers," *Problems of Communism*, Mar.-Apr. 1955, p. 5.

sions of America in a personal manner."[11] In China Kao Kang
was accused of conspiratorial activity against the Party. In
1954 he committed suicide. The communists were displeased
because he did not admit his guilt and his suicide was "an expression of his ultimate betrayal of the party."[12]

INTERNATIONAL MOVEMENT

In 1938 in its Constitution the Party in the United States
stated its adherence to the teachings of Marx-Engels-Lenin-
Stalin as "embodied in the Communist International."[13] The
Communist Party in America was a branch of an international
movement led by the Party in the U.S.S.R. As Alex Bittelman
wrote: "The proletarian vanguard of the United States can
justly take pride in the fact that it participated actively in the
building of the Communist International . . . a *mutual collaboration* of the revolutionary proletariat of all countries, organized in a world party, for the victory of the Dictatorship of
the Proletariat, for the establishment of a World Soviet Republic. The leading role of the Communist Party of the Soviet Union
in the Comintern needs neither explanation or apology . . .
the leaders of that Party—first Lenin and now Stalin—are proudly
followed as the leaders of the proletariat and of all oppressed
in every country of the world."[14] ". . . by building the revolutionary movement in the United States we are also building
the world power of the proletariat for the victory of the world
revolution."[15] On August 2, 1935, Georgi Dimitroff, General
Secretary of the Communist International, stated that Stalin
was the pilot of the International and that their historical mission was "to sweep fascism off the face of the earth and, together with it, capitalism!"[16]

---

[11] *I Chose Justice*, p. 34.

[12] As quoted by Peter S. H. Tang, "Power Struggle in the Chinese CP:
The Kao-Jao Purge," *Problems of Communism*, Nov.-Dec. 1955, p. 19.

[13] *The Constitution and By-Laws of the Communist Party of the United
States of America.* New York: Workers Library Publishers, Aug. 1938, pp.
5-6. Also p. 21.

[14] "Milestones of Comintern Leadership," *The Communist*, Mar. 1934,
p. 235.

[15] *Ibid.*, p. 248.

[16] *The United Front against Fascism*, p. 93.

THE POSITION OF THE U.S.S.R.

Comrade Kuusinen made clear that the International was subservient to the Soviet Union. "The fight against the war danger, for the defence of the Soviet Union, this is our central international task. Yet, as I did at the VIII. Plenum of the E.C.C.I., I should like to emphasize here that the best defence of the Soviet Union is the overthrow of the bourgeoisie in one's own country."[17]

Although for propaganda purposes the Communist International was dissolved, the Communist Party in America still considers itself a part of an international movement. The Party accepts the *Communist Manifesto* which views communism as an international movement, in which communists work for the welfare of the world movement.[18] Palmiro Togliatti, of the Italian "fraternal" party wrote: "As an organization the Communist International no longer exists, but its cause lives on."[19] B. Ponomarev, a Russian communist, said: "In our time it is the Soviet Union that demonstrates to other countries their 'morrow.' The history of the Communist Party of the Soviet Union is a source of knowledge for the fraternal parties, from which they can derive theoretical and practical lessons."[20] One communist in America, who seemed to be a bit disillusioned by the revelations concerning Stalin's crimes, said: "Not so long ago we had a slogan, 'What's good for the Soviet Union is good enough for the American Communists.' "[21] John Gates, who was also upset somewhat by Stalin's crimes, spoke of their having accepted "a concept of Soviet infallibility."[22] The Subversive Activities Control Board documents the non-deviation of the Party in America from the line, or lines, laid down in Russia. "Underlying all the evidence showing that petitioner followed

---

[17] "The International Situation and the Tasks of the Communist International," *International Press Correspondence*, Aug. 20, 1929, English Edition, p. 851.

[18] pp. 45, 71.

[19] "History of the Communist International—Some Problems," *World Marxist Review*, Nov. 1959, p. 52.

[20] "The Inheritance of the World Communist Movement," *World Marxist Review*, Aug. 1959, p. 23.

[21] *Daily Worker*, Nov. 30, 1956, p. 4.

[22] "Time for a Change," *Political Affairs*, Nov. 1956, p. 52. It should be noticed that those who could not go along completely with the new line from the U.S.S.R. left the Party, but the Party did not change.

the directives of the Soviet Union prior to 1940, and has continued its efforts to effectuate its policies since that time, is its complete and unquestioning adherence to the doctrines of Marxism-Leninism."[23] The Party still views the U.S.S.R. as the "new social order" and sends fraternal greetings from time to time.[24] They are "working class internationalists."[25] They adhere "to the great principle of working class internationalism . . . international solidarity. . . ."[26] ". . . proletarian internationalism . . . serving the best national interests of its people and thereby the common interests of all progressive humanity."[27] *International Affairs*, in its issue of July 1959, informs us that the interests of the U.S.S.R. and the international working class are identical. *World Marxist Review* tells us that "Lenin founded the Party on the principles of proletarian internationalism. He was irreconcilable to any attempts to bring the spirit of nationalism into the Party, or to split the Party branches on the basis of nationality."[28] We must remember that communists read their publications for guidance[29] and they must study Marxism-Leninism.[30]

IT IS NOT A GENUINE AMERICAN PARTY

According to Liu Shao-chi, "the most fundamental and common duty of us Communist Party Members . . . is . . . to transform the present world into a Communist world."[31]

Gus Hall is the present general secretary of the party. In 1934 while on trial he stated that he was willing "when the time comes" to take up arms and overthrow the constituted au-

---

[23] Brief for the Respondent, "Communist Party of the United States of America, Petitioner *vs.* Subversive Activities Control Board." In the Supreme Court of the United States, October Term 1960, p. 236. See also pp. 236-253.

[24] *Daily Worker*, Nov. 7, 1957, p. 3.

[25] Eugene Dennis, *Is Communism Un-American?* New York: New Century Publishers, 1947, p. 5.

[26] *Draft Resolution for the 16th National Convention of the Communist Party, U.S.A.*, New York: New Century Publishers, 1956, p. 57.

[27] *Ibid.*, pp. 58-59.

[28] May 1960, p. 24.

[29] Betty Gannett, *The Communist Party and You*, pp. 44-46.

[30] *Ibid.*, p. 46.

[31] *How To Be A Good Communist*, p. 37.

thorities in America.[32] Gus Hall is "strongly pro-Russian."[33] His article, "The Heartland of Imperialism Faces the Future," in the *World Marxist Review*,[34] is anti-American. Its very title indicates, in communist jargon, that the United States is the main enemy.

J. Edgar Hoover explains that "The Party in this country remains an inseparable arm of the treacherous, atheistic, international conspiracy which is being directed against the free world from Moscow."[35]

The Party carries on illegal work as well as legal work.[36] There is a secret Party as well as the open Party.[37]

The Communist Party does not try to be a mass party, but a party of the revolutionary elite. It is the General Staff of the revolution. It is the vanguard of the working class, "the most class-conscious section of the working class."[38] Stalin calls the Party "the advanced detachment of the working class;"[39] "The political leader of the working class";[40] "the General Staff of the proletariat."[41] He explains that it centralizes "the leadership of the struggle of the proletariat, thus transforming each and every non-Party organization of the working class into an auxiliary body and transmission belt linking the Party with the class,"[42] and that "the proletariat needs the Party first of all

---

[32] As quoted in J. Edgar Hoover, *An Analysis of the 17th National Convention of the Communist Party, USA*, p. 1. Statement made to the Senate Internal Security Subcommittee and released on Jan. 17, 1960.

[33] *Ibid.*, p. 2.

[34] Sept. 1960, pp. 10-15. James E. Jackson indicates that the Party in America accepts the line laid down at the Communist Summit meeting in Nov. 1960. *World Marxist Review*, Jan. 1961, pp. 38-45.

[35] "The Path of Democratic Justice," Oct. 3, 1960, p. 10.

[36] Stalin, *Leninism*, p. 93.

[37] For some of their secret practices see the Subversive Activities Control Board. Herbert Brownell, Jr., Attorney General of the United States *vs.* Communist Party of the United States of America. *Report of the Board*, Washington, D.C.: Government Printing Office, 1953, pp. 105-117. Senate Internal Security Sub-Committee, *The Communist Party of the United States of America*. Washington, D.C.: Government Printing Office, 1955.

[38] Marxist Study Series, *Theory and Practice of the Communist Party*, New York: New Century Publishers, 1948, p. 41.

[39] *Problems of Leninism*, Moscow: Foreign Languages Publishing House, 1954, p. 96.

[40] *Ibid.*, p. 97.

[41] *Ibid.*, p. 98.

[42] *Ibid.*, p. 103.

as its General Staff, which it must have for the successful seizure of power."[43]

It is not a genuine political party for it abolishes all other parties when it comes to power. As *Pravda*, April 5, 1956, said: "The party cannot permit that the freedom to discuss problems should be taken as a freedom to propagandize views alien to the spirit of Marxism-Leninism because this would contradict the party's rules and its principles."[44] B. Ponomarev writes: "From a force for overthrowing the system of exploitation the Party became a force for building the new, socialist society." ". . . that proletarian dictatorship is necessary first of all to suppress the resistance of the overthrown exploiters and of all the anti-socialist class forces in the country."[45]

When the Party is in power it is afraid to hold elections which are not rigidly controlled. In fact, a communist country is the type of country where a thief could break into Party headquarters and steal the results of next week's election!!

The Party is anti-parliamentarian. It represents itself and its dogma, and power lusts, and not its so-called constituents.

A LARGE PARTY NOT SOUGHT

The fact that the Party is not large in numbers does not mean that it is not dangerous. A conspiracy, although but a small minority, which is well organized and a part of an international movement, does not need many members in order to be exceedingly dangerous. They were a small minority when they took over Russia.[46] As an undercover agent, Armando Penha, pointed out they are interested in quality, not numbers.[47] As J. Edgar Hoover put it: "To that I can only say that numbers mean nothing and that those nations which have attempted to assess the threat of communism on the basis of numerical strength alone are eating the bitter bread of slavery for their short-sightedness."[48] Hoover stated that from its 17th National

---

[43] *Ibid.*, p. 104.

[44] As quoted in the *National Guardian*, April 16, 1956, p. 10. This publication is sympathetic to Communism.

[45] B. Ponomarev, "The Inheritance of the World Communist Movement," *World Marxist Review*, Aug. 1959, p. 26.

[46] *History of the Communist Party of the Soviet Union*, p. 196.

[47] *U.S. News and World Report*, Mar. 16, 1959, p. 8.

[48] "Communist 'New Look' a Study in Duplicity," *The Elks Magazine*, Aug. 1956.

Convention, December 10, 1959, "The Communist Party, USA, emerged from this convention more powerful, more unified and even more of a menace to our Republic."[49]

One of the things which can destroy the Party in America is exposure.[50] Government investigating committees can do this as nothing else can. J. Edgar Hoover considered this aspect of their work, which is a by-product of their investigation work in gathering information on the basis of which to recommend legislation, as their most important service to America.[51]

---

[49] *An Analysis of the 17th National Convention of the Communist Party, USA*, p. 1.

[50] Sidney Hook, "Introduction" in Simon Wolin, *Communism's Postwar Decade*, New York: The Tamiment Institute, 1955.

[51] Testimony before the House Committee on Un-American Activities, Mar. 26, 1947.

CHAPTER TWELVE

Conclusions

In spite of the flexibility and diversity embraced in dialectical materialism, and in spite of the fact that inconsistencies and contradictions have been in Marxism from the beginning, there are certain basic concepts to which communists of all generations have held. These include at least the following: *First,* atheism. *Secondly,* dialectical materialsm. *Thirdly,* that all things are in a state of change, i.e., nothing is absolute, all is relative. *Fourthly,* the class nature of all social institutions, ideals, ideas, morality, religion and laws. *Fifthly,* the irreconcilability of the class interests of the capitalists and of the proletariat. *Sixthly,* the necessity of revolution. *Seventhly,* the necessity and absolute supremacy of the Communist Party. *Eighthly,* the inevitability of Communism.

It should be obvious that if a person actually accepts the world view of communism, one should expect him to act in harmony with the basic concepts of communism and not in harmony with the concepts of a basically different world view. In other words, if the communist really believes in communism we should expect that his actions will be in harmony with his beliefs and not, for example, in harmony with the actions of a devout Christian. The Christian would be deceiving himself, but not the communist, if he thinks that the communist will act even somewhat like a Christian.

Communists maintain that they believe in communism. They spend countless dollars and innumerable man-hours in spreading their doctrines. Their actions have been in harmony with the basic assumptions which we listed in the first paragraph of this chapter. Therefore, reason tells us to believe that a *communist is a communist and that he will act like a communist.* We have no reason to believe that he is not a communist, or to believe that he will act like a Christian. To think that he is something other than he is, is a refusal to face reality and is an invitation to disaster![1]

To recognize that a communist is a communist, and to understand the philosophy of communism, will not automatically enable us to solve the problems which have been brought into the world, or intensified, by communism. However, it is the author's conviction that such an understanding is essential if the world is to escape enslavement by the communists. For the non-communist world to plan and to act as if communists are not communists, will not change them into non-communists but will contribute to the communist's conquest of the world. And this conquest, be it remembered, will not result simply in the change of one form of government for another, but the enthronement of a government and a way of life which are determined to destroy all the morals, mores, values, and ideals of pre-communist societies.

---

[1] William Henry Chamberlin, "Meeting of Giants," *Wall Street Journal*, Aug. 19, 1959. Adm. L. H. Frost, Director of Naval Intelligence, *Congressional Record*, Aug. 14, 1959, p. A7033.

SUBJECT INDEX